Polly Clingerman's
Dinner Companion

POLLY CLINGERMAN'S
Dinner Companion

Glorious, Easy Meals in Less Than an Hour!

The American Cooking Guild
Boynton Beach, Florida

Acknowledgements
—Project Management by Karen Perrino
—Edited by Joanne Leonard
—Recipe testing by Joan Patten
—Design and Typesetting by Clara Graves Graphic Design
—Illustrations by Jim Haynes, Graphics Plus
—Photographs by Burwell and Burwell

Printed in the United States of America

ISBN 0-942320-56-5

For a catalog of cookbooks write to:
The American Cooking Guild
3600-K South Congress Avenue
Boynton Beach, FL 33426-8488

To my father who was everyone's favorite dinner companion, to my mother, who taught me that food was sacred and to be treated with respect, and to John, taster and critic extraordinaire, without whom none of this would be so much fun.

Contents

✣ Try Pasta Tonight ✣

✣ Try Seafood Tonight ✣

❧ Try Poultry Tonight ❧

❧ Try Beef Tonight ❧

❧ Try Pork Tonight ❧

❧ Try Lamb Tonight ❧

❧ Try a Meatless Meal Tonight ❧

❧ Try Soup Tonight ❧

❧ Try Salad Tonight ❧

❧ Don't Cook Tonight ❧

❧ The Pantry ❧

✿ Guide to Hidden Treasures ✿

Here is a guide to the extra treats I tossed into the book—the boxed recipes not listed in the Contents—in categories that will help you with meal planning. In the Salad Dressings and Sauces lists I've included not only stand-alone recipes but also ones that are parts of other recipes. (There's no reason a good sauce should stay chained to a single dish.) I put an asterisk (*) by those titles so you'll know to read the recipe and lift out just the sauce.

*part of another recipe

*part of another recipe

Introduction

At the end of a busy day, making decisions is the last thing you want to do. You want to relax, you want to eat something good, you want to have someone spoil you a little. But no one is going to peel you a grape while you languish on the chaise longue. If you're going to eat, someone has to make dinner and that someone is you.

Hence **The Dinner Companion**, whose goal is to greet you in the kitchen with ways to make getting dinner a pleasant experience that adds a nice cap to the day rather than a final exhausting whack. Kitchen time can be restorative. When you come home, stop, take a deep breath and change gears. If the kids are hungry or cranky or just racing around in alarming displays of energy, calm them down with crackers and peanut butter. Give them a glass of juice or a mug of cider heated in the microwave. Then fix yourself a glass of wine or a soothing herb tea to sip slowly as you stir and unwind.

There are prep and cooking times at the beginning of each recipe, but don't take these as gospel. They are approximate. No two people work at the same speed or have the same equipment. I don't know how big your kitchen is, or whether you store onions in the cupboard or the garage. I can't factor in the phone that rings or the search for the jar of olives that hid behind the chicken soup. The timings give you an idea of what work is involved. Is it mostly slicing and chopping ingredients, or is it free time to enjoy while the dinner bubbles?

I couldn't resist sprinkling the pages with boxes, charts and tables—what a friend calls little windows and doors to go in and out of. The boxes are full of hints and tips, things that struck me funny, and a bevy of quick recipes for side dishes to make the meal fun. There are special breads to make from refrigerator biscuits, French and Italian loaves, English muffins and pita; interesting salads and vegetables, and quickly made desserts that run from light and luscious to sinfully rich. The charts are designed to give you recipes at a glance: splendid pasta sauces, creative pizzas, ideas for glamorizing chicken cutlets, toppings to adorn grilled meats and poultry, and a host of imaginative stir-fries to beguile your taste buds. They also give suggestions for zipping up rice, noodles, couscous, polenta and potatoes, and for sauces and toppings to jazz up vegetables. There are charts to tell you how to turn canned soups into house specials and how to make salads interesting. Flip through the book and wake up your taste buds as you read these recipes, most of which you can make in minutes and eat in leisurely bliss.

Be sure to look for the chef's hints tucked at the end of many recipes. *The Speedy Chef* offers quick tricks to save time. *The Clever Chef* gives tips on technique or an explanation of unusual ingredients. *The Adventurous Chef* suggests fun variations.

The Unhurried Chef tells you how to make the recipe even better if you have time. *The Skinny Chef* shows how to make the dish lighter. *The Vegetarian Chef* adapts recipes for meatless nights.

The Dinner Companion contains several recipe lists to help you use the book and plan your meals. At the front, the Contents pages give you the locations of the main dish recipes and the recipe charts. The other recipes for things like desserts, vegetables, and breads which are randomly strewn throughout the pages, are listed in the Guide to Hidden Treasures which follows the Contents. Do you hanker for a midnight snack or a wee indulgence? Check the Guide for inspirations. When you plan your next cocktail party, check the hors d'oeuvres list. Many recipes in the book make wonderful cocktail food.

Entertaining can be a source of frustration for the cook who loves people but leads a hectic life. Just about every recipe in **The Dinner Companion** is a marvelous dish for a party, be it casual or fancy. To make a recipe into a party, add a soup or starter. Pick a dessert, one of the wickedly rich ones or something sophisticated with fruits. Choose a festive coffee from the coffee boxes. You'll dazzle guests with the meal and breeze out of the kitchen cheery, unfrazzled, and ready to do it again next Friday. You'll get a reputation as an unflappable, kitchen-savvy host.

You may be a busy gourmet who enjoys reading about food but for one reason or another doesn't cook much. That's okay. In the Don't Cook Tonight chapter you'll find epicurean dinners to assemble from deli and off-the-shelf ingredients. In one glance you will see that this is serious stuff, the answer to impressive dinner parties when you are time-and-energy challenged. You shop, you assemble, you feast. This chapter alone could change your social life.

Whatever you serve, and whether you serve it to family or company, make the meal pretty. An attractive dish encourages us to relax and savor. A pretty centerpiece invites lingering. **The Dinner Companion** has a page of easy garnishes to make with little brain drain. If a bit of artistry would relax you, give the napkins a fancy fold. Set a potted plant in the center of the table or have someone pick flowers from the garden. Now and then light candles—they make any meal feel like an occasion and the soft lighting soothes and flatters.

Did I mention the nights when you are sick of being trendy or gourmet? Sometimes you want to say the heck with it, take down your hair, kick off your shoes and dig into something as un-chic as a can of chili. Don't apologize—we all need an occasional rest from the unbearable lightness of being proper. **The Dinner Companion** is at your service with a few casual, zesty recipes made from canned chili, tamales, all that stuff we love to eat when we let go.

Perhaps the biggest boon to the time-challenged cook is a pantry shelf meal. This is a soul saver when you haven't had time to shop. Take a minute to read the Pantry List. Strike out the things the family hates, make a shopping list and head for the market. With a well-stocked pantry, you have a wealth of dinners waiting for you. Why settle for takeout pizza when a homemade dinner is almost as easy—and a lot cheaper?

Remember, you aren't expected to prepare a fantastic meal every night; who wants that sort of pressure? With **The Dinner Companion** at your elbow, every night can be a happy experience. Cooking is a creative time when your soul expands and sheds the dents and spatters of the day. Invite the kids to help chop and stir. Hash over the day's events with your spouse while you sip a glass of wine and share the cooking chores. Or dream quietly by yourself as you measure and stir.

Play. Try things. Recipes aren't grim commandments, but friendly guides to combinations that taste good. Fool around with them. If feta cheese and tomatoes taste so good on top of beef steaks (page 89), how would they be on lamb or pork? Wonderful. If you can bake cornbread in the waffle iron (page 163) would cake batter work? Oh yes! Topped with a smidge of raspberry jam and cream cheese, it makes a delectible little morsel to savor in small, slow bites over a steaming cup of coffee.

It's your kitchen, and you can do whatever you want. It's great to be in charge.

Bon Appetit!

Polly

Try Pasta Tonight

Pasta is quickly made. It is soothing and versatile. You can have your pasta homey, sophisticated, light, robust, or ethnic. You'll find a sampling of all of these in this chapter along with three pasta tables which I thought you would have fun with as you dump and pour in the rapid dash toward dinner. You may not notice that pasta sauces fall in a few basic categories. The main ones are tomato based, cream based and, the boon to the speedy chef, uncooked. To show how simply they go together without too much thought and fuss, I put in a table of sauces of each type. Just because each of these recipes doesn't star on its own page, doesn't mean that it's ordinary or just okay for a busy night. There are some devastatingly good sauces in the tables that you'll make over and over. Look through the simple rules in the table headers, make the sauces to see how they work; then come up with your own creations and dazzle yourself and the family.

"Have your pasta homey, sophisticated, light or robust. There are devastatingly good sauces in the tables in this chapter that you'll make over and over."

Turkish Spaghetti

This has all the wonderful Turkish flavors: a meat sauce redolent of sweet and hot paprika topped with smooth, garlicky yogurt. A seductive combination.

Prep Time: 5 minutes
Cooking Time: 15 minutes

1 pound spaghetti, cooked and drained

2 cups plain yogurt

4 to 5 fat cloves garlic, minced

1 large onion, chopped fine

1 tablespoon vegetable oil

1 pound lean ground beef

⅔ cup tomato sauce

2½ teaspoons sweet paprika

½ teaspoon hot paprika or cayenne pepper (or to taste)

salt and pepper to taste

While the pasta cooks, mix the yogurt, garlic and salt to taste in a small bowl. Set in a warm place so it will be room temperature by serving time.

In a 10" skillet over medium heat, sauté onion in the oil until softened. Add the ground beef. Cook and stir until the beef loses its pink color. Add the tomato sauce, sweet and hot paprika and salt and pepper to taste. Cook for 8 minutes over low heat, stirring occasionally.

Divide the pasta among 4 heated plates. Top each portion with one fourth of the meat sauce. Ladle about ¼ cup of yogurt onto each serving. Serve the remaining yogurt separately at table for those who want more.

Yield: 4 servings.

The Adventurous Chef: To give the dish an authentic Turkish finish, add 1½ teaspoons paprika and a pinch of cayenne to 2 tablespoons melted butter. Drizzle over the yogurt topping.

❧ Pita Crisps ❧

2 6" pita rounds
2 tablespoons melted butter
2 teaspoons sesame seeds per disk (optional)

Split each pita into 2 flat disks. With kitchen scissors cut each into 4 triangles. Brush the cut side of each with melted butter and sprinkle with optional sesame seeds. Place on baking sheet and bake at 350° for 7 to 10 minutes or until crisp. Serve warm.

Yield: 4 servings.

Korean Noodles

I learned this dish when I studied Oriental cooking and it has been one of our favorites ever since. In the summer pour cold, defatted broth over the meat and noodles. It sounds odd, but it's delicious and fresh tasting on a hot day.

Prep Time: 5 minutes
Cooking Time: 10 minutes

1 pound yaki mein (Chinese dried noodles) or vermicelli, cooked and drained
2 teaspoons vegetable oil
2 eggs, lightly beaten
2 cups beef broth
½ pound ground beef
1½ tablespoons soy sauce
½ teaspoon sugar
1 clove garlic, minced
2 teaspoons toasted sesame seeds
2 teaspoons Oriental sesame oil
few drops hot sesame oil
½ teaspoon salt
¼ cup chopped green onions

While the noodles cook, heat the oil in a medium skillet. Add the eggs and cook them in a flat sheet until they are set and the top is no longer shiny. Remove the omelet from the skillet and cut it in thin strips.

Heat the broth in a small saucepan.

For the topping, sauté the beef in a medium skillet until it loses all pinkness. Add soy sauce, sugar, garlic, toasted sesame seeds, sesame oils and salt. Cook for 1 minute.

Divide the noodles among 4 individual soup bowls and spoon the beef sauce over them. Sprinkle each with ¼ of the eggs and green onions and pour heated broth over.

Yield: 4 servings.

The Clever Chef: To toast sesame seeds, heat a dry skillet over medium heat. Add the seeds and toast for 1 to 2 minutes, watching carefully and shaking the pan, until lightly browned.

Perciatelli with Turkey Olive Sauce

Perciatelli is a fat spaghetti whose chewy texture is perfect with this full-flavored sauce. The olives give a nice tang to the slightly sweet suaveness of onion, pepper and tomato.

Prep Time: 10 minutes
Cooking Time: 25 minutes

1 pound perciatelli, cooked and drained

2 tablespoons olive oil

1 large onion, chopped fine

2 large green peppers, stemmed, seeded, chopped coarse

2 cloves garlic, chopped fine

1 pound ground turkey

2 cans (14 to 16 ounces each) Italian style tomatoes, undrained

1 teaspoon meat glaze such as Bovril

1 cup pitted Kalamata olives

2 tablespoons tomato paste

2 teaspoons sugar

4 2" sprigs oregano or ½ teaspoon dried

2 2" sprigs thyme or ½ teaspoon dried

1 2" sprig rosemary or ¼ teaspoon dried

salt to taste

grated Parmesan cheese as a garnish

While the pasta cooks, heat the oil in a large skillet over medium heat. Add onion, peppers and garlic and sauté until tender, about 5 minutes. Add the turkey. Raise the heat a little and sauté until turkey is no longer pink. Add tomatoes with their juice, breaking them up with your fingers (see note). Stir in Bovril, olives, tomato paste, sugar, oregano, thyme and rosemary. Add salt to taste. Simmer uncovered until the liquid has cooked down and the sauce thickens, about 15 minutes. Check and correct seasoning. If you used fresh herbs, add a bit more just before serving.

Serve pasta and sauce separately so everybody gets a fair share of both. Pass the Parmesan to sprinkle on top.

Yield: 4 servings.

The Clever Chef: Canned tomatoes are convenient, but the seeds are annoying. To add tomatoes to a mixture without also adding the seeds, place a sieve over the pan and hold the tomatoes over it as you break them open. Lift them out and add them to the pan—the seeds remain in the sieve. To pit the olives, press down on them with the heel of your hand. The pits pop out.

Freeze Leftover Pasta

Italians, who adore their pasta, say it must be eaten the moment it is drained. If you are Italian, you should read no further. For the rest of you, I find that unsauced pasta freezes very well. If you boil too much, stick it in a freezer bag, press out all the air, and freeze. It will thaw in the microwave in 1 to 2 minutes.

Hong Kong Noodles

This isn't an authentic Chinese dish, but it has the flavors we all love: sweet, tangy hoisin sauce, smoky sesame oil—and of course, the indispensable garlic and ginger. This is one of my drop-in-guest meals. There is always ground turkey or beef in the freezer and the rest of the ingredients are pantry items.

Prep Time: 10 minutes
Cooking Time: 20 minutes

12 ounces vermicelli, cooked and drained
3 tablespoons vegetable oil
2 teaspoons minced garlic
1½ teaspoons minced fresh ginger
¼ teaspoon crushed red pepper flakes
1½ cups chopped onion
1 pound ground turkey or beef
½ cup chicken broth, divided
3 tablespoons hoisin sauce
3 tablespoons soy sauce
3 tablespoons dry sherry
2 tablespoons cornstarch
¼ to ½ teaspoon hot chili oil
2 tablespoons toasted sesame oil
3 green onions, sliced diagonally

While the vermicelli cooks, heat a wok or large skillet. Add oil, garlic, ginger, and red pepper. Sauté for 4 to 5 seconds. Add the onion and stir-fry until transparent. Crumble in the ground turkey or beef. Continue to stir-fry until the meat is no longer pink and is lightly browned.

In a small dish mix ¼ cup of the chicken broth with the hoisin sauce, soy sauce and sherry. Stir into the meat. Cover the skillet, reduce the heat, and simmer for 10 minutes. Stir once or twice while it cooks.

In a small bowl mix the cornstarch with the remaining chicken broth. Slowly stir the mixture into the meat. Cook and stir until the sauce thickens. Add hot chili oil.

Put the pasta into a hot serving bowl and toss with the sesame oil. Pour the sauce over the pasta and toss gently. Top with green onions.

Yield: 4 servings.

The Adventurous Chef: Serve with a dish of bean sprouts and let the diners put a handful on their pasta. This adds a nice crunch.

Some Nifty Tomato Sauces for Pasta

These tomato pastas are simple and informal. Most of them taste best on a sturdy pasta rather than a delicate one like fettuccini. You'll want to try all of them. For each recipe you'll need two 28-ounce cans of whole tomatoes, drained and chopped; or one 28-ounce can of crushed tomatoes, plus a few extras.

The Basic Steps:	In a large skillet over medium heat sauté the items below in 2 tablespoons olive oil.	Add tomatoes and the following ingredients. Simmer uncovered for 15 minutes or until sauce has thickened.	Stir in the items below. Then toss with 1 pound cooked pasta. Garnish as suggested.
Amatriciana *This sauce is hot with red pepper.*	1 clove garlic, crushed; ¼ teaspoon red pepper flakes. Cook 30 seconds.	A good dose of black pepper; salt to taste.	4 ounces (6-7 slices) bacon cut in pieces, cooked crisp and drained. Garnish with chopped parsley.
Tomato Basil *Fresh and herby. Do use fresh basil.*	Same as above.	Salt to taste.	Garnish with 30 basil leaves, chopped; ¼ cup Romano cheese.
Puttanesca *Tangy with black olives and capers.*	2 cloves garlic, crushed; ¼ teaspoon red pepper flakes; 4-6 anchovy fillets. Cook 30 seconds.	1 teaspoon dried oregano; salt and pepper.	¼ cup oil-cured olives, pitted (or any black Kalamata olives); 2 tablespoons capers. Garnish with chopped parsley.
Eggplant *A thick, luscious sauce.*	2 cloves garlic, crushed; 3 cups eggplant in ½" cubes; ⅓ cup dry red wine. Cover, cook 5 minutes	½ teaspoon dried crushed red pepper; 1 teaspoon oregano; 1 canned roasted red pepper in ½" dice; salt and pepper.	¼-½ cup halved Kalamata olives. Garnish with parsley and pass the Parmesan.

The Basic Steps:	In a large skillet over medium heat sauté the items below in 2 tablespoons olive oil.	Add tomatoes and the following ingredients. Simmer uncovered for 15 minutes or until sauce has thickened.	Stir in the items below. Then toss with 1 pound cooked pasta. Garnish as suggested.
Sausage *Use fusilli or rotini to hold the sauce.*	1 large onion, sliced; 3 garlic cloves, chopped. Sauté 6 minutes. Add 1 pound Italian sausage without casings. Cook till no longer pink, breaking up with a fork.	⅓ cup tomato paste; 2 bay leaves; 2 teaspoons dried basil; 1 teaspoon dried oregano.	Garnish with parsley. Pass the Parmesan.
Red Clam *A delight for clam lovers. Try it with fresh ones!*	3 cloves garlic, crushed; ¼ teaspoon red pepper flakes. Cook 30 seconds.	2 teaspoons dried marjoram; 2 tablespoons parsley.	2 cans (7 ounces) clams with juice. Cover, cook 5 minutes more. Then toss with parsley.
Tomato Gorgonzola *Buttery and cheesy.*	4 cloves garlic; 1 cup minced onion. Cook, stirring, until softened.	½ cup butter and 6 ounces Gorgonzola cheese, whisked together.	Pass lots of Romano or Parmesan (or stir 1 cupful into the sauce).

The Clever Chef: If your tomato sauce tastes sharp, add a little sugar (½ to 1 teaspoon). Garlic burns easily; watch it during that quick sauté. Soaking anchovies for 3 to 5 minutes in milk removes some of the saltiness and gentles the flavor.

✣ *Ethel's Apple Snickers Delight* ✣

If your soul feels a little dented or you deserve a reward for cleaning the garage, treat yourself to this blissful set of contrasts from my sister-in-law: velvety cream laced with Snickers bars and crispy apple. A dynamite combination.

3 tart apples like Granny Smith
3 Snickers candy bars (2.07 ounce)
1 package (3.4 ounces) instant French
  vanilla pudding mix
1 cup milk
1 container (8 ounces) whipped topping

Peel, core and coarsely chop the apples. Coarsely chop the Snickers bars. Place pudding mix and milk in a medium bowl and beat with a rotary beater. Fold in the whipped topping, then the chopped apples and Snickers bars. Chill in the refrigerator until serving time.

Yield: 6 servings.

Macaroni and Cheese

Everyone grew up on macaroni and cheese. It is the ultimate comfort food. It is also the perfect pantry-shelf meal because you always have the ingredients on hand.

Prep Time: 5 minutes
Cooking Time: 10 minutes

1 cup elbow macaroni, cooked and drained
2 tablespoons butter
2 tablespoons flour
1½ cups milk
2 cups grated sharp Cheddar cheese
½ teaspoon onion, grated
1 teaspoon A-1 sauce
½ teaspoon salt, or to taste
pepper to taste
crumbs from 2 slices of white bread
1 tablespoon melted butter

While the macaroni cooks, melt the butter in a large saucepan over medium heat. Add flour and cook, stirring, for 1 minute. Add the milk and cook and stir until thick. Blend in the cheese, onion, A-1 sauce and salt and pepper, stirring until the cheese melts. Stir in the macaroni and place in a buttered 10" pie plate.

Mix the crumbs with the melted butter and sprinkle them over the top. Broil for about 2 minutes or until the crumbs are brown.

Yield: 4 servings.

The Speedy Chef: Instead of elbows, look for the small sea shell pasta that cooks in 3 to 4 minutes. Top with packaged grated cheese instead of crumbs.

The Adventurous Chef: Go Italian by reducing the Cheddar to ¾ cup and adding ¾ cup diced mozzarella and ½ cup grated Parmesan. Or make it hearty by adding a cup of diced ham and ½ cup of frozen green peas, thawed. The kids would probably like it if you stirred in half a package of sliced frankfurters now and then.

❧ Ginger Pears ❧

This is a delicious quickie right off the pantry shelf. It looks and tastes very French.

1 can (1 pound) pear halves, drained
6 gingersnaps, crushed
1 jar raspberry jam (about 1 cup)
juice of 1 lemon, approximately
port wine (optional)

Roll the pear halves in the gingersnap crumbs. In a small pan heat the raspberry jam and thin it to taste with lemon juice to make a sauce. Add port to taste. Place the pears in individual dessert dishes. Top with enough raspberry sauce to half cover. Sprinkle generously with remaining crumbs. Pass the remaining sauce at table.

Yield: 4 servings.

Pasta Frittata

This makes a pleasant lunch or supper dish. Serve it with tomato sauce spooned on top, or with sliced tomatoes in season. If you have leftover pasta, here's your dish. A cup and a half of cooked pasta would be about right.

Prep Time: 10 minutes
Cooking Time: 10 minutes

4 ounces angel hair pasta, broken up, cooked and drained

4 eggs

⅓ cup milk (whole or skim)

¾ cup shredded mozzarella cheese

½ cup chives or thinly sliced green onions

¼ cup grated Parmesan cheese

1½ tablespoons chopped fresh basil or 1½ teaspoons dried

¼ teaspoon salt

¼ teaspoon onion powder

⅛ teaspoon cayenne

2 teaspoons cooking oil

1 jar (7 ounces) sliced roasted red pepper, drained

While the pasta cooks, beat the eggs lightly with the milk in a medium bowl. Add mozzarella, chives, Parmesan cheese, basil, salt, onion powder and cayenne. Whisk to blend well.

Heat the oil in a 10" non-stick skillet over medium heat. When it is hot, add the pasta and pimento. Stir and sauté for 1 minute. Pour the egg mixture over the pasta. Turn the heat to medium low and cook for 3 minutes or until just set. If the handle of the skillet is not oven-safe, cover it with foil. Place the frittata under the broiler to cook the top. (You don't want it to brown; 2 to 5 minutes should do it nicely.)

Cut into wedges and serve hot.

Yield: 4 servings.

The Clever Chef: Substitute ⅓ cup very finely chopped onion if you don't have chives or green onions. If you forget to break up the pasta before cooking, snip through the cooked pasta a few times with your kitchen scissors so it will be easier to combine with the egg mixture.

Pasta
Likes Moisture

When draining pasta, don't drain it too thoroughly or it will dry out and stick together. A little water should cling, which will keep the pasta absorbent and mix in with the sauce.

Fettuccine with Peas and Ham

If you're feeling really casual, you can use frankfurters in this. Any leftover meat would also work. If you use chicken or pork, which have a less pronounced flavor, add a little tarragon or oregano.

Prep Time: 6 minutes
Cooking Time: 22 minutes

1 pound fettuccine, cooked and drained

5 tablespoons butter, divided

10 ounces mushrooms, sliced thin

2 cups peas, fresh or thawed frozen

4 ounces prosciutto or other well-flavored ham, diced

6 tablespoons Parmesan cheese

3 tablespoons whipping cream, or more to taste

salt and pepper to taste

While the fettuccine cooks, heat 3 tablespoons of the butter in a medium skillet and add the mushrooms. Cook and stir over medium heat until they sweat, then turn up the heat and cook 5 or 6 minutes more. Add peas and prosciutto. Lower heat to medium and cook for another 5 minutes. Season with salt and pepper to taste.

Put 2 tablespoons of butter in the pasta serving bowl and put it in a warm place. Place the fettuccine in the heated bowl as soon as it is cooked and toss to coat with butter. Add the Parmesan cheese and toss again. Stir in the vegetable-ham mixture and cream. The pasta should not be dry. If it seems so, stir in more cream—up to 3 or 4 tablespoons. Serve immediately on very hot plates. Remember, pasta cools off quickly.

Yield: 4 servings.

❧ Savory Slices ❧

1 loaf (1 pound) unsliced French bread
⅓ cup butter, softened
1 teaspoon Worcestershire sauce
2 tablespoons minced parsley
½ teaspoon dried basil
¼ teaspoon garlic powder

Slice bread into 1" slices, cutting almost but not quite through to the bottom. Mix butter with Worcestershire sauce, parsley, basil and garlic powder. Spread each cut surface with butter mixture. Wrap loaf in heavy-duty aluminum foil. Bake at 350° for 15 minutes or until heated through. Serve warm.

Yield: 8 to 10 servings.

Fusilli with Italian Sausage and Cream

Yου can use any sturdy pasta with this sinfully rich sauce. Admittedly, it will not lower your cholesterol. My rule is, if you are going to indulge, be sure it's worth it. This dish is.

Prep Time: 5 minutes
Cooking Time: 18 minutes

1 pound fusilli, cooked and drained

3 tablespoons chopped onion

1 tablespoon vegetable oil

1 tablespoon butter

1 pound sweet or hot Italian sausage, casing removed

1½ cups whipping cream

½ teaspoon salt

¼ teaspoon pepper

½ cup Parmesan cheese, to be passed as a garnish

While the pasta cooks, sauté the onion in the oil and butter in a large saucepan until golden. Add the sausage and crumble with a fork. Sauté, stirring now and then, for 10 minutes. Stir in the cream, salt and pepper and cook until the sauce thickens, about 5 minutes. Toss the sauce with the hot pasta. Pass the Parmesan to sprinkle on top.

Yield: 4 to 6 servings.

The Skinny Chef: Instead of cream, use 1½ cups milk and 1 tablespoon of cornstarch or 1½ tablespoons flour. To avoid lumps, first make a paste of the thickener and a small amount of the milk, then stir into the rest of the milk. There's not a lot of difference between this and the rich original. You can also substitute light cream for the whipping cream.

A New Way to Cook Pasta

I have found a marvelous way to cook pasta which was recommended by the president of one of Italy's biggest pasta companies. Bring the water to a fast boil in a big pot. Add the pasta and boil furiously for 2 minutes. Then turn off the heat, cover the pot with a towel and put the lid on top. Let the pasta stand for the cooking time given on the box directions, usually 10 to 12 minutes or so. That's it! Pasta cooked this way has a silky texture. See what you think.

Some Nifty Cream Sauces for Pasta

These are lovely with delicate pastas like fettuccine and linguini, although the lusty Carbonara will hold its own with anything. Use whipping cream, light cream, half-and-half or milk in these wonderful sauces. Hint: A generous amount of freshly ground black pepper adds the right zing.

The Basic Steps:	In a large skillet cook these for 5 minutes over medium heat.	Add the following and bring to a boil over medium-high heat.	Stir in the following cheese until it melts. Then stir in 1 pound of cooked pasta and top with garnishes.
Carbonara *Richly flavored with bacon, onion and cheese.*	8 ounces (8-9 slices) bacon, diced; ¼ cup minced onion. Drain off fat when cooked.	⅓ cup cream; ⅓ cup chicken broth; ¼ teaspoon (or more) black pepper.	½ cup grated Parmesan cheese; salt to taste. Garnish with parsley and black pepper.
Crab Artichoke *A delicate sauce worthy of an occasion.*	1 tablespoon butter; 1 clove garlic, minced; 1 cup chopped fennel (or celery); ½ teaspoon fennel or anise seed.	1 cup cream; 8 ounces cooked crabmeat; 1 cup sliced cooked artichoke hearts.	½ cup grated Swiss cheese; salt to taste. Garnish with chopped parsley.
Romana *Pretty with nuggets of ham, peas and mushrooms.*	1 tablespoon butter; ½ cup chopped ham or prosciutto; 3 cups sliced mushrooms.	1¼ cups cream; 1 cup cooked green peas.	½ cup grated Parmesan cheese. Garnish with chopped parsley.
Walnut Basil *A dynamite combination of flavors.*	1 tablespoon butter; 2 cloves garlic, minced; 1 cup chopped fresh basil. *Cook only 1-2 minutes.*	1¼ cups cream; 1 cup chopped, toasted walnuts.	½ cup grated Parmesan cheese. Garnish with basil.
Alfredo *A rich and silky combination.*	2 tablespoons butter.	1 cup half-and-half; ¼ teaspoon nutmeg; ¼ teaspoon black pepper. Cook and stir 5 minutes or until slightly thickened.	¾ cup Parmesan. When melted, stir in 6 ounces half slices of pepperoni. Garnish with chopped parsley.

The Basic Steps:	In a large skillet cook these for 5 minutes over medium heat.	Add the following and bring to a boil over medium-high heat.	Stir in the following cheese until it melts. Then stir in 1 pound of cooked pasta and top with garnishes.
The Skinny Chef Alfredo *This one won't make your arteries ache.*	1 tablespoon butter; 2 tablespoons minced onion; 1 clove garlic, minced.	3 tablespoons flour; 2 cups skim milk; 1 cup chicken broth; ½ teaspoon salt; ¼ teaspoon pepper. Simmer until thickened (5 to 8 minutes).	½ cup Parmesan. Garnish with parsley. Pass more Parmesan at the table if you like.
Spinach Ricotta *The ricotta melts into the sauce for a delightful texture.*	3 tablespoons butter; 10-ounce package frozen spinach, cooked, squeezed dry; ¼ cup finely chopped walnuts; 1 teaspoon dried rosemary.	⅔ cup milk mixed with ⅔ cup cream, ½ cup ricotta cheese; ¼ teaspoon nutmeg.	Garnish with 4 ounces cooked ham cut in thin slivers. Pass the Parmesan.

The Skinny Chef: If you use light cream or half-and-half in these recipes, boil the sauce about 2 minutes after adding to thicken it a little. If you use milk, add 1 tablespoon flour or 1½ teaspoons cornstarch for every cup of milk. Put the flour in a little dish, add enough of the milk to make a thin paste, then stir the paste into the rest of the milk.

❧ Chocolate Chip Cookie Torte ❧

Chewy and crisp, topped with a satiny pillow of chocolate cream, here is your ultimate chocolate chip cookie dessert.

¼ cup sweetened condensed milk
2 tablespoons cream cheese
2 tablespoons unsweetened cocoa
¼ teaspoon vanilla
pinch salt
1 cup frozen whipped topping, thawed
½ package (16 ounces) refrigerated choco-
   late chip cookie dough
Garnish: chopped nuts, shaved chocolate

Preheat the oven to 375°.

In a small mixing bowl beat the condensed milk, cream cheese, cocoa, vanilla and salt with an electric mixer until smooth. Fold in the whipped topping. Place in the refrigerator to chill.

Press the cookie dough into an 8-inch round on a cookie sheet. Bake until done, 8 to 12 minutes. Let the cookie sit for a minute, then remove from the cookie sheet to a cooling rack.

When the cookie is cool, place it on a serving plate. Heap the chilled filling on top. Sprinkle with chopped nuts and a little shaved chocolate. To serve, cut in wedges.

Yield: 4 servings

Smooth and Spicy Macaroni and Sausage

Sausage, tomatoes, onions and a lacing of hot pepper. Yum! Even better, the macaroni cooks in the same pot as the sauce, which gives you time to make a salad of oranges with romaine and some other crunchy green.

Prep Time: 8 minutes
Cooking Time: 30 minutes

1 pound hot breakfast sausage or chorizo

1 onion, chopped

1 green or red bell pepper, chopped

1 tablespoon oil, if needed

1 can (14 to 16 ounces) diced tomatoes, undrained

8 ounces elbow macaroni or small bow ties, uncooked

1 cup sour cream

1 ¼ cups milk

1 - 2 tablespoons sugar

1 tablespoon chili powder

1 teaspoon salt

parsley as a garnish

In a Dutch oven brown the sausage, onion and pepper, using the oil if needed. Pour off the fat. Add tomatoes, macaroni, sour cream, milk, sugar, chili powder and salt. Bring to a boil. Reduce the heat to low. Cover and simmer for 20 to 25 minutes or until the macaroni is tender. The dish should be a little saucy and soupy. Sprinkle with parsley.

Yield: 4 to 6 servings.

Note: You can use mild sausage, of course. It's your kitchen. But try the hot version first. The cream softens the fiery peppers and turns them into something special.

❧ Viennese Torte ❧

Keep a pound cake in the freezer and you'll never find yourself without a dessert. Here is a delicious cake that's made in minutes and looks like you spent hours.

1 pound cake, thawed
3 tablespoons rum or orange juice
3 to 4 tablespoons raspberry preserves
3 to 4 tablespoons apricot preserves
1 cup frozen whipped topping, thawed
¼ cup toasted slivered almonds

Cut the cake into 3 layers horizontally. Sprinkle one cut side of each with 1 tablespoon rum. Place the bottom layer on a serving plate. Spread with raspberry preserves. Add the middle layer and spread with apricot preserves. Put on the top layer. Frost the cake with whipped topping. Sprinkle with nuts. Keep in the refrigerator until serving time.

Yield: 8 servings.

The Adventurous Chef: You can use almost any preserves. Orange marmalade is good, too. Fresh strawberries or raspberries are a delicious garnish.

Vermicelli with White Clam Sauce

This has to be one of the easiest and most luscious sauces for pasta. The flavor combination is perfect: clams, fruity olive oil, oregano, and garlic. I have known normally well-behaved guests to fight over the last bites, so be warned.

Prep Time: 4 minutes
Cooking Time: 17 minutes

1 pound vermicelli, cooked and drained
½ cup olive oil
1 clove garlic, peeled and halved
½ cup bottled clam juice
½ teaspoon dried oregano
¼ teaspoon salt
a few grinds of black pepper
1 can (7½ ounces) minced clams, undrained
2 tablespoons flat Italian parsley, chopped

While the pasta cooks, heat the olive oil in a 10" skillet over medium heat until the oil looks wavy. Add the garlic halves and sauté, turning now and then, until they are golden. Press on each clove with a fork to release all the flavor, then remove. Slowly add the clam juice, sliding it into the oil gently so the oil doesn't pop and bubble up. Add oregano, salt and pepper. Simmer uncovered over medium heat for 5 minutes. Add the clams and their juice. Mix well and cook, uncovered, for about 10 minutes or until the sauce thickens and gets a little syrupy. Stir in the parsley.

Toss hot pasta with half the sauce. Divide it among four bowls and spoon the remaining sauce over each.

Yield: 4 servings.

The Clever Chef: Italian parsley has more flavor than the curly kind.

The Adventurous Chef: Add a cup of shredded Monterey Jack cheese at the very end. Stir just until the cheese starts to melt.

French Bread Sticks

Cut off one third of a fat 1-pound loaf of French bread. Cut this piece lengthwise into 3 layers and each layer into 4 sticks. Dip the sticks into ⅓ cup of melted butter. Arrange them on a baking sheet and broil 6" from the heat for about 8 minutes or until golden brown, turning often. Serve warm.

Yield: 12 bread sticks.

Rigatoni with Tuna in Roasted Red Pepper Garlic Sauce

This uncooked sauce has the enticing flavors of the garlicky rouille that accompanies Mediterranean fish soups. A grooved pasta grabs and hangs onto the sauce.

Prep Time: 4 minutes
Cooking Time: 10 minutes

*1 pound rigatoni, cooked al dente and
    drained*

*1 jar (7 ounces) roasted red peppers,
    undrained*

*2 anchovies, soaked 5 minutes in milk and
    patted dry*

2 large cloves garlic, coarsely chopped

2 teaspoons dried oregano

¼ teaspoon salt

½ teaspoon freshly ground pepper

¼ cup olive oil

*1 can (7 ounces) chunk light tuna in
    water, drained and flaked*

1 tablespoon capers, drained

While the pasta cooks, place roasted peppers with their liquid, anchovies, garlic, oregano, salt and pepper in food processor or blender and process until smooth. Pour in the olive oil and process again just to blend. Scrape the sauce into a serving bowl. Add the tuna and capers and mix well.

The minute the pasta is done, drain it, return it to the still-hot pot and toss with the tuna sauce. Serve immediately.

Yield: 4 servings.

❧ Herbed Cheese Italian Bread ❧

1 loaf (1 pound) Italian bread
*8 ounces Monterey Jack cheese, in thin
    slices*
½ cup melted butter
1 tablespoon parsley
1 teaspoon minced onion
1 teaspoon poppy seeds

Cut the loaf into 1" slices down to but not through the bottom. Put cheese slices in the slits. Mix melted butter, parsley, onion, poppy seeds. Drizzle mixture over the top of the loaf. Wrap in foil. Bake at 350° for 15 minutes. Remove foil and bake 15 minutes more.

Yield: 8 to 10 servings.

Linguini with Squash and Curry Coconut Sauce

Y ou'll want to serve this Thai-inspired coconut curry sauce over everything from chicken to fish fillets. It's smooth as velvet, punched up with a kick of ginger and a tang of lemon.

Prep Time: 12 minutes
Cooking Time: 22 minutes

8 ounces linguini, cooked and drained
1 tablespoon vegetable oil
1 medium onion, chopped fine
1 clove garlic, crushed
grated rind of ½ lemon
1½ tablespoons grated fresh ginger
1 tablespoon curry powder
1 tablespoon turmeric
2 cups canned unsweetened coconut milk
1 acorn squash (1½ to 2 pounds) peeled,
*   cut into 1" cubes*
1 teaspoon salt
⅔ cup plain yogurt
1 tablespoon finely chopped fresh cilantro

While the linguini cooks, heat the oil in a heavy saucepan and cook the onion over medium-low heat until transparent. Add garlic, lemon rind, ginger, curry powder and turmeric. Cook and stir for 3 minutes. Add the coconut milk and cook for 15 minutes over low heat, stirring occasionally.

While the sauce cooks, sprinkle squash with salt, put it in a steamer and cook covered over boiling water for 15 minutes or until tender. Stir the yogurt into the sauce and cook gently for a minute or two to heat through. Don't let the sauce boil.

Divide pasta among four plates; top with cooked squash and spoon the sauce over the top. Sprinkle with chopped cilantro.

Yield: 4 servings.

The Clever Chef: Unsweetened coconut milk is available where Oriental groceries are sold. Coconut milk may separate at the beginning of cooking. Just give it a stir and it will smooth out. If you don't have cilantro, substitute flat-leaf parsley.

Some Nifty Uncooked Sauces for Pasta

Here are some uncooked pasta sauces to make in minutes and savor at leisure. Use any pasta for these. They make delicious main dishes jazzed up with a fancy bread. Many are also perfect accompaniments for a simple grill.

The Basic Steps:	Combine as directed.	Cook 1 pound pasta, drain, toss with the sauce to heat and serve immediately. Also note the following:
Pesto *Features the heavenly, deep-green blend of garlic and basil.*	Purée in blender or processor: 2 cups firmly packed basil leaves; ¾ cup Parmesan cheese; ¼ cup pine nuts; 4 cloves garlic. With motor running, add about ½ cup of oil in steady stream until consistency of thick mayonnaise.	Before draining pasta dip out 2 tablespoons cooking water and blend with the sauce. All the pestos are also good on potatoes and vegetables.
Garlic Spinach Pesto *Essence of fresh spinach and parsley with lots of garlic.*	Purée in blender or processor: 3 cups spinach leaves (no stems, lightly packed); 2 cups parsley; 1 cup Parmesan; ½ cup salad oil; ¼ cup blanched almonds; ¼ cup melted butter; 2 tablespoons pine nuts; 3 cloves garlic, crushed.	Before draining the pasta, dip out ⅓ cup cooking water and blend it into the sauce. Serve with Parmesan cheese.
Mint Pesto *Wonderful with grilled lamb or chicken.*	Purée in blender or processor: 4 cups loosely packed mint leaves; 4 cloves garlic, crushed; 1 tablespoon lemon juice; 2 tablespoons olive oil; ⅓ cup water. Put in bowl. Fold in ½ cup Parmesan; 2 tablespoons pine nuts.	Toss with hot pasta.
Roasted Pepper Dill *Right off the pantry shelf. Use a robust pasta.*	Purée in blender or processor: ⅔ cup olive oil; 5 medium canned roasted peppers; ⅔ cup fresh dill; 1½ teaspoons lemon juice; 1¼ teaspoons salt, ¾ teaspoon pepper; ½ teaspoon sugar. Stir in 2 tablespoons Parmesan cheese.	Toss with hot pasta. Top with broiled scallops or shrimp or strips of broiled chicken—or serve plain and pass the Parmesan.

The Basic Steps:	Combine as directed.	Cook 1 pound pasta, drain, toss with the sauce to heat and serve immediately. Also note the following:
Herbed Cream Cheese *Delicious on fettuccine!*	Mix in blender or processor 4-5 ounces herbed cream cheese; 6 tablespoons fresh chives; 6 tablespoons parsley.	Toss until the cheese melts.
Roasted Pepper Ricotta *Has a seductive and creamy texture.*	1 jar (6-7 ounces) roasted red peppers, drained; 2 cups ricotta cheese; enough milk to make a medium-thick sauce (1½ to 1¾ cups).	Toss over heat. Try tossing in ¼" diagonal slices of Italian or Polish sausage, sautéed and drained.
Fresh Tomato Mozzarella *Gourmet fare for the height of tomato season.*	Cut 4 large, ripe tomatoes into 1" cubes and mix with 16 ounces ounces mozzarella (or feta) cheese in ½" cubes; 1 cup basil leaves, cut into strips; 3 cloves garlic, finely minced; 1 cup olive oil; ½ teaspoon salt; pepper to taste.	Let sauce stand as long as is possible (2 hours is ideal, 30 minutes is fine). Toss with cooled pasta. Serve with grated Parmesan.
Tomato with Fresh White Cheese *Uses tangy feta or goat cheese along with basil and olive oil.*	Mix 1 pound fresh plum tomatoes, skinned, seeded, chopped coarse; 12 ounces feta or mild goat cheese (crumbled or in ½" dice); ⅓ cup packed basil leaves; 6 tablespoons lemon juice; ¼ cup olive oil; 1 teaspoon sugar; salt and pepper.	Let stand at room temperature for 30 minutes or longer. Toss with hot pasta. Serve immediately.
Fresh Tomato *Celebrates the arrival of ripe tomatoes.*	Put 2 pounds room-temperature ripe tomatoes in blender or processor with 2 cloves garlic; ⅓ cup loose-packed basil leaves; ¼ cup loose-packed parsley; ⅓ cup olive oil; salt and pepper. Blend smooth.	Toss with hot pasta.

Artichoke Linguini

This lovely, light, lemony sauce can be made from pantry-shelf ingredients. It is fare for a party.

Prep Time: 10 minutes
Cooking Time: 15 minutes

1 pound linguini, cooked al dente and drained

4 tablespoons olive oil, divided

5 tablespoons butter, divided

1 tablespoon flour

1 cup chicken broth

3 cloves garlic, crushed

2 teaspoons lemon juice

1 teaspoon grated lemon rind

2 teaspoons parsley, chopped

8 canned artichoke hearts, chopped

2 tablespoons Parmesan cheese

2 teaspoons capers, drained

salt and pepper to taste

While the linguini cooks, heat 2 tablespoons of the oil and 3 tablespoons of the butter over low heat in a heavy skillet. Add the flour and cook and stir until smooth. Stir in chicken broth and cook for 1 minute. Add garlic, lemon juice, lemon rind, parsley, and salt and pepper to taste. Cook for 5 minutes. Add the artichokes, Parmesan cheese and capers. Cover and cook over low heat for 8 minutes.

In a 10" skillet over medium heat melt the remaining 2 tablespoons of butter with the remaining 2 tablespoons olive oil, and add Parmesan cheese to taste. Add the drained linguini and toss well. Place the pasta on a platter and pour the sauce over all. Serve with more Parmesan.

Yield: 4 servings.

The Social Chef: This is a good meal for vegetarian guests. Use vegetable instead of chicken broth.

Garlic Press & Clean-Up

Cleaning the garlic press is no bother if you remember to put it in water at once. The water puffs the garlic so that instead of sticking like glue to the holes it all but floats off.

Try Seafood Tonight

Seafood cookery has to be quick. By the time shrimps turn pink (about 3 minutes) they are done, fillets and steaks need only 5 minutes per ½ inch thickness. If you cook seafood longer than that it is dry, flavorless and unworthy of your time or your tummy. This chapter runs the gamut from delicate, perfectly-broiled sole fillets to robust catfish bouillabaisse. For your sophisticated nights try the salmon topped with ginger, carrots and leeks on angel hair pasta. When you want rich flavor, make the orange roughy with souffléed-cheese topping or the classic Greek celebration of shrimps oozing with tomato and Feta. Give a look at the sauces in this chapter: coconut curry sauce for catfish, avocado and chutney dipping sauces—a fun idea for crispy, oven-fried fish.

Don't flip past a recipe because you don't have the fish it calls for. If your mouth waters, use a different one. Fish is infinitely adaptable. You can almost always substitute one of a similar thickness and be just fine. Once you taste the exciting flavor combinations in these pages you will see that they will adorn a variety of fish gorgeously.

"For your sophisticated nights try the salmon topped with ginger, carrots and leeks on angel hair pasta."

Chio's Broiled Sole

My friend Chio learned this from her fish seller in Rehobeth. It's incredibly simple and totally delicious. You can substitute flounder or another lean white fish for the sole.

Prep Time: 5 minutes
Cooking Time: 8 minutes

4 fillets of sole
2 to 4 tablespoons butter
salt and lemon pepper to taste

Preheat the broiler. Use a broiler pan without its rack. Place the sole in the pan and add just enough water to film the bottom of the pan.

Dot the sole with butter and sprinkle with salt and lemon pepper.

Place 3" below the heat and broil for 8 minutes exactly, without turning. The fish will be moist with delicately browned edges.

Yield: 4 servings.

❧ Maggie's Cole Slaw ❧

This is an extraordinary combination of the crisp crunch of cabbage, the sturdy crunch of almonds and the soft crunch of ramen noodles.

½ head cabbage
1 package (3 ounces) ramen soup noodles
¼ cup sugar
5 green onions, chopped
½ to ¾ cup chopped almonds
½ cup white vinegar
¼ cup vegetable oil
salt and pepper to taste

Chop the cabbage fine in the food processor using on/off pulses. You should have 3 to 4 cups. Break up the ramen noodles and set aside the flavor packet for another use.

In a large bowl mix the cabbage, noodles, sugar, green onions, almonds, vinegar and oil. Add salt and pepper to taste.

Yield: 4 to 6 servings.

Catfish Bouillabaisse

This is catfish gone Mediterranean. To make it a memorable meal place a slice of hot garlic bread in your bowl before ladling on fish and broth or float toasted rounds of rouille-topped French bread on top.

Prep Time: 10 minutes
Cooking Time: 35 minutes

¼ cup vegetable or olive oil

6 medium onions, cut into ¼" slices

5 cups water plus 2½ fish or chicken bouillon cubes

2 cups dry white wine

1 teaspoon dried thyme

½ teaspoon saffron threads

1 bay leaf

salt, pepper and cayenne pepper to taste

4 medium boiling potatoes (about 1 pound), peeled and cut into ¼" slices

1 to 1½ pounds catfish fillets, cut into 1" to 1½" cubes

Heat oil in a heavy pan over medium heat. Add the onions and cook, stirring frequently, until soft, about 8 minutes. Add the water, bouillon cubes, wine, thyme, saffron, and bay leaf. Add salt, pepper and cayenne to taste. Bring to a boil. Reduce heat, cover, and simmer for 5 minutes. Add the potatoes. Cover and simmer until they are tender, 10 to 12 minutes. Add the fish. Cover and simmer 10 more minutes. Taste. The broth should be highly seasoned. Add salt, pepper or cayenne if needed. Remove the bay leaf and serve in soup bowls.

Yield: 4 servings.

❧ Rouille Sauce ❧

Garlicky, and as fiery as you like, this deep orange mayonnaise adds the final touch of "wonderful" to French fish soups and stews. If you haven't eaten it before you are in for a treat.

6 cloves garlic, pressed
⅛ teaspoon salt
1 teaspoon oregano
⅓ cup canned pimento, drained
2 tablespoons olive oil
⅓ cup fresh bread crumbs, lightly packed
1 cup mayonnaise
hot pepper sauce

In a blender or food processor bowl place the garlic, salt, oregano and pimento. Purée. With the motor running add olive oil. Pour into a bowl. Stir in bread crumbs and mayonnaise.

Season highly with hot pepper sauce. This sauce should be nippy.

Yield: 1 cup.

Salmon with Ginger and Vegetables

The salmon is topped with pale green and orange ribbons and flavored with ginger, sherry and butter. Serve it with a light white wine, a delicate salad of Boston lettuce and crusty rolls.

Prep Time: 10 minutes
Cooking Time: 25 minutes

4 salmon steaks, 8 ounces each

¾ cup fennel, thinly sliced crosswise (about 4 ounces)

2 carrots, cut into matchsticks

1 small leek (white and 2" of green), cut into matchsticks

3 tablespoons dry sherry

3 tablespoons butter, softened

2 teaspoons grated fresh ginger

salt and pepper to taste

cooked angel hair pasta, as an accompaniment

Preheat the oven to 375°. Place salmon in a shallow ovenproof dish and season with salt and pepper.

Blanch the vegetables in boiling salted water for 3 minutes, drain and place on top of the salmon. Sprinkle with sherry.

In a small bowl mix the butter and ginger. Dot it over the vegetables. Season with salt and pepper. Cover the dish with foil, tenting the foil if it looks like it will touch the butter. Cover. Bake for 20 to 25 minutes or until cooked.

Place each salmon steak on a portion of pasta and spoon the juices over all.

Yield: 4 servings.

❧ Some Fun Dessert Coffees ❧

These coffees, with a little cookie to nibble, can stand in for dessert and look very glamorous. Brew strong coffee. Your guests will probably thank you if you make it decaffeinated. For each serving use ½ cup hot coffee, then:

Cappuccino Style: Sweeten each cup with 2 teaspoons of sugar (optional) and top with whipped cream and a little cinnamon or nutmeg.

Almond: Add 2 tablespoons Amaretto liqueur to each cup. Top with whipped cream.

Viennese: Top each cup with whipped cream.

Orange Mocha: Add 2 tablespoons chocolate syrup and 2 tablespoons orange liqueur to each cup.

Spiced: Put in with the ground coffee 8 whole cloves and a 3" cinnamon stick. Add 2 teaspoons sugar to each cup. Top with whipped cream.

Espresso Style: Top each cup with a twist of lemon peel.

Salmon with Onions and Soy

Salmon cooked on a bed of sweet onions, flavored with soy sauce. A lovely combination.

Prep Time: 5 minutes
Cooking Time: 16 minutes

2 tablespoons vegetable oil
2 cups diced onion
4 salmon steaks
½ cup soy sauce

Heat the oil in a skillet large enough to hold the salmon steaks in one layer. Add the onions and sauté over medium heat until softened, 5 to 6 minutes. Lay the salmon steaks over the onions, pour the soy sauce on top and cover. Cook over medium low heat for 10 minutes or until the salmon is done.

Remove the salmon steaks to a serving platter or individual plates. Raise the heat and boil the sauce rapidly until it thickens. Pour over the salmon.

Yield: 4 servings.

❧ Joan's Fruit and Brie in Parchment ❧

My neighbor often serves this to end her elegant dinners. It's light, it's sophisticated, and the combination of melting brie, brown sugar and still slightly crisp fruit is irresistible.

parchment paper or foil
1 medium pear, sliced
1 medium apple, sliced
*half an 8-ounce round Brie cheese cut in
    ¼" thick slices*
1 tablespoon brown sugar
1 tablespoon toasted sliced almonds

Cut 4 pieces of cooking parchment or foil into heart shapes 12" wide and 9" long. Place 2 or 3 pear slices and 2 or 3 apple slices on half of each heart. Top each with some of the cheese slices. Sprinkle each with brown sugar.

Preheat the oven to 400°. Fold the unused half-heart over the fruit and cheese. Starting at the top, fold the edges over twice, making a little hem. Go all around the opened edge until it is sealed tight. This takes only a minute once you see what you are doing. Place the packets on a large baking sheet.

Bake for 3 to 5 minutes or until the cheese just starts melting. To serve, cut a cross through the top of each packet and fold the corners back. Sprinkle cheese with almonds and serve hot and melting.

Yield: 4 servings.

Look What You Can Do with a Cup of Rice!

Cook it in Something Different: For all or part of the cooking liquid use chicken, vegetable or beef broth or tomato juice. For ¼ of the liquid use wine, beer, sherry, or a fruit juice (apple, orange, pineapple).

Stir in Something Different: To start, cook 1 cup of rice in 1½ cups water and fluff it with a fork. Then add any of the combinations given below and heat through.

Caribbean Coconut Fruit Rice:

1 can (11 ounces) mandarin oranges, drained and chopped
1 can (8 ounces) crushed pineapple, drained
½ cup chopped bell pepper
½ cup slivered almonds, toasted
⅓ cup packaged sweetened coconut, toasted
2 tablespoons mango chutney
¼ teaspoon powdered ginger

Coconut Rice:

⅓ cup packaged sweetened coconut
3 tablespoons butter

Oriental Rice:

½ can (7-ounce size) water chestnuts, sliced
½ jar (4-ounce size) roasted red pepper, chopped
¼ cup soy sauce
¼ cup chopped green pepper
3 tablespoons butter
2 green onions, chopped
1 tablespoon pine nuts

Green Rice:

½ bunch watercress, minced
½ cup spinach leaves, minced
3 green onions, minced
1 tablespoon parsley, minced
1 tablespoon butter
Tabasco sauce

Other Possibilities:

- *Chopped dates and nuts*
- *Sliced mushrooms, green onions and shallots*
- *Chopped tomato, bell pepper, broccoli, onion, asparagus, green beans, celery, or grated carrot*
- *Leftover vegetables*
- *Chopped ham, crisp fried bacon, cooked pork, or seafood*
- *Chutney and peanuts*
- *Salsa*
- *Water chestnuts and soy sauce*
- *Chopped cilantro, parsley, or other fresh herbs*
- *Sliced mandarin oranges, chopped apples, or raisins*
- *Sliced black or green olives*
- *Grated cheese, any type.*

Broiled Salmon Steaks with Mustard Sauce

First marinated then broiled, the salmon comes out deliciously moist with crusty edges and a flavor that keeps you reaching for one more bite.

Prep Time: 5 minutes
Marinating Time: 15 minutes
Cooking Time: 15 minutes

4 salmon steaks
¼ cup dry white wine
¼ cup milk
1 cup sour cream, at room temperature
½ cup minced green onions, both white and green parts
1½ tablespoons Dijon mustard
1 tablespoon chopped parsley
¼ teaspoon dried thyme, crushed
¼ teaspoon dried marjoram, crushed
salt and pepper to taste

In a shallow dish big enough to hold the salmon, mix wine, milk and salt and pepper to taste. Marinate salmon in this mixture at room temperature for 15 minutes. Preheat the broiler.

In a small bowl mix sour cream, green onions, mustard, parsley, thyme, marjoram and salt and pepper to taste. Set aside.

Drain the salmon. Place it in a foil-lined, shallow, ovenproof dish. Season with salt and pepper. Broil 6" from the heat for 5 to 7 minutes. Turn the salmon, spread with the sauce and return to the broiler for 5 minutes. If there is any sauce left, serve it separately.

Yield: 4 servings.

The Unhurried Chef: Marinate the salmon up to 4 hours in the refrigerator.

❧ New Potatoes With Caviar ❧

This is a dynamite accompaniment to any simple fish dish. It's also a great cocktail appetizer.

8 new potatoes
1 cup sour cream
1 jar (2 ounces) black or red caviar

Peel potatoes and boil in lightly salted water for 15 to 20 minutes or until done. Drain. Slice a thin piece from the bottom of each. Scoop a little out of the top of each with a melon baller. Fill the cavities with a little sour cream and a dab of caviar.

Yield: 4 servings.

Orange Roughy with Mustard Souffle Topping

This will suit any gourmet occasion. The creamy mayonnaise topping browns and puffs like a soufflé and the mustard gives a lovely flavor.

Prep Time: 6 minutes
Cooking Time: 10 minutes

½ cup mayonnaise
½ cup Dijon mustard
1 ½ pounds orange roughy

Preheat broiler. In a small bowl mix mayonnaise and mustard. Place fish in a shallow, oven-proof pan. Spread mayonnaise mixture over it to cover completely. If you don't have enough topping make more, using equal parts mayonnaise and mustard.

Place the fish 6" below source of heat and broil until the topping puffs and browns and the fish is done, 6 to 10 minutes. If the topping browns before the fish is ready, turn off the broiler, set oven to 350°, and bake for a few minutes more. Lift the fish out of the accumulated liquid and serve hot.

Yield: 4 servings.

The Adventurous Chef: Use any firm, white-fleshed fish such as flounder, sole or catfish.

❧ Betsy's Tart ❧

This is all but instant and looks like a magazine picture. As to taste, the combination of velvety pudding and juicy, slightly tart fruit is pure sorcery.

1 baked pie crust or prepared crumb crust
1 package (3.4 ounces) instant vanilla
  pudding
1⅓ cups whole milk or half-and-half
sliced kiwifruit, strawberries and bananas

Make the pudding according to package directions, but use only 1⅓ cups milk so it will be thick. Pour it into the pie crust and arrange the sliced fresh fruit on top.

Yield: 6 to 8 servings.

The Adventurous Chef: Use any flavor pudding: chocolate, lemon, or pistachio. Top with other fruits. For the Fourth of July what about blueberries, strawberries and bananas? Kiwi fruit and pears, with a dusting of coconut and cinnamon, would be delicious after an Indian meal.

The Skinny Chef: Use low-calorie pudding on a layer of lady fingers or angelfood cake instead of pie crust.

Shrimp Scorpio Style

Feta cheese and tomatoes are the key to the glorious flavor of this dish. The feta melts into the sauce, giving a creamy texture and rich flavor. We like it over pasta, but you could serve it with rice or bulgur wheat as well.

Prep Time: 15 minutes
Cooking Time: 25 minutes

4 tablespoons fruity olive oil, divided

1 teaspoon finely chopped garlic

2 cups chopped tomatoes, canned or fresh

½ cup dry white wine

¼ cup basil leaves, chopped finely

1 teaspoon dried oregano

1 ½ pounds medium shrimp, peeled and deveined

⅛ teaspoon hot red pepper flakes

8 ounces crumbled feta cheese

salt and pepper to taste

cooked fusilli, rigatoni or other short, sturdy pasta, as an accompaniment

Preheat oven to 400°. In a 10" skillet, heat 2 tablespoons of the oil and add the garlic. Cook over medium heat for only a second or two—if it gets brown it will be bitter. Add the tomatoes and cook for 1 minute. Add the wine, basil, oregano, and salt and pepper to taste. Cook over medium heat for 10 minutes.

Sprinkle the shrimp with salt and pepper. Heat the remaining oil in a large skillet and add the shrimp. Cook for 1 minute or just until the shrimp turn pink. Sprinkle with red pepper flakes.

Spoon the shrimp and any pan juices into a baking dish that holds them in no more than two layers. Top with the feta cheese, then the tomato sauce. Bake for 10 minutes or until hot and bubbling and the cheese is melted. Spoon shrimp over hot pasta.

Yield: 4 servings

The Clever Chef: Except in summer when you have red-ripe tomatoes, canned are best for this dish. I snip them up with kitchen scissors while they are still in the can.

Parmesan · Cheese Bread

1 loaf (1 pound) crusty French or Italian bread
½ teaspoon finely minced garlic (optional)
⅓ cup olive oil
⅓ cup grated Parmesan cheese

Preheat oven to 450°. Split bread horizontally. Add garlic to the oil, if desired. Brush cut sides of the bread with equal amounts of the oil. Sprinkle each with half the cheese. Arrange on a baking sheet, cut sides up, and bake for 10 minutes.

Yield: 4 servings.

Scallops Provençal

Tomato and garlic are enhanced with butter in this dish, resulting in a rich texture and heady flavor. Heaped on thick pieces of toasted French or Italian bread, it makes a wonderful meal with salad, black Mediterranean olives and white wine.

Prep Time: 10 minutes
Cooking Time: 25 minutes

1 pound scallops
2 tomatoes, peeled, seeded and coarsely chopped, canned or fresh
8 tablespoons butter, divided
4 teaspoons chopped garlic, divided
6 tablespoons chopped shallots, divided
4 thick slices French or Italian bread
olive oil
salt and pepper to taste

🍂 Scallop Alert 🍂

The little crescent-shaped muscle on the side of sea scallops is like pure rubber when you bite into it. It takes just a second to remove it and makes the scallop a lot nicer to eat.

Preheat oven to 400°. If you are using sea scallops (the large ones), cut each in half horizontally.

Place the tomatoes in a heavy pan with 6 tablespoons of the butter. Add salt and pepper. Simmer uncovered for 10 minutes. Add 3 teaspoons of the garlic and 4 tablespoons of the shallots. Simmer for another 3 minutes.

In another heavy pan or skillet heat the remaining butter until it is quite hot. Add the scallops. Cook over high heat, stirring often, for 3 to 4 minutes or until the scallops turn opaque. Don't overcook or they will be tough. Add the remaining teaspoon of garlic and 2 tablespoons of shallots.

Brush the bread slices with a little olive oil, place them on a baking sheet and bake for 4 to 5 minutes or until lightly browned and crusty. Place a piece of toast on each plate. Using half the sauce, spoon equal amounts on each toast. Top with the scallops, then the remaining sauce. Serve piping hot.

Yield: 4 servings.

The Adventurous Chef: Make Snails Provençal by substituting 2 cans of snails (each holding about 18) for the scallops.

Fire and Ice Avocado Crab Tart

Hot, creamy sauce poured over a baked tart shell heaped with cold crab and avocado equals fire and ice. The contrasts of flavor, texture and temperature are utterly seductive in this wonderful summer dish.

Prep Time: 8 minutes
Cooking Time: 10 minutes

2 ripe avocados
2 tablespoons lemon juice, divided
1 tablespoon minced green onion
1 tablespoon minced parsley
1 teaspoon salt
¾ cup lump crabmeat
1 9" baked pie crust
3 tablespoons butter
¼ cup minced onion
3 tablespoons flour
1 cup chicken broth
½ cup half-and-half
1 teaspoon soy sauce
1 teaspoon Worcestershire sauce
6 tablespoons Parmesan cheese

In a small bowl mash 1 of the avocados and add 1 tablespoon of the lemon juice with the green onion, parsley and salt. Mix gently. Fold in the crab. Spoon the mixture into the pie shell. Slice the second avocado and arrange it on top. Sprinkle with 1 tablespoon of lemon juice. Set aside.

Preheat the broiler.

In a small saucepan melt the butter. Sauté the onion until softened. Add flour and stir and cook for 1 to 2 minutes. Whisk in the stock, half-and-half, soy sauce and Worcestershire sauce. Cook and stir until thickened. Taste and adjust the seasoning if necessary.

When you are ready to serve, pour the hot sauce over the tart. Sprinkle with Parmesan. Run the tart under the broiler for 30 to 60 seconds—just long enough to melt the cheese. Serve immediately.

Yield: 4 to 6 servings.

The Adventurous Chef: Substitute shrimp, cooked ham or chicken for the crab—whatever you have that you want to turn into witchery.

Mackerel with Rosemary and Garlic

I learned this from Marcella Hazan and it's just plain wonderful. The fish soaks up garlic, rosemary and lemon flavors as it cooks. When you eat it, arm yourself with lots of crusty bread so you can mop up every bit of the juices.

Prep Time: 6 minutes
Cooking Time: 15 minutes

2 whole mackerel or croakers, 1 pound each, cleaned and pan-ready
¼ cup olive oil
3 cloves garlic, peeled
1 teaspoon dried rosemary, crumbled
2 tablespoons lemon juice
1 teaspoon salt
½ teaspoon freshly ground pepper
lemon wedges as a garnish

Wash the fish under cold running water and pat dry with paper towels.

Heat the oil in a 10" skillet over medium heat. Add the whole garlic cloves and the rosemary. Sauté until the garlic colors lightly.

Add the fish to the pan. Brown one side, sprinkle with salt and pepper, and turn to brown the second side. When both sides are browned, add the lemon juice.

Lower the heat to medium-low. Cover the pan tightly. Cook about 6 minutes, uncover, turn the fish, cover and cook 5 to 6 minutes more.

Yield: 2 servings.

❧ It's Olive Oil ❧

Agreed, this dish isn't low-fat, but consider that the fat here is olive oil, which is credited with lowering heart-disease rates in the Mediterranean. Another thought—the fatty acids in fish are also considered healthful. So enjoy.

Fish in Coconut Curry

These are wonderful flavors: coconut, garlic, hot peppers, ginger, curry. As they say, what's not to like? For festive occasions use large shrimp.

Prep Time: 10 minutes
Cooking Time: 12 minutes

¼ cup butter or margarine

1 cup chopped onion

3 large garlic cloves, minced

1 jalapeño pepper, minced

1 tablespoon grated fresh ginger

2 teaspoons paprika

2 tablespoons curry powder

8 plum tomatoes, peeled, seeded and cubed, canned or fresh

1 cup clam juice or chicken broth

½ cup canned sweetened coconut cream

1 teaspoon grated lemon rind

1½ pounds flounder, catfish, halibut or monkfish fillets cut into 2" squares

salt and pepper to taste

cooked rice as an accompaniment

In a large skillet melt the butter and sauté the onion, garlic, jalapeño, ginger, and spices with salt and pepper to taste until the onion is soft and transparent. Add the tomatoes, clam juice, coconut cream and lemon rind. Stir well and bring the mixture to a boil. Add the fish, cover and simmer 5 minutes per half inch of thickness, turning the pieces once. Serve over rice.

Yield: 4 servings.

The Clever Chef: Coconut cream is the stuff used in piña coladas. You'll find it with drink mixes in the grocery store. Don't confuse it with unsweetened coconut milk, which is sold in the Oriental section. The recipe needs the added sweetness.

The Adventurous Chef: If you use shrimp in this dish, cook them for 3 to 5 minutes or until they turn pink.

❧ Rice Tips ❧

Don't get nervous about whether your rice will be ready too early. Rice holds up to an hour with no problem.

Don't throw out leftover rice. In fact, you might consider making twice what you will eat in one meal and freezing the extra in a plastic bag. When you want to serve it give it 3 or 4 minutes in the microwave and it's as good as freshly made.

Look What You Can Do with Ice Cream, Sherbet and Frozen Yogurt!

Make a Topping

Fruit Toppings

Pineapple Mint: Drain a 9-ounce can of crushed pineapple. Mix with 2 tablespoons crème de menthe or melted mint jelly.

Melba: Thaw a 12-ounce package of frozen raspberries. Whirl in blender or processor and strain. Add 3 tablespoons of sugar. Place in a saucepan over medium heat until sugar dissolves, then boil rapidly for 3 minutes. Cool. Makes 1 cup.

Hot Raspberry: When we lived in Germany a few years ago, this was a popular dessert. Ladle hot Melba Sauce over vanilla ice cream. The sauce turns the surface into a gooey, pink-swirled sauce.

Oriental: Cut up undrained preserved kumquats. Super on chocolate ice cream.

Peach: Frozen or sweetened sliced fresh peaches.

Fruit-Pie Filling: Canned pineapple, cherry, peach, blueberry—season with a little cinnamon or nutmeg.

1000 and One Nights: Moisten chopped dates with honey thinned with a little hot water or orange juice.

Easy Orange: Top chocolate or vanilla with thawed, orange juice concentrate.

Summer Fruit: Equal parts orange segments, sliced bananas, blueberries.

Other Toppings

Hot Caramel: Melt ½ pound caramels with 2 tablespoons water over hot water.

Mincemeat: This always topped off our Christmas dinner when we lived in Africa. Add a little brandy or rum to bottled mincemeat to loosen it up. Heat it and serve hot on vanilla ice cream. You'll never go back to plum pudding and pumpkin pie.

Liqueurs: Cointreau, crème de menthe, crème de cacao, or any coffee or fruit flavored liqueurs. Amaretto is lovely. Suit the flavor to the ice cream.

Maple Rum: Top coffee ice cream with hot maple syrup flavored with rum or rum extract.

Chocolate Mint: Melt thin chocolate mints over hot water.

Tropical: Add coconut, golden raisins and nuts to commercial butterscotch sauce.

Coconut Snowballs: Roll balls of ice cream in coconut, top with chocolate syrup. For a party, add a spoonful of anisette and set it on fire.

Ginger: Ginger marmalade or chopped preserved ginger in syrup.

Oreo and Friends: Crushed Oreos, coconut bars or macaroons.

Make a Parfait

Use This Ice Cream	Layer in a Parfait Glass With	Top With Whipped Cream and...
Chocolate Cinnamon: To softened chocolate ice cream add cinnamon to taste.	Chocolate fudge sauce.	A sprinkle of cinnamon.
Two-Tone Cherry: To softened vanilla ice cream add a little juice from a can of black cherries. Fold in some chopped cherries.	Pistachio ice cream.	A whole cherry or chopped nuts.
Mocha: Coffee ice cream.	Chocolate fudge sauce.	A few chocolate-covered coffee beans.
Strawberry: Vanilla ice cream.	Thawed frozen strawberries.	A berry.
Blueberry: Vanilla ice cream.	Blueberry sauce.	Whole blueberries.

❦ Brie with Almonds and Raspberries ❦

This is an elegant dessert, pretty and drop-dead delicious: warm, oozy Brie under a layer of toasty almonds with a fruity raspberry center.

1 wedge (12 ounces) Brie
2 tablespoons seedless red raspberry jam
1 tablespoon raspberry-flavored liqueur
   (optional)
1½ teaspoons brown sugar
3 tablespoons sliced almonds
1 tablespoon light honey
crisp cookies as an accompaniment

Preheat the oven to 350°. Cut the Brie in half horizontally and place the bottom half on an ovenproof serving plate. In a small bowl com-bine the jam and optional liqueur. Spread the mixture on the cheese half, leaving a 1" margin around the edge. Put on the top. Sprinkle with brown sugar and almonds and drizzle with honey. Bake for 4 to 5 minutes or until the cheese is soft. Serve immediately with the cookies.

Yield: 4 to 6 servings.

The Social Chef: This is also a lovely hors d'oeuvre. Serve it with fancy unflavored crackers.

Risotto with Shrimp and Tomatoes

How can I persuade you to stop everything and prepare this dish? The rice is creamy, richly flavored, and spoons up soft and warm. The shrimp, tomatoes, peas and tinge of garlic make it pure sensuous pleasure.

Prep Time: 10 minutes
Cooking Time: 25 minutes

3½ to 4 cups chicken broth
1 tablespoon olive oil
1 clove garlic, pressed
8 ounces raw shrimp, shelled and deveined
¾ to 1 cup plum tomatoes, peeled, seeded and chopped, canned or fresh
2 to 3 tablespoons butter
¼ cup chopped onion
2 cups arborio or long grain rice
½ cup frozen peas, thawed
¼ cup chopped basil or parsley

Put the broth in a pan and bring to a boil over high heat. Turn heat to low.

In a medium skillet over medium heat, heat the olive oil. Add the garlic and shrimp and cook and stir until shrimp turn pink, 1 to 2 minutes. Add the tomatoes and cook for 1 minute. Set aside.

In a 4-quart pan or 12" skillet over medium-high heat, melt 2 tablespoons of butter, add the onions and stir and cook for 2 minutes. Add the rice and stir until the grains are well coated. Reduce the heat to medium. Add ½ cup of the hot broth and stir until it is absorbed. Add another ½ cup. Cook until it is absorbed, stirring occasionally (or steadily if you need soothing. I like to stir and ponder.) Continue to add liquid in ½-cup amounts until the rice has lost its hard center. Stir in the shrimp, peas and parsley—and another tablespoon of butter if you want real luxury.

Yield: 4 servings

The Vegetarian Chef: Omit the shrimp and stir ¼ cup Parmesan cheese into the finished risotto.

Pita Wedges
with Herb Butter

⅓ cup butter, softened
1 tablespoon finely chopped parsley
1 teaspoon lemon juice
1 clove garlic, crushed
⅛ teaspoon salt
⅛ teaspoon pepper
2 6" pita rounds

Preheat oven to 350 °. In a small bowl combine butter, parsley, lemon juice, garlic, salt and pepper. Split the pita rounds to form 4 flat discs. Spread the inner sides of each with herb butter. With kitchen scissors, cut each into 6 wedges on the baking sheet. Bake for 3 minutes or until crisp. Serve warm.

Yield: 24 wedges.

Cod with Garlic-Butter Crumbs

You can use any white fish fillets—catfish, cod, flounder, sole—whatever looks good at the market. Every bite is a combination of crisp topping and moist, tender fish, and the flavors of browned butter, garlic and lemon.

Prep Time: 5 minutes
Cooking Time: 20 minutes

2 slices white bread

2 tablespoons butter or margarine

1 clove garlic

4 small cod fillets, about 6 ounces each

2 tablespoons lemon juice

¾ teaspoon salt

*parsley sprigs and lemon wedges as a
    garnish*

Preheat the oven to 450°. In the blender or processor whirl bread until you have fine crumbs. Set aside.

In a 10" skillet over medium heat, heat butter or margarine until hot. Using your garlic press, press the garlic directly into the skillet and cook until very lightly browned (don't let it turn dark brown or it will be bitter). Stir in the reserved bread crumbs and cook, stirring frequently, until the crumbs are very lightly toasted. Remove the skillet from the heat (the crumbs will continue to fry for a minute, even off the heat).

In a 9" x 13" glass baking dish arrange the fillets. Sprinkle them with lemon juice and salt. Press the crumb mixture on top. Bake, uncovered, for 10 to 15 minutes, until the fish is starting to flake when you test it with a fork.

Garnish the fish with parsley sprigs and lemon wedges.

Yield: 4 servings.

✿ Sesame Broccoli ✿

1 medium bunch broccoli
*⅓ cup sesame seeds, toasted quickly in a
    hot, dry skillet*
3 tablespoons sake or dry sherry
1 tablespoon soy sauce
1¼ teaspoons sesame oil
1½ teaspoons honey

Cook broccoli in boiling salted water until crisp-tender, 5 to 8 minutes. Drain thoroughly and let cool to room temperature. In a medium bowl mix sesame seeds, sake, soy sauce, sesame oil and honey. When broccoli is tepid, add it to the bowl of seasonings and mix well to coat. Serve at room temperature.

Yield: 4 servings.

Mussels Marinières

When we lived in Brussels every restaurant served Moules Marinières—some served only that. They came in a huge pot accompanied by a bowl of the best French fries you'd ever taste, a green salad, and of course, bread to sop up the juices your soup spoon missed.

Prep Time: 12 minutes
Cooking Time: 8 minutes

3 to 4 pounds mussels, scrubbed
3 tablespoons butter
½ cup thinly sliced onion
1 clove garlic, pressed
1 rib celery, sliced
1 cup vermouth
½ cup minced parsley
⅛ teaspoon dried thyme
⅛ teaspoon pepper

Discard any mussels that don't close when you tap them with your finger. Tear off the fibers around the shells.

Melt the butter in a 4 to 6 quart pot, over medium heat. Add onion, garlic and celery and cook, stirring occasionally, until softened, about 2 to 3 minutes. Add wine, parsley, thyme and pepper and bring to a boil over high heat. Add the mussels. Lower the heat, cover the pot and simmer until the mussels open, about 5 minutes. Discard any that don't open.

With a slotted spoon transfer the mussels to individual serving bowls and give everyone a share of the cooking broth.

Yield: 4 servings.

The Adventurous Chef For **Thai-Style Mussels**, omit butter, thyme and celery. Bring wine, onion and garlic to a boil. Add mussels and cook as above. Separately mix one 14-ounce can unsweetened coconut milk and 3 to 4 tablespoons Thai red curry paste (or 1 tablespoon minced fresh ginger, 1 teaspoon curry powder and 1 teaspoon chili powder). Lift mussels out into soup bowls and stir coconut mixture into the pot. Add ¼ cup slivered fresh basil leaves and heat to simmering. Ladle onto the mussels. ♦ **American Style:** Use clams in the shell instead of mussels.

❧ Ginger Iced Tea ❧

5 tea bags
1½ cups sugar
¾ cup lemon juice
1 tablespoon vanilla extract
1 teaspoon almond extract
1 quart chilled ginger ale

Put the tea bags in a pan or bowl and pour 1 cup boiling water over them. Cover and steep for 5 minutes. Remove the tea bags, squeezing them gently to get out all the flavor. Stir in sugar, lemon juice, vanilla and almond extracts and 4 cups water. Chill if you have time. Before serving stir in the ginger ale. Serve in tall glasses over ice.

Yield: 3 quarts.

Easy Stuffed Shrimp

Better than easy, these crab-topped shrimp are moist, buttery and delicious.

Prep Time: 15 minutes
Cooking Time: 20 minutes

12 jumbo shrimp, shelled and deveined

1½ cups soft breadcrumbs

1 tablespoon chopped parsley

*½ teaspoon chopped fresh garlic or
⅛ teaspoon garlic powder*

*1¼ cups fresh or canned crabmeat, flaked
(6 ounces)*

3 tablespoons melted butter or olive oil

2 tablespoons sherry or dry vermouth

Preheat the oven to 450°.

Rinse shrimp, pat dry with paper towels. Split the shrimp down the inside of the curve, cutting not quite through so you can spread them out butterfly fashion. Arrange them in a greased 9" x 13" baking dish. In a bowl combine bread crumbs, parsley, garlic, crabmeat, melted butter and sherry. Place an equal portion of stuffing on each shrimp. Bake for 20 minutes or until shrimp are opaque and the stuffing lightly browned.

Yield: 4 servings.

The Adventurous Chef: Because jumbo shrimp are so expensive, I often use large shrimp instead. If you do this, you have to bake them a little differently to compensate for their relative thinness. Place shrimp close together, overlapping the thin ends, and pat the topping over the entire surface. This way they will stay juicy. ♦ The crab topping is also delicious on fish fillets. Bake them for 15 to 20 minutes, depending on the thickness of the fish.

Some Quick Potato Ideas

Canned tiny whole potatoes, sitting there ready-cooked on your pantry shelf, can be surprisingly good in a pinch. My father, who never went a day without eating potatoes, loved them sliced and fried golden with a big sprinkle of coarsely ground pepper.

Parsley Potatoes: Drain a 1-pound can of tiny whole potatoes. Dry thoroughly with paper towels. Cook gently in 2 to 3 tablespoons butter and 1 to 2 tablespoons chopped parsley until the potatoes are heated through and well coated with parsley butter. Salt and pepper them well.

Oregano Sautéed Potatoes: Prepare the same as Parsley Potatoes but substitute 2 teaspoons dried oregano for the parsley and sauté them until they are golden brown and slightly crisp.

Oven-Fried Fish with Two Sauces

These sizzle nicely in the oven and get a golden crust on the bottom; the sauces are just right to show the fish off. Don't miss the avocado sauce—it has the fresh, bright taste of gazpacho.

Prep Time: 15 minutes
Cooking Time: 10 minutes

1 ½ pounds lean fish fillets such as catfish
¾ cup dry breadcrumbs
¾ teaspoon paprika
1 teaspoon chopped fresh dill weed or
    ¼ teaspoon dried
½ teaspoon salt
⅛ teaspoon pepper
⅓ cup milk
¼ cup butter or margarine, melted

Avocado Sauce:

1 large avocado, peeled and chopped
    coarsely
2 medium tomatoes, peeled and chopped
    coarsely
½ green pepper, coarsely chopped
2 cloves garlic
1 teaspoon tomato paste
1 teaspoon salt
⅛ teaspoon pepper

Chutney Sauce:

½ cup sour cream
⅓ cup mayonnaise
3 tablespoons minced mango chutney
2 tablespoons lemon juice
hot pepper sauce, to taste

Place the oven rack slightly above the center. Preheat the oven to 500°.

Cut each fillet into several pieces. On a piece of wax paper mix crumbs, paprika, dill, salt and pepper. Pour the milk into a plate. Dip the fish in the milk, then coat with the crumb mixture. Place in a shallow 13"x 9" pan. Drizzle melted butter over the fish. Bake uncovered for 10 minutes or until the fish just starts to flake when you test it with a fork.

Place the Avocado Sauce ingredients in the blender and purée until smooth.

In a small bowl, mix the Chutney Sauce ingredients.

Place the fish on a platter and serve hot. Serve the sauces separately.

Yield: 4 servings.

Crumbed Oysters

O ysters are delicious in crispy, buttery crumbs. For a party, bake them in individual scallop shells.

Prep Time: 10 minutes
Cooking Time: 15 minutes

¼ cup butter, divided

¾ cup soft breadcrumbs (about 2 slices)

¾ teaspoon chopped garlic

3 tablespoons minced parsley, plus more for garnishing

24 oysters, shucked

1 tablespoon grated Parmesan cheese

Preheat oven to 400°.

In a heavy skillet over medium heat, melt 2 tablespoons of the butter. Add the crumbs and garlic and toss for 2 to 3 minutes or until golden. Stir in 3 tablespoons of parsley. Spread ⅔ of the crumb mixture in a shallow, greased ovenproof glass dish or 4 scallop shells. Top with the oysters.

Mix the Parmesan cheese with the remaining crumb mixture and pat over the oysters. Cut the remaining butter into small pieces and dot them over all. Bake on the top shelf of the oven for 10 to 15 minutes, depending on the size of the oysters, until the juices are bubbling. Sprinkle with parsley and serve piping hot.

Yield: 4 servings.

❧ Pears in Chocolate Fluff ❧

Ever since a chef was inspired by la Belle Hélène, whoever she was, pears and chocolate have been a favorite combination. This one is special—pear cubes in a fluff of chocolate cream made crunchy with toasted almonds.

1 can (29 ounces) pear halves

½ cup semisweet chocolate chips

¼ cup light corn syrup

½ teaspoon vanilla

1 cup thawed frozen whipped dessert topping

¼ cup sour cream

½ cup slivered almonds, toasted

Drain pear halves well. Cut them into large pieces and set aside. In a small saucepan combine chocolate chips and corn syrup. Heat, stirring constantly, just until chocolate melts. Stir in vanilla and set aside to cool to lukewarm. Stir together the whipped topping and sour cream. Fold in the cooled chocolate mixture, the pears and ⅓ cup of the almonds. Spoon the fluff into dessert dishes and chill well. Garnish with remaining almonds.

Yield: 4 servings.

Italian Seafood Stew

S eafood stew is an aromatic mix of tomatoes, onion, garlic, basil and thyme. Like most good recipes, this one need not be followed slavishly—use whatever seafood is available or suits your mood.

Prep Time: 15 minutes
Cooking Time: 30 minutes

1 tablespoon olive oil

1 cup chopped fennel or celery

1½ cups chopped onion

4 large cloves garlic

1 can (14 to 16 ounces) tomatoes with juice, cut up

⅓ cup tomato paste

¾ cup vermouth

¾ cup chicken broth or bottled clam juice

2 teaspoons dried basil

1 teaspoon dried thyme

¼ teaspoon red pepper flakes

4 littleneck clams, scrubbed

4 ounces white fish fillet, cut in 1" cubes

4 ounces sea scallops

4 ounces medium shrimp, peeled and deveined

salt to taste

crusty French bread or cooked pasta or rice as an accompaniment

In a medium Dutch oven or stew pot heat the oil over medium heat. Add fennel, onion and garlic and cook, stirring occasionally, for 6 to 8 minutes or until onion is transparent.

Add the tomatoes, tomato paste, vermouth, broth, basil, thyme and red pepper flakes. Cook over medium heat for 5 minutes. Add the clams, cover and cook over medium low heat for 5 minutes. Add fish cubes, scallops and shrimps. Cook 5 to 7 minutes more. The clams should be open, the fish firm but not rubbery. Taste for salt. Serve the stew in large shallow soup bowls with crusty French bread or over pasta or rice.

Yield: 4 servings.

The Adventurous Chef: Instead of mixed seafood, use 36 clams in the shell. Increase the 5 minutes cooking time to 10 before adding them, then cook covered until they open. ♦ To make an all-fish stew, add 5 minutes to the initial cooking time and use 1½ pounds fish fillets, cubed. Continue as in the recipe. ♦ To make a real feast, serve the stew with Aioli (p. 216) or Skordalia (p. 209) and oven-toasted, ¼" slices of French bread. Heap a little sauce on the toast and munch with the soup.

The Pantry-Shelf Chef: For the seafood substitute two 7½-ounce cans of clams. Increase the cooking time after the tomatoes are added from 5 minutes to 15. Add clams and their juice and cook uncovered only until all is well heated.

Tuna Rockefeller

This delectable quickie is right off the pantry shelf. Neither the tuna, the spinach nor the cheese dominates—they just make each other taste better. The chewy texture is pure delight. Everyone will love this, including the kids.

Prep Time: 6 minutes
Cooking Time: 20 minutes

2 cans (7 ounces) solid water-packed tuna
2 packages (10 ounces) frozen chopped
  spinach, thawed
⅔ cup mayonnaise
½ cup chicken-flavored stuffing mix
¼ cup Parmesan cheese
yogurt as an accompaniment

Preheat the oven to 350°. Drain and flake the tuna. Press any extra liquid out of the spinach.

In a medium bowl, combine all the ingredients. Place the mixture in a buttered 9" pie plate. Bake for 20 minutes. Pass a bowl of yogurt to serve as a sauce.

Yield: 4 servings.

Peach Cream with Sherry Caramel Sauce

Fresh peaches are warmed in a thick, sherry-flavored caramel and topped off with whipped cream that melts into the caramel in a heavenly fashion.

4 fresh peaches
¾ cup bottled caramel sauce
½ cup sweet sherry
whipped cream or ice cream as an
  accompaniment

Plunge the peaches into rapidly boiling water for 20 seconds. Remove and slip off the peels. In a small saucepan heat the caramel sauce and the sherry over medium heat until it reaches a

boil. Let it bubble over low heat for 1 minute. Add the peach halves and turn them over several times, spooning the sauce over them so they warm and soak up some of the flavor.

Serve warm or at room temperature in glass dishes with plenty of sauce. Top with whipped cream or vanilla ice cream or pass a bowl of whipped cream at the table.

Yield: 4 servings.

Try Poultry Tonight

*T*his chapter is jammed with delectable tastes, textures and combinations. Chicken's mild taste makes it friendly to every flavor and sauce it meets: light, rich, spicy or delicate. This chapter pairs chicken with almonds and dates, with ginger, with cheese and sherry, with garlic and lemon, with orange. To ease the bother of choosing dinner when your brain refuses to make one more decision, I tossed some fun tables in among the standard recipe pages. They give you easy and imaginative ways to prepare grilled chicken fillets, chicken scallops, and stir-fries. Chicken breasts are dear to the heart of the quick cook, but boned thighs and cut-up wings cook almost as fast. You can use them instead of chicken breasts in most recipes for a change of pace and texture. The same with Cornish game hens. If you cut them in half, neck to tail, and flatten them gently with your hand, you can use them in any of the recipes. You'll have to add 5 to 10 minutes to the cooking, though, so this wouldn't be for your fast-as-a-speeding-arrow nights. For nights when you are running late, there are recipes to turn rotisserie chickens from the deli into gourmet dishes that taste like hours of loving care.

"Chicken's mild flavor makes it friendly to every flavor and sauce it meets: light, rich, spicy or delicate. Be sure to check the tables for dozens of quick recipes."

Chicken with Rosemary

A light dish, heady with rosemary and garlic. Serve it with rice or small pasta, a crunchy salad and chewy French bread.

Prep Time: 15 minutes
Standing Time: 30 minutes
Cooking Time: 20 minutes

9 teaspoons fruity olive oil, divided

2 large cloves garlic

3 3" sprigs of rosemary or 1¼ teaspoons dried, plus ½ teaspoon minced leaves or ¼ teaspoon dried

4 skinless, boneless chicken breast halves, pounded ½" thick (see box on p. 50)

¼ cup minced shallots

⅓ cup dry vermouth

3 tablespoons chicken broth

1 teaspoon Dijon mustard

¼ teaspoon freshly ground black pepper

¼ cup whipping cream

salt to taste

Rub 2 teaspoons of the oil on the bottom of a dish that can hold the chicken in two layers. Cut the garlic cloves into thin, lengthwise slivers and the rosemary sprigs into 1" pieces. Scatter ⅓ of the garlic and rosemary in the dish. Top with half the chicken. Repeat: oil, garlic, rosemary, chicken. Top with 2 teaspoons oil and the remaining garlic and rosemary sprigs. Cover with plastic wrap and set aside to marinate for 30 minutes.

Heat 3 teaspoons (1 tablespoon) of oil in a skillet over medium-high heat. Add shallots and minced rosemary. Cook and stir until golden, about 2 minutes. Lift out the shallot mixture and set aside.

Raise the heat to high. Add the marinated chicken breasts and brown lightly on both sides, about 2 minutes per side. Remove the chicken to a plate. Add the vermouth, scrape up the browned bits, and boil until the wine has reduced to a thickish glaze, 2 to 3 minutes. Return the shallots and rosemary to the skillet. Stir in the broth, mustard and pepper. Boil, stirring, for 2 to 3 minutes or until the sauce is reduced by two thirds. Add the cream. Boil again to reduce the sauce by half, about 2 minutes. Taste and add salt. Return the chicken to the pan along with any accumulated juices. Cook over medium-low until chicken is warmed, spooning the sauce steadily over the top, 1 to 2 minutes.

Yield: 4 servings.

Quick Broth for Recipes

When a recipe calls for broth I often use water and chicken bouillon granules which come in a little jar. It is quick and the results are good. This is especially handy in recipes that call for a small quantity.

Chicken Breasts with Sesame and Green Chilies

Cinnamon and clove season this wonderful sauce of onions, green chilies and sesame seeds. Serve with rice or polenta.

Prep Time: 5 minutes
Cooking Time: 20 minutes

2 tablespoons olive oil

4 skinless, boneless chicken breast halves

1½ cups thinly sliced onion

2 tablespoons chopped parsley

1 tablespoon sesame seeds

1 1" stick cinnamon

⅛ teaspoon ground cloves

1 bay leaf

1 tablespoon cider vinegar

⅓ cup dry sherry

*2 whole canned green chilies (mild or hot)
    cut into strips*

salt and pepper to taste

In a skillet over high heat, heat the oil. Brown the chicken breasts lightly, about 2 minutes per side. Remove them to a platter and season with salt and pepper. To the skillet add the onion, parsley, sesame seeds, cinnamon stick, cloves, and bay leaf. Stir over medium heat until the onions are nicely coated with oil and spices. Cover and cook over medium-low heat until the onion is transparent and very soft, 10 to 12 minutes. Stir several times. Add vinegar, sherry, and chilies. Raise the heat to high and cook, stirring, until most of the liquid is gone, 4 to 5 minutes. Season with salt and pepper to taste, then add the chicken and any accumulated juices. Cook over medium-low heat, basting continuously with the onion mixture, until the chicken is heated through.

Yield: 4 servings

❧ Carrots and Broccoli Supreme ❧

This is very pretty, a perfect companion for a delicate chicken breast or fish entrée.

2 cups carrots cut on the bias in ¼" slices

2 cups broccoli florets

½ cup olive oil

¼ cup white wine vinegar

*2 teaspoons chopped fresh basil or
    ½ teaspoon dried*

salt and pepper to taste

Drop carrots into 1 cup of boiling, salted water. Cover. Steam for 5 minutes. Remove cover. Add broccoli and cook uncovered for another 5 minutes. Drain well. Immediately toss with oil, vinegar and basil. Add salt and pepper to taste. Serve warm or at room temperature.

Yield: 4 servings.

Fruited Saffron Pilaf

P ass a bowl of yogurt to spoon over this savory chicken pilaf, studded with raisins, bananas, pine nuts and tomatoes.

Prep Time: 10 minutes
Cooking Time: 15 minutes

1 cup rice

2 cups chicken broth

2 tablespoons golden raisins

¼ teaspoon saffron

1 medium banana, sliced

1 medium onion, sliced

2 tablespoons pine nuts or almonds

2 tablespoons oil or butter, divided

1 small clove garlic, minced

2 skinless, boneless chicken breast halves, pounded ¼" thick (see box on p. 50)

1 medium tomato, peeled, seeded and coarsely chopped

yogurt and oil-cured olives as accompaniments

Cook the rice in the broth with the raisins and saffron.

Sauté the banana, onion and pine nuts in 1 tablespoon oil until the onion softens, about 5 minutes. Add the garlic and cook, stirring, for another 2 minutes.

Brown the chicken in 1 tablespoon oil for about 1 minute per side. Cut the chicken into 1" squares. Save any juices that accumulate.

When the rice is done fold in the tomatoes, the banana-pine nut mixture and the chicken with its juices. Serve with yogurt and olives.

Yield: 3 to 4 servings.

❧ Chocolate Bar Pie ❧

This frozen pie is almost chewy before melting into a thick velvet cream. While it's almost an instant dish to prepare, it needs to freeze overnight to be perfect.

1 9" chocolate crumb or graham cracker pie crust

1 bar (7 to 8 ounces) milk chocolate

1 teaspoon vanilla extract

1 carton (8 ounces) frozen whipped topping

Cut chocolate into pieces and melt in the top of a double boiler over hot, not boiling water. Cool. Fold chocolate and vanilla extract into whipped topping. Pour into pie shell and freeze overnight.

Yield: 6 to 8 servings.

The Adventurous Chef: Pipe or spoon whipped topping around the edges of the pie and grate chocolate over the top.

The Speedy Chef: Spoon the filling into individual serving dishes and freeze for 30 minutes. It becomes a sinfully yummy chocolate mousse.

Chicken in Green Chili Cream

T he sauce that bathes these quickly-cooked chicken breast scallops is creamy, hot and delicious. Serve the dish with rice or pasta and a crisp green salad.

Prep Time: 10 minutes
Cooking Time: 20 minutes

2 tablespoons vegetable oil, divided

4 skinless, boneless chicken breast halves, pounded ¼" thick (see box p. 50)

⅔ cup finely chopped green pepper

⅔ cup finely chopped onion

1 large clove garlic, minced

2 tablespoons chopped canned green chilies

1 cup canned tomato wedges, undrained

3 ounces Neufchatel or light cream cheese, cubed

salt and pepper to taste

In a 10" skillet heat 1 tablespoon of the oil over medium-high heat and brown the breast halves lightly, about 1 minute per side. Salt and pepper them and remove to a plate as they brown.

Reduce the heat to medium-low. Add to the skillet the remaining tablespoon of oil. Sauté the green pepper, onion and garlic until softened, 3 to 4 minutes. Add the chilies and the tomatoes with their juice. Chop the tomatoes coarsely with a wooden spoon. Stir over low heat until the mixture starts to bubble. Add the cubed cheese. Stir and mash the cheese into the vegetable mixture to make a creamy sauce. Add salt and pepper to taste.

Add the chicken breasts to the skillet and spoon the sauce over them. Cover and simmer gently for 5 minutes.

Yield: 4 servings.

ﻬ Bulgur 101 ﻬ

Bulgur is cracked wheat that has been partially processed. The little grains boil up light, fluffy, moist and chewy with a delightful nutty taste. Serve it as you would rice.

2 tablespoons butter
½ cup chopped green onions
⅔ cup bulgur
1 cup boiling broth or water

In a medium saucepan melt the butter. Add the green onions and bulgur and cook and stir for 10 minutes. Add the boiling broth, cover and simmer gently for 15 minutes or until most of the liquid is absorbed. Uncover. Raise the heat to medium and stir until dry.

Yield: 4 or more servings.

Pilaf: Sauté ½ cup celery and ½ cup chopped nuts along with the bulgur. Stir 1 to 2 tablespoons raisins into the cooked bulgur.

Spiced Bulgur: Add 1 teaspoon cumin seeds, ½ teaspoon cardamom seeds, 6 crushed peppercorns, 1½ teaspoon crushed coriander seeds and 2 teaspoons grated orange peel to the broth. Boil for 3 minutes *before* adding to the bulgur mixture.

Chicken Scallops with Portobello Mushrooms and Cheese

These juicy chicken scallops are topped with fat, meaty portobello mushrooms under a blanket of melting Swiss cheese.

Prep Time: 5 minutes
Cooking Time: 15 minutes

4 skinless, boneless chicken breast halves, pounded ⅓" thick (see box)

4 tablespoons butter, divided

8 to 10 ounces portobello mushrooms, thickly sliced

1 tablespoon fresh lemon juice

¼ cup dry sherry

4 to 8 thin slices Swiss cheese, or enough to cover chicken

salt and pepper to taste

Preheat the oven to 350°.

In a 10" skillet, sauté the chicken scallops in 1 tablespoon of the butter over medium-high heat until lightly browned, about 1 minute per side. Salt the pieces and place them in a shallow ovenproof dish. Don't overlap.

Sauté the mushrooms in the remaining butter over medium heat for 2 to 3 minutes. Add the lemon juice and salt and pepper to taste. Cook, stirring gently, for 1 to 2 minutes. Add the sherry and bring the mixture to a boil. Ladle the mushroom sauce over the chicken. Top pieces with overlapping slices of cheese to cover each completely. Bake uncovered until cheese is melted, 4 or 5 minutes.

Yield: 4 servings.

❧ Chicken Scallops ☙

You can buy veal, turkey and pork already cut into thin scallops, but chicken breast halves need to be flattened. Here's how: Place a breast half between sheets of waxed paper or plastic wrap. Whack it with the flat part of a wide knife blade or the bottom of a small skillet until it is ¼" thick, or whatever thickness the recipe calls for.

Chicken Breasts Moroccan Style

My friend Monique, a beautiful French woman who grew up in Morocco, served this chicken stuffed with spiced couscous, ground almonds, raisins and dates. I had to have the recipe. She kindly obliged and our guests have enjoyed it ever since.

Prep Time: 15 minutes
Cooking Time: 30 minutes
Standing Time: 10 minutes

⅓ cup couscous

1 tablespoon plus 1 teaspoon butter, divided

1 teaspoon honey

¾ cup ground almonds

¾ cup golden raisins

⅛ teaspoon ginger

⅛ teaspoon nutmeg

⅛ teaspoon allspice

⅛ teaspoon cumin

⅛ teaspoon cinnamon

3 medium onions, sliced

4 boneless chicken breast halves with the skin intact

8 to 10 dates, pitted

¼ cup chicken broth or water

salt to taste

Bring ⅔ cup water to a boil in a small pan. Add the couscous, salt, 1 teaspoon of the butter, and cook for 2 minutes. Cover and let it stand for 10 minutes. Mix the couscous with the honey, ground almonds, raisins, the spices, and salt and pepper to taste. Set aside. Preheat the oven to 400°.

In a large skillet over high heat, brown the onions in 1 tablespoon butter until golden, 5 to 8 minutes. Season them with salt and pepper. (Add a light sprinkle of the spices used for the couscous if you like.)

Push as much couscous stuffing under the skin of each breast half as will fit easily. Use the remaining couscous to stuff the dates.

Place the sautéed onions in a shallow, ovenproof dish that will hold the chicken in one layer. Place the chicken on the onions and poke the stuffed dates into the empty spaces. Pour the chicken broth around the breasts. Bake for 30 minutes or until the breasts are golden brown and done.

Yield: 4 servings.

❧ Menu ❧

Chicken Breasts Moroccan Style

Green Salad with Sliced Oranges

Bananas in Yogurt

Chicken Stir-Fries You May Not Have Tried

All recipes are for 1 pound boneless, skinless chicken or turkey breast cut in strips or 1" cubes. You can also make these recipes using boneless beef, pork, lamb, or raw whole shrimp, shelled and deveined. Use the same amounts. Serve the stir-fries with rice, pasta, couscous, bulgur wheat, polenta, flour tortillas or pita pockets. All recipes serve 4.

The Basic Steps:	Mix and reserve for use in Column 4:	Heat 2 tablespoons oil in wok or skillet. Add poultry. Stir-fry over high heat for 4 minutes. Salt and pepper. Then add:	Stir the sauce from column 1 and add it along with the items below. Cook and stir until thickened. Check seasonings.
Oriental BBQ *An irresistible sweet-sour combination.*	½ cup hoisin sauce; 2 tablespoons balsamic vinegar; 2 teaspoons brown sugar; ¼ teaspoon garlic powder; ¼ teaspoon black pepper; 2 teaspoons cornstarch; 3 tablespoons water.	1 green pepper in strips; 1 large onion, sliced; 1 large carrot, sliced thin. Stir-fry 3 to 4 minutes.	Add 2 cups coarsely chopped cabbage. Cook until cabbage is bright green and heated through.
Indian Curry *Has few vegetables, so add one to the meal.*	½ cup chicken broth; 2 tablespoons chopped chutney; 2 teaspoons cornstarch.	2 cloves garlic, minced. Fry 30 seconds. Add 1-2 teaspoons curry powder; 1 large sweet red pepper cut in strips. Stir-fry 3 minutes.	Serve with rice, yogurt and maybe a dish of lentils.
Mexican *Loads of chili flavors along with black beans and sour cream.*	½ cup chicken broth; 2 teaspoons cornstarch. Rub 2-3 tablespoons chili powder into the raw chicken.	1 cup corn; 2 tomatoes, diced. Stir-fry 2 minutes.	1 cup canned black beans, drained and rinsed. Serve with sour cream, tortillas and salsa.

The Basic Steps:	Mix and reserve for use in Column 4:	Heat 2 tablespoons oil in wok or skillet. Add poultry. Stir-fry over high heat for 4 minutes. Salt and pepper. Then add:	Stir the sauce from column 1 and add it along with the items below. Cook and stir until thickened. Check seasonings.
Ginger Peach *Sensational! Sliced peaches in soy and ginger sauce.*	½ cup chicken broth; 2 tablespoons soy sauce; 2 tablespoons grated ginger; 2 teapoons cornstarch; ⅛ teaspoon black pepper.	2 cloves garlic, minced; ½ cup slivered almonds. Stir-fry 1 minute.	When thickened add 3 peeled, sliced peaches; 6 green onions with tops, in 1" pieces. Heat through. Delicious!
Salad *Stir-fried chicken tossed with crisp vegetables and a sesame-flavored vinaigrette.*	3 tablespoons seasoned rice vinegar; 1 tablespoon soy sauce; ¼ teaspoon dried red pepper flakes; 2 tablespoons olive oil; ⅛ teaspoon Oriental sesame oil (optional).	½ teaspoon ginger; 1 large green onion in 2" match-sticks. Stir-fry 1 to 2 minutes.	In bowl, place 1 large head Romaine in pieces; 8 ounces blanched bean sprouts; 1 large red pepper in match-sticks; 2 bunches radishes, quartered. Top with the chicken, sprinkle with sauce. Toss.

❧ Elegant Ice Cream Dessert ❧

½ cup crumbled almond macaroons

3 tablespoons kirsch or Grand Marnier, divided

¾ cup whipping cream

1 pint vanilla ice cream, softened

⅓ cup chopped toasted blanched almonds

1 cup fresh or frozen whole strawberries

Put the macaroons in a small dish and sprinkle them with 1½ tablespoons kirsch. In a medium bowl whip the cream until stiff and beat in the remaining liqueur. In a large, chilled bowl beat the soft ice cream until it is light and forms mounds when dropped from the beaters. Quickly fold in the whipped cream, almonds and soaked macaroons.

Spoon into individual dessert glasses. Cover with plastic wrap and freeze. Thirty minutes will give you a soft set which is delightful. Freeze longer for a firm set. Garnish with whole strawberries before serving.

Yield: 6 servings.

Ginger Chicken

C hicken breast strips in a velvety garlic-ginger cream. This is delicious served with boiled new potatoes and sliced tomatoes in vinaigrette sauce.

Prep Time: 10 minutes
Standing Time: 15 minutes
Cooking Time: 10 minutes

1 teaspoon salt

¼ teaspoon freshly ground black pepper

1½ teaspoons ground ginger

1 clove garlic, crushed

2 skinless, boneless chicken breast halves

1 cup light cream

¼ cup minced parsley

Mix together the salt, pepper, ginger and garlic. Flatten the chicken breasts slightly with a rolling pin or the bottom of a heavy jar and slice them lengthwise into ½" strips. Place the chicken on wax paper and sprinkle with the seasoning mixture. Mix it well into the chicken and let it stand for 15 minutes.

In a medium skillet bring the cream to a boil. Add the chicken pieces and simmer them for 1 to 2 minutes on each side.

Remove the chicken to 4 warm plates. Boil the cream briefly to thicken it. Then pour the sauce over the chicken and sprinkle with parsley.

Yield: 4 servings.

❧ Instant Chocolate Mousse ❧

This one's not only super quick, but unlike the classic recipe, it doesn't use uncooked egg. So you can eat chocolate mousse once again!

1 can (14 ounces) sweetened condensed milk

1 package (4 ounces) instant chocolate pudding

1 cup cold water

1 cup whipping cream

Put the condensed milk, the pudding mix and water in a medium-sized mixing bowl and beat with a mixer until well combined. Chill in the freezer for 5 minutes. Whip the cream until it

makes soft peaks and fold into the pudding. Spoon into serving dishes.

Yield: 6 servings.

The Adventurous Chef: Add 2 to 3 tablespoons orange or apricot liqueur and 1 teaspoon grated orange peel. **To make a parfait:** Crush enough vanilla or chocolate wafers to make 1 cup and layer the mousse with the wafer crumbs into 6 4-ounce parfait glasses. Also, try freezing chocolate mousse when you have some left over. The texture is almost chewy.

Company Chicken Surprise

Open your foil packet and find a plump chicken breast stuffed with ham and cheese in a sauce of leeks, sherry and tarragon. This makes a great impression, and it's dead easy.

Prep Time: 10 minutes
Cooking Time: 20 minutes

4 skinless, boneless chicken breast halves

4 thin slices ham

4 thin slices Swiss cheese

2 leeks, white part with 2 inches of green, thinly sliced

4 tablespoons dry sherry

1 tablespoon fresh tarragon or 1 teaspoon dried

2 tablespoons butter

salt and pepper to taste

Preheat the oven to 350°. Slit each chicken breast horizontally, insert a slice of ham and cheese and close it up.

Blanch the leek strips in boiling water for 1 minute. Drain well.

Cut 4 pieces of foil, each large enough to enclose a breast. Divide the leeks evenly among the pieces of foil. Sprinkle with half the tarragon, top with the chicken. Sprinkle with salt and pepper and the remaining tarragon. Curl up the edges of the foil to hold the wine in and pour 1 tablespoon of sherry over each. Dot with butter. Close the packets tightly, place them on a baking sheet and bake for 20 minutes or until done. Delicious with jasmine rice.

Yield: 4 servings.

The Social Cook: When you make these for a party, you can assemble them in the afternoon. Keep refrigerated until baking time.

❧ Garlic Bread ❧

½ cup butter, softened
2 cloves garlic, mashed
¼ cup Parmesan cheese
1 loaf (1 pound) French or Italian bread

Preheat oven to 375°. Combine butter, garlic and Parmesan. Slice bread into 1" slices, cutting almost but not quite through to the bottom. Spread each cut surface with butter mixture. Wrap loaf in heavy-duty aluminum foil and bake for 15 minutes or until heated through. Serve warm.

Yield: 8 to 10 servings.

Chicken Livers on Garlic Crostini

These chicken livers are cut into small pieces so they almost melt into the rich sauce of garlic, rosemary and tomato, and are served on crisp, golden, garlicky slabs of toasted bread. Even people who don't much like chicken livers adore this dish.

Prep Time: 10 minutes
Cooking Time: 20 minutes

4 whole garlic cloves

⅓ cup olive oil

2 2" sprigs fresh rosemary or ½ teaspoon dried

1 pound chicken livers, cut into very small pieces

1 large onion, sliced thin

4 plum tomatoes, peeled, seeded and chopped, canned or fresh

½ cup white wine

4 tablespoons capers

salt and pepper to taste

Crostini (see box)

Lightly smash each garlic clove with the flat of a knife so it opens but remains whole. Heat the olive oil in a skillet over medium heat. Add the garlic and rosemary and fry until the garlic is dark gold and the oil well flavored. Discard garlic and rosemary. Add the chicken livers, onion, tomatoes and salt and pepper to taste. Cook over low heat for 15 minutes.

Add wine and capers. Raise the heat and continue cooking until the wine has evaporated. Heap the mixture on *crostini*, or serve plain with a crisp green salad.

Yield: 4 servings.

The Adventurous Chef: You can substitute mixed giblets for the chicken livers. Also, try the mixture on pasta—or rolled up in crepes, heaped on polenta or in a rice ring.

❧ Crostini ❧

1 loaf Italian or French bread
1 clove garlic, cut in half
Olive oil, to taste

Preheat the oven to 400°. Cut the bread into 1" slices and rub each with a garlic clove half. Brush slices lightly with olive oil. Place directly on the oven rack and bake for 6 to 8 minutes or until the *crostini* start to crisp but are not brown.

Chicken Breasts with Feta

C reamy feta cheese melted into a garlicky tomato sauce bathes these chicken breasts.
It's heavenly. Serve with rice or pasta and a romaine salad.

Prep Time: 10 minutes
Cooking Time: 25 minutes

4 tablespoons butter, divided

*2 medium tomatoes, peeled, seeded,
  coarsely chopped*

1 tablespoon finely minced onion

2 large cloves garlic, minced

4 skinless, boneless chicken breast halves

6 ounces feta cheese, thinly sliced

salt and pepper to taste

In a small saucepan place 3 tablespoons of the butter and the tomatoes, onion and garlic. Add salt and pepper to taste and simmer uncovered over medium-low heat for 10 minutes.

Meanwhile, in a medium skillet over medium heat, sauté the chicken breasts in the remaining tablespoon of butter for 3 minutes on each side.

When the sauce is ready, pour it over the chicken. Cover the chicken with thin slices of feta cheese. Cover the pan and simmer gently for 10 minutes, basting several times.

Yield: 4 servings.

Dress It Up
with Grapes

Eat grapes hot? Yes, indeed. Heated in a skillet with a dab of butter, they burst in your mouth warm and juicy, sweet and tart. Hot grapes make a delicious accent to heap around grilled poultry, or top any sort of fish. Try them mixed with Italian or Polish sausages.

Hoisin Hens

C ornish hens in a thick, dark, Oriental sauce are sweet, hot, garlicky, and utterly delicious. This recipe gets raves from guests.

Prep Time: 8 minutes
Cooking Time: 46 minutes

2 tablespoons vegetable oil
2 Cornish hens
1½ cups diced onion
2 teaspoons minced garlic
1½ teaspoons minced fresh ginger
¼ cup soy sauce
¼ cup hoisin sauce
¼ cup dry sherry
¼ teaspoon hot pepper flakes
½ cup chicken broth
thin, cooked pasta as an accompaniment
Oriental sesame oil for pasta

Place a wok or heavy pot that will just hold the hens over high heat. Add the oil. When it is hot add the game hens, breast down. Reduce the heat to medium, cover, and cook for 3 minutes. Turn the hens and cook for another 3 minutes. Add the onion, garlic, ginger, soy sauce, hoisin sauce, sherry, hot pepper flakes and chicken broth. Cover and simmer over medium-low heat for 20 minutes, turn the hens and cook for 20 minutes more.

Remove the hens from the wok. The sauce should be thick and syrupy. If it isn't, cook uncovered for a few minutes.

Cut each hen in half through the backbone and serve on a bed of thin pasta, like capellini, which you have tossed with sesame oil (use 1 tablespoon oil for 12 ounces pasta).

Yield: 4 servings.

Sesame Toast Slices

6 tablespoons butter, melted
1 teaspoon Oriental sesame oil (optional)
½ loaf French or Italian bread
1 egg, slightly beaten with ¼ teaspoon salt
¼ cup sesame seeds

Preheat oven to 375°. Cut bread into ½" slices, slightly on the diagonal (to give a bigger slice).

If you are using the sesame oil, mix it with the melted butter. Brush butter on both sides of each slice. Brush *one side only* with the beaten egg and dip immediately into sesame seeds. Place seed-side-up on a baking sheet and bake for 20 minutes or until golden and crisp. Serve warm.

Yield: 4 servings.

Cornish Hens with Olives and Grapes

The hens are cooked in white grape juice and green grapes, and nipped with black Greek olives. This is company fare. A mix of wild and white rice would be nice with this.

Prep Time: 10 minutes
Cooking Time: 40 minutes

2 tablespoons olive oil

2 Cornish hens, halved down the spine and breast

1 clove garlic, minced

⅓ cup thinly sliced celery

¾ cup white grape juice

3 ounces black Kalamata olives, pitted (about 14)

4 teaspoons tomato paste

¾ cup chicken broth

½ cup seedless green grapes

salt and pepper to taste

In a skillet that will hold the hen halves in one layer, heat the oil over medium high heat. Dry the hens thoroughly with a paper towel, place them in the pan and brown them on both sides for about 10 minutes. Salt and pepper them. Turn the heat to medium low. Add the garlic and celery with ¼ cup water and stir, spooning the mixture over the hens. Cover and cook over medium-low heat for 25 minutes or until tender.

Uncover and add the grape juice and olives. Cook over high heat until the liquid looks syrupy and is making big bubbles. Add the tomato paste, chicken broth and grapes. Cook uncovered over high heat for 5 minutes. Taste for salt and pepper.

Yield: 4 servings.

❧ Chocolate Fondue ❧

This is easy and wonderful for parties. Guests dip fruits or bits of pound cake into the warm, creamy chocolate.

1½ cups whipping cream

16 ounces semisweet chocolate, chopped

1 tablespoon orange or raspberry liqueur

dippers: *strawberries, grapes, chunks of kiwifruit, pineapple, banana, papaya, apple, pear, or chunks of pound cake.*

In a medium pan heat the cream just to the boiling point. Off the heat, stir in the chocolate until it is melted. Add liqueur. Heat gently if necessary.

Arrange the fruit and cake on a big platter and place in the center of the table. Pour the chocolate into 12 small dessert bowls.

Yield: 12 servings.

The Adventurous Chef: Melt 4 ounces of cream-filled chocolate mint patties along with the chocolate.

Chicken Wings in Port and Tarragon

You'll serve these to company, you'll serve them to the family. In fact, once you taste this combination of port, tarragon and garlic, you'll be making them once a week.

Prep Time: 12 minutes
Cooking Time: 25 minutes

6 tablespoons flour

1 teaspoon garlic salt

½ teaspoon pepper

2 pounds chicken wings, tips removed, cut at joints

2 tablespoons oil

1 medium onion, sliced

2 cloves garlic, minced

1 cup port wine

2 teaspoons dried tarragon

On a piece of wax paper, mix flour, garlic salt and pepper. Coat the wing sections with the mixture.

In a large skillet heat the oil. Add the wings and brown them on all sides (about 10 minutes), removing them as they brown. Add the onion and garlic to the skillet and cook and stir over medium heat for 5 minutes. (If the skillet is too dry, add a little more oil.) Return the chicken to the pan. Add the Port and tarragon. Raise the heat to high, bring the wine to a boil, then lower the heat to medium low. Cover and simmer gently for 25 minutes or until the wings are tender. Stir halfway through the cooking time so sauce will be distributed evenly.

Yield: 4 servings.

❧ Flavor Combinations ❧

Garlic, tarragon and port are a delicious combination. Chefs have their heads full of flavor combinations that work. Here are some winning combos to help you wing it deliciously.

Wine and herbs ♦ Wine, herbs and garlic

Soy sauce, dry sherry and ginger ♦ Soy sauce, dry sherry and sugar ♦ Soy sauce, garlic and sugar ♦ Soy sauce, garlic, sugar and peanut butter

Lemon and parsley ♦ Lemon, garlic and parsley ♦ Lemon and oregano ♦ Lemon, Parmesan cheese and parsley

Tomato and garlic ♦ Tomato and herbs ♦ Tomato, cinnamon and cumin ♦ Tomato, cumin, chili pepper and cilantro

Lime and cilantro

Sour cream and paprika ♦ Sour cream or yogurt and dill ♦ Yogurt and mint

Chili Chicken with Dumplings

L ight-as-a-feather corn dumplings in a thick, spicy mix of chili beans and chicken. Sour cream is delicious with this dish.

Prep Time: 15 minutes
Cooking Time: 35 minutes

Dumplings:

1 ½ cups biscuit mix
½ cup cornmeal
⅔ cup milk

Chicken:

2 teaspoons cooking oil
4 skinless, boneless chicken thighs or
*   breast halves, cut into 1 ½" pieces*
1 can (15 ounces) tomato sauce
2 cans (15 ounces) spicy chili beans,
*   undrained*
1 can (15 ounces) corn, undrained
¼ teaspoon dried oregano
1 cup Cheddar cheese, shredded
sour cream as a garnish, if desired

In a medium bowl combine the biscuit mix and cornmeal. Add milk and stir with a fork only until the dry ingredients are dampened. Set aside.

Heat the oil in a 4-quart Dutch oven or other pot that is at least 9" in diameter. Add the chicken and brown quickly over medium-high heat. Add the tomato sauce, the chili beans and corn with their liquid and the oregano. Bring to a boil. Drop the dumplings in by rounded teaspoonfuls. Lower the heat to medium low and cook uncovered for 10 minutes. Cover and cook for 10 minutes more. Sprinkle with cheese. Cook covered for 2 to 3 minutes more or until the cheese melts.

Serve right from the pot at the table.

Yield: 4 servings.

The Vegetarian Chef: Omit the chicken and add another can of any sort of beans.

Mediterranean Oranges

4 navel oranges
1 can (11 ounces) mandarin oranges,
*   undrained*
¼ cup red currant jelly
¼ cup sugar
1 teaspoon kirsch (or to taste)

Peel the oranges down to the flesh so no white pith remains. Cut in half crosswise, then cut

each half into 3 round slices. Reassemble the halves on a flat, shallow dish. In the food processor place mandarin oranges and their syrup, currant jelly and kirsch. Process smooth. Taste and add more kirsch if you like. Pour the sauce over the oranges. Serve chilled.

Yield: 4 servings.

Look What You Can Do With Broiled Chicken Breasts!

Coat Them And Top Them With Something Delicious

These toppings are enough for 4 skinless, boneless chicken breast halves. Broil them 6" from the heat, 4 minutes to a side. Don't overcook them. They're done as soon as there is no pink left in the center. Cut one to test. All recipes serve 4.

The Basic Steps:	Sprinkle both sides with salt and pepper. Then coat as follows.	Broil both sides, turning once, until done to taste. Baste if required. Mix topping and finish as follows.
Sesame Almond *Has a crisp, crunchy coat of sesame seeds.*	In shallow dish lightly beat 1 egg and 1 teaspoon sesame oil. Mix 1 tablespoon sesame seeds and ¾ cup finely chopped sliced almonds on a piece of wax paper. Dip in egg, then almonds.	Serve immediately, garnished with a slice of lemon and a sprig of mint.
Far-East Style *The classic flavors of soy, sherry, garlic and sugar.*	Dip in a mixture of 3 tablepoons soy sauce; 2 tablespoons sherry; 1 clove garlic, minced; and 4 teaspoons brown sugar.	Baste often with soy mixture. **Topping:** 1 tablespoon minced green onion and 2 tablespoons sesame seeds. Return to broiler until seeds are brown.
Italian *Topped with ham and melting cheese.*	Rub with olive oil and sprinkle with dried oregano.	**Topping:** a thin slice of prosciutto or ham and a slice of mozzarella. Return to broiler until cheese melts. Garnish with basil leaves. You could serve with a ribbon of tomato sauce or puréed roasted peppers across the top.
Cheese Puff *An airy little Parmesan soufflé topping.*	Brush with oil, salt and pepper.	**Topping:** a paste of 4 tablespoons Parmesan cheese; 4 tablespoons mayonnaise; 4 tablespoons chopped green onions and 3 tablespoons parsley.

Raspberry Chicken

This has a velvety sauce with an intriguing flavor you can't readily identify. Serve it for an elegant little dinner when you want something understated and sophisticated. Serve with rice, snow peas, and a green salad.

Prep Time: 7 minutes
Cooking Time: 15 minutes

4 skinless, boneless chicken breast halves
2 tablespoons butter
¼ cup finely chopped onion
¼ cup raspberry vinegar
¼ cup chicken broth
¼ cup whipping cream
salt and freshly ground pepper
watercress or parsley as a garnish

Pound each breast several times with your fist to flatten slightly. Season on all sides with salt and pepper.

Melt the butter in a large skillet over medium heat. Add the chicken breasts and cook for 3 minutes. Turn and cook for another 3 minutes or just until lightly colored. Remove to a plate. Add the onion to the fat in the pan. Over low heat, cook until tender, 2 to 3 minutes. Add vinegar, raise the heat to medium high and let bubble until reduced to about a tablespoonful and the mixture is syrupy. Lower the heat to medium low and whisk in the broth and cream. Simmer for 1 minute.

Return the chicken breasts to the skillet. Simmer gently, basting often with the sauce, until they are just done and the sauce is reduced and slightly thickened, about 5 minutes. Don't overcook. Remove the chicken with a slotted spoon to a heated serving platter. Pour the sauce over. Garnish with watercress or parsley.

Yield: 4 servings.

Ice Cream Pudding

Make this in minutes. Since it needs to chill for an hour, prepare it before you start the rest of the meal. By the time you've cooked and finished eating dinner, it's ready.

1 package (3.4 ounces) instant pudding mix, any flavor
1 cup cold whole milk
2 cups ice cream, any flavor, softened
fresh fruit as a garnish, if desired

Using a mixer beat the pudding mix and milk on low speed for 1 minute. Fold in ice cream until mixture is smooth. Spoon into individual dishes. Chill for 1 hour or more. Garnish with fresh fruit if you like. A mint sprig is pretty.

Yield: 4 servings.

Chicken Lebanese Style

I got this recipe from a Lebanese chef when John and I were living in Africa. The chef grilled his chicken and you can do that too, but my recipe is for broiling. This is too good to go out of season.

Prep Time: 5 minutes
Marinating Time: 15 minutes
Cooking Time: 10 minutes

6 large cloves garlic

1 teaspoon salt

½ cup lemon juice

¼ cup olive oil

4 boneless chicken breast halves

*soft pita bread or flour tortillas as an
   accompaniment*

Make a paste of the garlic and salt (for how to do this, see the box on p. 67). In a small bowl mix the garlic paste with the lemon juice and oil. Put the chicken in a flat dish, pour the marinade over, and turn the pieces to coat them evenly. Leave them for 15 minutes.

Scrape the marinade off the chicken into a small pan, leaving the chicken as dry as possible so it will brown. Place the chicken on a broiler pan and broil 6" from the heat for 4 minutes on each side.

In a small saucepan, boil the marinade for at least 2 minutes to kill any microbes from the raw chicken.

Place the chicken on individual plates or a platter and pour the hot marinade over it. Serve with the pita bread or tortillas, letting diners tear off a piece of bread to wrap a piece of chicken.

Yield: 4 servings.

The Unhurried Chef: If you have time, marinate the chicken longer—up to 24 hours in the refrigerator.

Mint Tea

This is fun to serve with Middle Eastern dishes; it's minty, sweet and refreshing.

1 tablespoon loose green tea leaves
¼ cup lightly packed fresh mint leaves
3 tablespoons sugar
3 cups boiling water

Rinse a 4-cup teapot with very hot tap water. Put tea, mint and sugar into the pot and pour in the boiling water. Stir to dissolve the sugar. Cover and steep for 5 minutes.

Yield: 3 or 4 servings.

The Clever Chef: Any plain loose tea may be substituted. If tea bags are all you have, open up two and use them.

❧ *A Fajita Party* ❧

Make Chicken Lebanese Style a party dish by turning it into *fajitas*. Cut the cooked chicken breasts into ¼" to ½" strips. Roll chicken strips in flour tortillas and serve them with Tomato and Olive Salsa, Kidney Beans with Cilantro, and Roasted Red Peppers, along with diced avocado, chopped onion, sour cream and other garnishes.

Tomato and Olive Salsa

1 pound large, ripe tomatoes
½ cup Kalamata olives, pitted and coarsely
*   chopped*
2 tablespoons chopped cilantro
½ cup thinly sliced green onions
1½ teaspoons white wine vinegar
1 small clove garlic, minced

Peel, seed and chop the tomatoes. Put them in a bowl and add the remaining ingredients. Taste and add salt if needed.

Yield: 4 servings.

Kidney Beans with Cilantro

3 cups canned Kidney beans, drained and
*   rinsed*
¼ cup chopped mint
¼ cup chopped cilantro
2 tablespoons finely chopped onion
¼ cup olive oil

2 tablespoons white wine vinegar
salt and pepper

Mix all ingredients and serve at room temperature. You can make this a day ahead; the flavor will improve on standing.

Yield: 6 servings.

Roasted Red Peppers

2 large red bell peppers
3 tablespoons olive oil
1 teaspoon rice wine vinegar
6 tablespoons chopped fresh basil or
*   3 teaspoons dried*
salt and pepper to taste

Preheat the broiler. Cut the peppers in half and lay them cut side down on a baking sheet. Place them 4" below the broiler heat and broil until blistered and charred. Seal peppers in a plastic bag to steam for 10 minutes. The peels will come off easily. Remove the seeds. Pat dry and cut in 1" strips. Place the strips in a bowl and add the oil, vinegar and salt and pepper to taste. Mix to coat well. Just before serving add the fresh basil.

Note: If you use dried herbs, add them with the oil. They'll improve with standing, whereas the fresh ones would wilt and lose flavor.

Yield: 4 servings.

Braised Orange Chicken

This is a glorified version of old-fashioned chicken and gravy—the kind Grandma cooked with dumplings—but this one adds a subtle hint of orange that is absolutely delicious. Don't forget the orange peel garnish. It makes this a truly lovely dish.

Prep Time: 15 minutes
Cooking Time: 30 minutes

4 skinless, boneless chicken thighs
1 tablespoon vegetable oil
1 large onion, thinly sliced
1 teaspoon salt
4 medium red potatoes, peeled
1 medium orange
1 tablespoon flour
⅓ cup chicken broth
1 teaspoon chopped fresh rosemary or
*   ½ teaspoon dried*

Cut each thigh in half lengthwise. Put oil in a 10" skillet over medium-high heat. When the oil is hot, add the thighs, onion and salt. Cook until the onions are soft and the chicken is browned and no longer pink inside. (Make a little cut in one to check.) This will take about 10 minutes. Remove the chicken to a plate, leaving the onions in the skillet.

While the chicken cooks, cut potatoes into 1" chunks. With a vegetable peeler, cut two 4" strips of peel from the orange, avoiding the white part, and cut the strips into little shreds. Or, use a zester. Squeeze the orange, measure ½ cup of juice and put into a small bowl. Stir the flour into the juice, then add the chicken broth and 1 cup of water.

Add potatoes and juice mixture to the onions in the skillet. Raise the heat to high and bring to a boil. Turn heat to low, cover and simmer for 15 minutes. Return the chicken to the skillet. Stir in the rosemary and cook uncovered about 5 minutes more, until the potatoes are done and the chicken is heated through. The sauce should be thickened and have a rich chicken flavor tinged with orange. If looks or tastes thin, remove the chicken from the pan, raise the heat to high and boil until the sauce thickens and the flavor becomes pronounced. Pour the sauce over the chicken and garnish with the orange peel.

Yield: 4 servings.

Herbed ❧ Butter Sticks ❧

½ loaf French or Italian bread
½ cup butter, softened
½ teaspoon dried chervil
½ teaspoon dried basil
¼ teaspoon garlic powder
¼ teaspoon onion powder

Preheat oven to 425°. Cut the bread in half lengthwise, then cut each piece lengthwise into thirds to make a total of 6 long wedges. In a small bowl combine the remaining ingredients. Spread herbed butter on the cut surfaces. Bake on an ungreased baking sheet for 7 to 9 minutes or until golden. Serve warm.

Yield: 6 large bread sticks.

Sophie's Super Lemon Chicken

This doesn't taste anything like you think it will when you read the ingredients. There is a slight tang of lemon but basically the lemon and garlic melt into a deliciously rich sauce that feels smooth on the tongue.

Prep Time: 8 minutes
Marinating Time: 15 minutes
Cooking Time: 35 minutes

2 cloves garlic

1 teaspoon salt

1 teaspoon thyme

3 tablespoons fresh lemon juice, divided

4 skinless, boneless chicken breast halves

1 tablespoon oil

1 tablespoon butter

3 tablespoons flour

1½ cups low-salt chicken broth

1 tablespoon minced fresh parsley

cooked rice, as an accompaniment

Garlic-Salt Paste

To mash garlic and salt to a paste, lay the garlic on your cutting board. Place the flat side of a wide-bladed knife on the cloves and whack the blade with your fist. You now have mashed garlic. Put the salt on the garlic. Place the flat side of the knife's point on the garlic and salt and mash and scrape until you have a creamy paste. This takes about 30 seconds.

Make a paste of the garlic and salt (see box). In a shallow dish mix the garlic paste, thyme, and 2 tablespoons of the lemon juice. Add the chicken and turn to coat well. Cover with plastic wrap and let it marinate for 15 minutes. Lift chicken out, pat dry, and save the marinade.

Heat the oil and butter in a 10" skillet over medium-high heat until the butter stops foaming. Add the chicken and sauté until golden, about 2 minutes on each side. Transfer to a plate.

Add flour to the skillet and cook over medium-low heat, stirring, for 2 to 3 minutes. Whisk in broth and remaining lemon juice in a thin stream. Continue to cook and whisk until smooth. Return the chicken to the skillet along with any accumulated juices. Cover and simmer for 15 minutes or until just cooked through (it will still be springy to the touch). Stir in the parsley. Place each portion on a mound of rice and top with the sauce.

Yield: 4 servings.

Look What You Can Do with Chicken Breast Halves—Or Veal or Turkey Cutlets!

Cutlets, or scallops, are thin pieces of meat or poultry that are cooked quickly over high heat so the outside browns before the inside dries out. Have your pan and oil or butter very hot. Slip in the meat and brown both sides, allowing only a minute or so per side. Add the sauce, cook for 8 minutes, and that's it. These recipes serve 2. You can double the recipe to serve 4, but you may have to use 2 skillets. The recipes are for half chicken breasts but you can use 4-ounce turkey, pork or veal cutlets.

Start This Way: Pound 4 skinless, boneless chicken breast halves to ¼" thickness. Mix 2 tablespoons flour, 1 teaspoon salt and ¼ teaspoon pepper on a piece of wax paper. Salt the cutlets on both sides and coat them with seasoned flour. In a 10" skillet over medium-high heat, heat 1 tablespoon oil and 1 tablespoon butter. Don't let the butter brown. When it stops foaming, slip in the cutlets and brown quickly for only 1 to 2 minutes per side. Then:

The Basic Steps:	Add these ingredients, cover and simmer for 8 minutes or until tender.	Remove scallops to a plate and keep warm. If the sauce is thin, boil it rapidly until it thickens slightly. Then add the following ingredients and taste for salt. Spoon sauce over scallops.
Piccata *The classic Italian scallopini.*	1 tablespoon minced onion or shallot; 1 tablespoon rinsed capers (optional); and ½ cup white vermouth.	2 tablespoons parsley; 1½ teaspoon grated lemon rind.
Latin American *Nippy, slightly sweet, and tinged with cinnamon.*	½ cup orange juice; 3 tablespoons raisins; 2 tablespoons chopped canned hot green chilies; a pinch cinnamon.	1 tablespoon chopped fresh cilantro. After spooning sauce over, garnish with toasted pine nuts or almonds.
Southwestern *The flavors of Tex-Mex chili.*	½ cup red wine; ¼ cup tomato purée; ¾ teaspoon dried oregano; ½ teaspoon chili powder.	After spooning sauce over, garnish with lime wedges and sour cream.
Roma *Has a topping of ham and melted cheese.*	Three ½" slices of portobello mushroom, in 1" pieces; ½ cup white wine; 2 ounces prosciutto or ham, in thin strips.	Top with 2 ounces thinly sliced Fontina. Wrap skillet handle with foil and run cutlets under broiler just long enough to melt cheese. Spoon sauce over.

The Basic Steps:	Add these ingredients, cover and simmer for 8 minutes or until tender.	Remove scallops to a plate and keep warm. If the sauce is thin, boil it rapidly until it thickens slightly. Then add the following ingredients and taste for salt. Spoon sauce over scallops.
Ruby *Creamy with a hint of sweetness.*	¼ cup dry white wine.	After mixing 2 tablespoons red currant jelly well into juices, stir in ½ cup sour cream.
Parmesan *With a scrumptious tomato garnish.*	Before coating with flour, coat with ½ cup grated Parmesan. When brown, add ¼ cup dry white wine. Sprinkle with a total of 1 tablespoon Parmesan.	Garnish with sautéed cherry tomatoes. Don't skip this garnish—it turns a tasy dish scrumptious.
Mustard Cream *An exquisite dish.*	1 tablespoon minced shallots; 2 tablespoons white wine; 1 teaspoon vinegar; pinch dried thyme; ½ cup cream. Make sure the heat is very low.	½ to 1 teaspoon Dijon mustard; salt and pepper to taste.

✿ Caramel Brie with Fresh Fruit ✿

The perfect ending for a meal: warm Brie under a blanket of rich caramel with little nuggets of pecans.

1 tablespoon butter
6 tablespoons firmly packed brown sugar
2 tablespoons light corn syrup
2 teaspoons flour
2 tablespoons milk
1 wedge (12 ounces) Brie, at room temperature
¼ cup coarsely chopped pecans, briefly toasted in a hot, dry skillet
***fruit** such as pear wedges, apple wedges, grapes or sliced peaches as an accompaniment*

In a small saucepan over medium-high heat melt the butter. Add the sugar, corn syrup and flour.

Mix well and bring to a boil. Lower the heat and simmer for 5 minutes, stirring constantly. Cool to lukewarm. Gradually stir in milk. Place the Brie on a serving plate and pour the sauce over it so it drips attractively down the sides. Sprinkle with pecans. Serve with fresh fruit.

Yield: 4 to 6 servings.

The Clever Chef: To insure that the Brie is at its best, leave it at room temperature for at least an hour before pouring on the caramel. If you are clever with your microwave, you could warm it that way in a pinch.

Chicken with Brie Sauce

T his chicken has one of the most delicious sauces you will ever taste. The Brie is
melted into a vinaigrette mixture—oil, wine vinegar and mustard—which makes
an utterly bewitching combination.

Prep Time: 8 minutes
Cooking Time: 10 minutes

¼ cup olive oil

*2 teaspoons shallots or green onions,
     minced*

1 teaspoon garlic, minced

¼ cup sherry wine vinegar

1 tablespoon fresh lemon juice

2 teaspoons Dijon mustard

5 ounce ripe Brie cheese, rind removed

1 tablespoon vegetable oil

4 skinless, boneless chicken breast halves

pepper to taste

Warm the olive oil in a large saucepan over
low heat. Add the shallots and garlic and
cook for 4 to 5 minutes or until softened,
stirring now and then. Stir in the vinegar,
lemon juice and mustard. Cut the cheese
into small pieces and stir into the mixture.
When the sauce is smooth (it will always
look a little grainy), season with pepper
to taste. Keep warm.

In a 10" skillet heat the vegetable oil over
medium-high heat. When it is hot, add the
chicken. Sauté for 2 minutes per side or
until browned and cooked through. Place
on serving plates and top with the warm
sauce.

Yield: 4 servings.

Dressing Up
Frozen Peas

Cook two 10-ounce packages of frozen peas.
Make one of the following variations by adding the suggested ingredients:

Peas and Water Chestnuts: 3 tablespoons
butter, ½ teaspoon celery salt, 1 can (8
ounces) water chestnuts, drained.

Orange Mint Peas: 3 tablespoons butter, 2
tablespoons chopped fresh mint leaves or 2
teaspoons dried, zest of half an orange.

Yield: 4 servings.

Sandy's Orange Chicken

Unbelievably easy, and unbelievably delicious. The subtly spiced chicken needs no browning; it just cooks with the orange rice. The result is spectacular.

Prep Time: 5 minutes
Cooking Time: 25 minutes

2 to 3 teaspoons curry powder
1¼ teaspoons salt, divided
¼ teaspoon pepper
4 skinless, boneless chicken breast halves
1½ cups orange juice
1 cup rice
¾ cup water
1 tablespoon brown sugar
1 teaspoon dry mustard
1 tablespoon butter (optional)
chopped parsley as a garnish

In a small bowl combine curry powder, ½ teaspoon salt and pepper. Sprinkle this over all sides of the chicken and rub in well. Set aside.

In a 10" skillet combine orange juice, rice, water, brown sugar, mustard, butter if desired, and ¾ teaspoon salt. Mix well. Place the chicken on the rice and bring to a boil over high heat. Cover, lower heat to medium low and simmer for 20 minutes.

Remove the pan from the heat and let stand, covered, for 5 minutes. If liquid still remains, remove the cover and cook over medium heat until it is absorbed. Sprinkle with parsley.

Yield: 4 servings.

The Adventurous Chef: Add 1 or 2 tablespoons each of nuts and raisins to the rice mixture before starting to cook.

❧ Peaches in Wine ❧

This is one of my favorite summer desserts. It provides a fragrant wine to sip with the meal and delicately wine-tinged peaches for dessert.

4 fresh peaches, peeled and sliced
fruity white wine, rosé, or sparkling
*   red wine*

Divide the peaches among 4 large-bowl wine glasses. Fill with wine. Replenish wine during the meal as needed. At dessert time, eat the peaches with a spoon. Butter cookies or champagne biscuits are good with this.

The Adventurous Chef: Use other fruits such as strawberries, plums, cantaloupe or honeydew. Half-fill each glass with fruit.

Roast Chicken in Cardamom Yogurt Sauce

On your way home buy a spit-cooked chicken and reheat it in this fragrant curry sauce. Serve with plain boiled rice and chutney. To be festive, offer little bowls of any or all of these garnishes: chopped peanuts, coconut, raisins, tomato, avocado, green pepper, onion.

Prep Time: 5 minutes
Cooking Time: 18 minutes

2 tablespoons olive oil

1 cup chopped onion

¼ teaspoon minced garlic

1 3" cinnamon stick

½ teaspoon crushed fennel seeds

½ teaspoon ground cardamom

¼ teaspoon ground ginger

1 tablespoon flour

1 chicken bouillon cube plus ½ cup water

1 cup yogurt

1 rotisserie-cooked chicken

Heat the olive oil in a large skillet. Sauté the onion, garlic, cinnamon, fennel, cardamom and ginger over medium-low heat until the onion is tender. Stir in the flour, bouillon cube and water. Cook until thickened. Stir in the yogurt, cover and simmer over low heat for 5 minutes. Quarter the roasted chicken. Add it to the sauce and cook, covered, for 10 minutes, or until it is well heated. Baste several times with the sauce.

Yield: 4 servings.

❧ Dishwasher Savvy ❧

I used to hate unloading the dishwasher. When I considered the work it saved—all the washing and rinsing and drying before you even got to putting the dishes away—I felt like an ungrateful grump. But that didn't make me dislike it any less. Then I discovered a trick that changed my attitude. Now I put the silverware in the basket handles up, like with like. In the morning I grab all the knife handles and put the knives away. Ditto with spoons and forks. I feel so clever that the euphoria sees me through the rest of the process.

Cape Malay Chicken

L ots and lots of onions half-melted into a ginger curry sauce with soft bits of to-mato, poured over a spit-cooked chicken. This is good with yellow rice mixed with chopped pecans. I like to stir yogurt into each bite; John, my husband, likes his yogurt separate as an accent.

Prep Time: 8 minutes
Cooking Time: 35 minutes

1 tablespoon vegetable oil

2 onions, sliced

3 tomatoes, peeled, seeded and chopped, canned or fresh

2 cups chicken broth

1 tablespoon curry powder, or to taste

2 cloves garlic, crushed

2 tablespoons apricot jam

1 teaspoon grated fresh ginger or ¼ teaspoon ground ginger

2 tablespoons golden or dark raisins

1 rotisserie-cooked chicken

2 to 3 tablespoons plain yogurt (optional) plus yogurt to serve at table

In a medium saucepan heat the oil and sauté the onions and tomatoes until soft. Add chicken stock. In a small bowl mix the curry powder with a little of the stock until smooth. Stir in garlic, jam, ginger and raisins and add the mixture to the pot. Bring to a boil, lower heat, and simmer uncovered for 10 minutes.

Preheat the oven to 350°.

Cut the chicken into serving pieces. Place in an ovenproof casserole and pour the hot sauce over it. Cover with foil and bake for 15 to 20 minutes or until the chicken is heated through. If you want a creamy sauce, stir in the yogurt.

Serve the chicken with a dish of yogurt as an accompaniment.

Yield: 4 servings.

❧ Perfect Iced Tea ❧

Put 1 family-size or 3 regular-size tea bags in a pan or heatproof pitcher. Pour in 2 cups of boiling water and let steep for 3 to 5 minutes. Remove the tea bags, squeezing them to get out all the flavor. Add 2 cups water. If you want to sweeten the tea, stir in ¼ to ½ cup sugar before adding the water. Pour the tea over ice. If you've got fresh lemons, pop a wedge onto each glass.

Anita's Paprika Chicken

A friend in Africa used to fix this dish and we lapped it up. It works perfectly with a rotisserie chicken. Be careful not to let the sauce boil; the sour cream might curdle, and the chicken become overdone. Just let it imbibe the wonderful sauce.

Prep Time: 5 minutes
Cooking Time: 15 minutes

¼ cup butter

2 tablespoons paprika

1 package onion soup mix

¾ cup water

1 rotisserie-cooked chicken, cut into
   serving pieces

2 cups sour cream

In a large skillet over medium heat, melt the butter. Add paprika, soup mix and water. Mix well. Add the cut-up rotisserie chicken. Bring the liquid to a boil. Lower the heat to medium low—you want a bare simmer. Stir in the sour cream, cover and simmer very gently, just to heat the chicken through, for 10-15 minutes.

Yield: 4 servings.

Caraway Loaf

1 loaf (1 pound) French or Italian bread
⅓ cup soft butter
1 teaspoon caraway seeds

Preheat oven to 350°. Cut bread into 1" slices, cutting almost but not quite through to the bottom. Mix butter and caraway seeds and spread each cut surface with the mixture. Wrap loaf in heavy-duty aluminum foil. Bake for 15 minutes or until heated through. Serve warm.

Yield: 8 to 10 servings.

Mediterranean Chicken

H ere is a delicious, olive-rich tomato sauce that will glorify a purchased cooked chicken. Of course, there's nothing to keep you from sautéing four chicken breasts and pouring the sauce over them.

Prep Time: 10 minutes
Cooking Time: 20 minutes

1 tablespoon olive oil

½ cup chopped onion

1 small clove garlic, crushed

½ large green pepper, cut into 1" squares

1 ¼ cups tomato sauce

½ cup sliced green olives

½ cup sliced black olives

pinch dried thyme

1 to 2 tablespoons parsley

3 peppercorns

1 rotisserie-cooked chicken, cut up

In a large, heavy pan, heat the olive oil. Add the onion, garlic and green pepper. Cook for 5 minutes or until softened. Stir in the tomato sauce, olives, thyme, parsley and peppercorns and stir. Add the chicken to the sauce. Cover and simmer gently for 10 to 15 minutes or until the chicken is well heated.

Yield: 4 servings.

Menu

Mediterranean Chicken

Polenta

Green Salad with Fennel

Raspberries with Whipped Cream
and Grated Chocolate

Zesty Chicken with Arabian Rice

A rotisserie-cooked chicken is sauced with an intriguing mixture of Oriental and Indian flavors and served with date-and-almond-studded rice. A sensational dish.

Prep Time: 10 minutes
Cooking Time: 30 minutes

Chicken:

1 ½ tablespoons butter, divided

½ medium onion, sliced

1 rotisserie-cooked chicken, cut into serving pieces

2 tablespoons soy sauce

2 tablespoons vermouth

4 teaspoons lime or lemon juice

½ teaspoon curry powder

½ teaspoon ginger

¼ teaspoon dried oregano

⅛ teaspoon black pepper

Rice:

1 cup rice

¼ cup toasted almonds

8 dates, pitted and sliced

In a large skillet heat 1 tablespoon of the butter. Add the onion and cook and stir over medium heat for 3 to 4 minutes or until softened. Add the chicken, soy sauce, vermouth, lime juice, curry powder, ginger, oregano and pepper. Bring the mixture to a boil. Turn the heat to low, cover and simmer for 20 minutes or until the chicken is well heated.

Meanwhile, prepare the rice according to package directions. When it is done, stir in almonds, dates and the remaining half tablespoon of butter. Serve with the chicken.

Yield: 4 servings.

Bananas in Yogurt

Here's a quick, light dessert. Perfect after a spicy meal.

1 cup plain yogurt
2 tablespoons brown sugar
4 large bananas

Mix the yogurt and brown sugar. Slice the bananas and toss them lightly with the yogurt mixture. Spoon into 4 dessert dishes.

Yield: 4 servings.

From top to bottom, clockwise: Sunflower Nacho Pizza, page 108; Chicken Lebanese Style, page 65; and White Beans with Cilantro, page 65.

From top to bottom, clockwise: Antipasto, page 213; Salmon with Ginger and Vegetables, page 24; and Rigatoni with Tuna in Roasted Red Pepper Garlic Sauce, page 16.

Indonesian Extravaganza

A spicy peanut sauce is poured over hot rotisserie-cooked chicken and jazzed up with a bevy of curry-type accompaniments. This is fun eating!

Prep Time: 10 minutes
Cooking Time: 20 Minutes

1 can (10 ½ ounces) chicken broth

½ cup chunky peanut butter

⅛ teaspoon cayenne pepper or more to taste

1 teaspoon sugar

1 rotisserie-cooked chicken

salt to taste

cooked rice, as an accompaniment

½ cup each of at least 5 curry accompaniments (see box)

Preheat the oven to 350°. In a saucepan combine broth, peanut butter, cayenne and sugar. Bring to a boil, reduce heat and simmer uncovered for 20 minutes, stirring occasionally. It will thicken. Season to taste with salt.

In the meantime, place the chicken in an ovenproof dish and reheat it in the oven. Pour the sauce over the chicken and serve with the rice and other accompaniments.

Yield: 4 servings.

The Adventurous Chef: Cut the chicken into serving pieces. Make the sauce in a large skillet and add the chicken after the first 5 minutes.

Traditional Curry & Accompaniments &

mango chutney

chopped green onion

chopped onion

chopped tomato (seeded and peeled)

orange segments, in ½" pieces

chopped dates

crumbled crisp bacon

coconut, sweetened or fresh

peanuts, coarsely chopped

chopped green and red bell pepper

flaked or powdered chili pepper

raisins

sesame seeds

chopped avocado sprinkled with lemon juice

chopped banana sprinkled with lemon juice

Turkey Roma

Delicate cutlets topped with cheese and tomato. This is delicious with Lemon Chive Pasta.

Prep Time: 8 minutes
Cooking Time: 20 minutes

2 tablespoons olive oil, divided

1 pound plum tomatoes, peeled, seeded, chopped, canned or fresh

1 tablespoon butter

1 pound boneless turkey breast cutlets, pounded ⅛" thick (see box p. 50)

1 tablespoon lemon juice

2 teaspoons coarsely chopped fresh sage

4 ounces mozzarella, sliced thin

1 tablespoon chopped fresh parsley

salt and pepper to taste

In a medium saucepan heat 1 tablespoon of the oil over medium-high heat until hot but not smoking. Add the tomatoes and cook, stirring, for 8 to 10 minutes or until slightly thickened. Season with salt and pepper. Cover and keep warm.

Preheat the oven to 425°.

In a large skillet heat the remaining oil and the butter over medium-high heat until hot but not smoking. Pat the cutlets dry and sauté them in batches for 1 minute only on each side, or until golden. Transfer them to a plate as they are done.

Arrange the turkey in a single layer in a large baking dish. Sprinkle with lemon juice, season with pepper. Top each cutlet with sage and mozzarella. Spoon tomato sauce evenly over all. Bake just until the cheese melts and the sauce bubbles, 1 to 2 minutes. Sprinkle with parsley.

Yield: 4 servings.

Lemon ❧ Chive Pasta ❧

1 pound pasta, cooked and drained
2 tablespoons butter
1 tablespoon chopped chives
2 tablespoons olive oil
1 teaspoon grated lemon rind

While the pasta is cooking, heat the butter and chives in a small saucepan for 1 minute. Stir in the olive oil and lemon zest and cook for 1 minute more. Pour over the pasta and combine.

Yield: 4 servings.

Turkey Tonnato

T his is an easy version of the classic Italian summer dish, *Vitello Tonnato*. Instead of cold roast veal, the tuna sauce tops slices of roasted turkey breast from the deli counter. The perfect accompaniment for this is thickly sliced tomatoes sprinkled with salt and pepper, a drizzle of olive oil and vinegar and a sprinkle of chopped fresh dill. Sesame pita toasts add the final touch. A word about temperature: Whereas the sauce can come directly from the fridge, the turkey must be at room temperature for the best texture and flavor.

Prep Time: 5 minutes
Soaking Time: 5 minutes
Cooking Time: None

*¾ pound roasted turkey breast, in
    ¼" slices*

¾ cup mayonnaise

½ cup canned white tuna, drained

*2 anchovy fillets, soaked in milk for 5
    minutes and drained*

1 clove garlic, minced

1 tablespoon drained capers, divided

thin lemon slices as a garnish

Overlap the turkey slices on a platter. In the blender or food processor blend mayonnaise, tuna, anchovies, garlic and half the capers until silky smooth. Spoon the sauce over the turkey. Sprinkle with the remaining capers and garnish with lemon slices.

Yield: 4 servings.

The Skinny Chef: Use half low-fat mayonnaise and half yogurt.

The Adventurous Chef: Leftover sauce also makes a delicious open-face sandwich. Spread your bread with *tonnato* sauce and top with turkey.

❧ A Summer Meal ❧

Instead of turkey use an assortment of vegetables for a lovely meatless meal.

*2 pounds green beans, cooked 5 minutes
    or until crisp-tender*
*2 pounds red-skinned potatoes, cooked,
    quartered*
4 to 6 hard-cooked eggs, sliced
Tonnato Sauce (see above recipe)

On a platter, arrange the vegetables and egg slices. Spoon some of the sauce over them. Serve the rest separately.

Yield: 4 servings.

Stacky-Uppy Turkey

This recipe, originally a glorious buffet-style treatment of holiday leftovers, has been in the family of my friend Maggie for 3 generations. The current generation has turned the eagerly-awaited feast into a year-round party dish (see box).

Prep Time: 10 minutes
Cooking Time: 20 minutes

3 cups cooked rice
2-3 cups chopped leftover turkey
3 cups turkey gravy

Condiments:

canned crisp Chinese noodles
chopped tomatoes
chopped green onions
coconut
raisins
drained crushed pineapple
chopped peanuts

Heat the rice, turkey and gravy separately; keep warm.

Set out small dishes of condiments.

The assembly of the meal is important; it makes a difference when you add what to the stack on your plate. So, assemble dishes in this order: Rice, turkey, Chinese noodles, gravy, tomatoes, green onions, coconut, raisins, pineapple, and peanuts.

Yield: 6 servings.

❧ Festive Chicken Stacks ❧

Once you have eaten Stacky-Uppy Turkey, you won't want to wait for the holidays to eat it again. To serve it for guests, give it a grown-up name and proceed as follows:

4 skinless, boneless chicken breast halves
3 tablespoons butter
3 tablespoons flour
2 cups chicken broth
2 cups cooked rice
condiments (choose from the above list)

Place the chicken breasts in a pan, cover them with water by 1 inch, bring to a boil and simmer gently for 5 minutes. Remove the pan from the heat, leave the cover on and let the chicken sit for 15 minutes.

In a small pan melt the butter, stir in the flour and let it bubble for 2 minutes. Slowly add the chicken broth and cook and stir until smooth. Continue as in the recipe above.

Yield: 4 servings

The Speedy Chef: Instead of the butter, flour and broth, use a can of chicken gravy or a package of gravy mix.

Turkey Sandwich Supreme

A sandwich for the gods: turkey on pumpernickel with Saga Blue cheese, a crunchy mustard whose grains burst deliciously in your teeth, and chutney.

Prep Time: 5 minutes

butter
2 slices of pumpernickel bread
1 tablespoon mango chutney
1 tablespoon rough-grain mustard
2 or 3 leaves Boston lettuce
¼" slice Saga Blue cheese
1 or 2 slices cold roast turkey breast
2 or 3 rings of a big sweet onion

Butter one slice of bread and spread it with chutney. Spread the second slice with mustard. On the chutney slice place the lettuce, cheese, turkey and sweet onion. Top with the mustard-coated bread. Eat blissfully.

Yield: 1 sandwich.

Kiwifruit and Whipped Cream

This is a fun dessert. You spear a piece of kiwi with your fork and dunk it into whipped cream, then brown sugar. The combination of tart, icy-cold fruit, mellow cream and caramelly brown sugar is irresistible.

6 fresh kiwifruits, icy cold if possible
1 cup whipping cream, whipped
½ cup brown sugar

Peel the fruit with a sharp knife. Cut each into quarters and arrange the pieces in a bowl. Whip the cream and put it in another bowl. Put the brown sugar in a third. Serve everything chilled. This is leisurely, help-yourself food.

Yield: 4 servings.

The Adventurous Chef: Serve other fruits this way. Apricots would be lovely.

The Social Chef: The classic way to serve this dish is on a bed of crushed ice in a shallow bowl. Arrange the kiwifruit on the ice, then hollow out a place to hold the bowl of whipped cream. The bowl of brown sugar is on its own. This is a neat thing to do when you are feeling cosmopolitan.

Try Beef Tonight

Quick beef recipes used to be a matter of a hamburger or big, fat steak. Now that you can buy "tenders" from formerly long-cooking cuts like chuck and shoulder, there is a whole new array of delicious possibilities. A lot of recipes in this chapter are streamlined updates of long-simmered dishes. They're delicious and I wonder why we didn't do this long ago. I also put in tables loaded with ideas for glamorizing grilled steaks and tossing off unusual stir-fries. The tables contain some of the tastiest, most imaginative recipes in the chapter. I keep harping on this theme because I don't want you to think that being in a table diminishes a recipe's standing. The table makes choosing and cooking a dish a little easier. The recipes in the lamb and pork chapters (tables included) also work deliciously with beef, so cruise the book, see what sets your tastebuds tingling and adapt. Recipe freewheeling will give you a sense of freedom and you will eat better than you ever did.

"A lot of recipes in this chapter are streamlined updates of long-simmered beef dishes."

Grilled Flank Steak, Teriyaki Style

Garlicky sweet-soy teriyaki flavors with an added nip of chutney—delicious. Serve with Hot Potatoes in Shallot Vinaigrette.

Prep Time: 15 minutes
Cooking Time: 16 minutes

½ medium onion, sliced thin

¼ teaspoon garlic powder

⅓ cup soy sauce

2 tablespoons rice vinegar

2 tablespoons mango chutney, chopped

1 flank steak, 1½ to 2 pounds

In a large zip lock bag place onion, garlic powder, soy sauce, vinegar and chutney. Close bag and squeeze to mix. Add the flank steak, close the bag tightly and squeeze again until all surfaces are coated with onions and liquid. Leave to marinate for 20 minutes at room temperature or up to 8 hours in the fridge.

Heat the grill or broiler. Remove meat from marinade, lifting off any onions that stick. Grill 4" from the heat source for about 8 minutes per side or to taste. Let the steak sit for 5 minutes to absorb back its juices. Then slice it against the grain at an angle.

The Adventurous Chef: To turn Grilled Flank Steak leftovers into fajitas, cut the meat into thin strips and singe it quickly in a very hot skillet. Roll the strips in flour tortillas along with sautéed onions and peppers, tomatoes, salsa, sour cream, guacamole or other trimmings.

Yield: 4 servings.

Hot Potatoes in Shallot Vinaigrette

Buy the smallest new potatoes you can. The almost creamy texture of the potatoes is beautifully offset by the crunch of shallots and the nippy sauce.

1 pound small new potatoes, well washed
1½ tablespoons white wine vinegar
1½ teaspoons Dijon mustard
⅓ cup olive oil
1 shallot, minced
2 tablespoons minced parsley
salt and pepper to taste
coarse salt as a garnish

In a saucepan, cover potatoes with salted water, bring to a boil and simmer for 20 minutes or until done. Drain.

While the potatoes cook, combine in a small bowl the vinegar, mustard, and salt and pepper to taste. Whisk in the oil in a thin stream to make a thick emulsion. Add shallot and parsley.

When the potatoes are done, put them immediately in a heated serving bowl and toss with the dressing. Serve with a little bowl of coarse salt to be added at will.

Yield: 4 servings.

Horseradish Beef

The flavor is elusive—neither curry nor horseradish predominates. Take the meat right from the freezer and half-thaw it in the microwave on ¾ power. Slice while it's still stiff, and you're on your way.

Prep Time: 10 minutes
Cooking Time: 20 to 25 minutes

4 boneless chuck top blade steaks, about
 1¼ pounds total (see box p. 86)
2 teaspoons cornstarch
½ teaspoon curry powder, divided
¼ teaspoon powdered ginger, divided
2 teaspoons Worcestershire sauce, divided
1 large onion, sliced thin
2 tablespoons oil, divided
½ teaspoon sugar
1 cup chicken broth
1 tablespoon horseradish
1 cup sour cream or yogurt
salt and pepper to taste
noodles or rice as an accompaniment

Cut the beef into ¼" slices. Toss it with the cornstarch, half the curry powder, half the ginger, and half the Worcestershire sauce. Set aside at room temperature.

In a medium frying pan sauté the onion in 1 tablespoon of the oil over medium heat for 5 to 8 minutes, until soft and transparent but not brown. Stir in sugar and the remaining curry powder, ginger, and Worcestershire sauce. Remove the onions from the pan and keep them warm.

Raise the heat to medium high. Add the remaining oil to the pan, and brown the beef. Add broth, the reserved onions, and salt and pepper to taste. Mix well. Cover and simmer over medium to medium-low heat for 10 to 15 minutes, until the meat is tender and the sauce thickened. Stir in the horseradish and sour cream. Serve hot with noodles or rice.

Yield: 4 servings.

❧ Fun Dessert Coffees II ❧

Irish Coffee: Into a warmed wine glass place 2 teaspoons sugar and fill glass ⅔ full of hot coffee. Mix. Add 2 tablespoons Irish whiskey and top with softly whipped cream.

Liqueur Coffee: Fill demitasse cups ¾ full of hot coffee. Add a dash of any of these liqueurs:

white Crème de Menthe, orange-flavored liqueur, anisette or crème de cacao.

Café Royale: Make Liqueur Coffee using Cognac or brandy. Bourbon or rum is good too.

Grilled Steak with Red Pepper Sauce and Pasta

This is a startlingly beautiful dish, especially when accompanied by snow peas. This is the dish for an elegant after-work dinner party. It needs no salad, just a good, crusty bread.

Prep Time: 12 minutes
Cooking Time: 20 minutes

4 beef steaks (see box p. 88)
1 tablespoon oil
1 teaspoon minced fresh ginger
1 clove garlic, minced
1 medium yellow onion, sliced thin
1 large sweet red pepper, seeded and cut
    into ¾" squares
1 cup chicken broth
3 tablespoons sweet sherry
1½ teaspoons soy sauce
2 tablespoons cold butter, cut into small
    pieces
cooked capellini as an accompaniment
cooked snow peas as an accompaniment
    (optional)

Grill the steaks to the desired degree of doneness.

In a heavy skillet, heat oil over medium heat. Stir in the ginger and garlic and cook, stirring, for 30 seconds. Don't let the garlic brown or it will be bitter. Add the onion and red pepper, lower the heat, cover, and cook gently for 8 - 10 minutes.

Add the broth and boil uncovered over medium-high heat for 5 minutes. Add sherry, soy sauce, and any juices that have collected around the meat. Cook the sauce for another 2 to 3 minutes to reduce it. Swirl in the butter and stir only until melted. Don't cook further.

If the steaks have cooled, warm them quickly in a 400° oven for 2 or 3 minutes. Place a bed of cooked cappellini on each plate and top with a steak. Spoon the sauce over. For a gorgeous effect, arrange snow peas beside them. And dine gloriously!

Yield: 4 servings.

Saigon Fillets

Despite the long ingredient list, this superb dish goes together in minutes because there's almost no chopping, just measuring. The steaks are served on a bed of rice with a heady curry sauce that blends with the meaty flavor rather than overpowering it.

Prep Time: 10 minutes
Cooking Time: 10 minutes

6 tablespoons butter
2 tablespoons minced onion
1 clove garlic, minced
1 tablespoon curry powder
1 tablespoon powdered ginger
1 tablespoon chili sauce
1 tomato, peeled, seeded, chopped coarsely
1 tablespoon soy sauce
1 teaspoon sugar
2 tablespoons flour
1 cup chicken broth
1 teaspoon Bovril or other meat extract
4 beef steaks (see box p. 88)
cooked rice as an accompaniment

In a small, heavy saucepan heat the butter, then add onion and garlic and sauté for 1 minute. Add curry powder, ginger, chili sauce, tomato, soy sauce and sugar. Mix well. Stir in flour, broth and Bovril. Cook for two minutes.

Grill or pan-fry the steaks to the desired degree of doneness. To serve, place steaks on a bed of rice and pour the sauce over.

Yield: Serves 4.

The Clever Chef: Start the rice before you do anything else because that is your time-taker. Then, approach the dish like a professional chef. Get out a bunch of little custard cups. Chop the onion, and place it in one cup. With a garlic press, mash garlic and put it on top of the onion. Measure curry and ginger into a second dish. In a third put the chili sauce and soy sauce, the tomato and the sugar. Place the flour in a fourth. In a glass measuring cup combine the chicken broth and Bovril. Cut 6 tablespoons from a stick of butter. You have now done the most time consuming part of your preparation.

Fussy Philosophers

Chinese philosophers seem to have been fussy eaters. It was said that Confucius wouldn't eat if his wife forgot to put the ginger on the table. His wife finally walked out on him when he refused to touch the meat because it was not "squarely sliced". And the great Chinese philosopher, Tsengtse, divorced his wife "over the matter of cooking peas". Which should serve as a warning to all cooks: do not marry a Chinese philosopher.

Steak with Garlic and Sherry

The sauce on these quickly prepared steaks is a delicious mixture of garlic, sherry, mustard and just enough cream to make it smooth and velvety.

Prep Time: 5 minutes
Marinating Time: 30 minutes
Cooking Time: 10 to 12 minutes

¼ cup plus 2 tablespoons dry sherry, divided

2½ teaspoons Dijon mustard

2 teaspoons Worcestershire sauce

4 beef steaks (see box below)

1 tablespoon vegetable oil

1 tablespoon butter

2 cloves garlic, smashed but intact

¼ cup sour cream

In a wide, flat dish combine ¼ cup of the sherry, the mustard and the Worcestershire sauce. Add the steaks, turn them to coat, and marinate for 30 minutes at room temperature, turning once or twice.

Remove the steaks from the marinade and pat them dry with paper towels. Save the marinade.

Over medium-high heat, heat oil and butter in a heavy skillet that will hold the steaks without letting them touch. Brown the meat on one side, lower the heat to medium and add the smashed garlic. Turn the steaks and cook until done to your taste.

Remove to a warm platter. Discard the garlic and add the reserved marinade to the pan along with the remaining sherry. Scrape up the browned bits stuck to the pan bottom. Stir in the sour cream and any juices that have accumulated with the steaks. Heat well but do not boil. Pour sauce over steaks.

Yield: 4 servings.

❧ Steaks No Longer Have to be Huge ❧

It used to be that a steak was a t-bone, rib eye or New York strip. It was big and fat and gloriously marbled. It cost a bunch and was often more food than you really wanted. Now come the small blade steaks or mock tenders from such improbable cuts as chuck and shoulder, sold in packs of 8 or 10.

These cuts from the hard-working muscles are usually more flavorful than the delicate fillet and rib steaks, and they cook up surprisingly moist and tender. They have opened up a whole new set of recipes in our house. I use the small steaks in fancy recipes that earlier would have been either too much food or too expensive. Since they are thinner than standard steaks they should be quickly sautéed over high heat. If you wish to broil or grill them, do it fast, about 3" from high heat, and watch carefully.

Look What You Can Do With Broiled Beef Steaks!

Coat Them And Top Them With Something Fun

The toppings are enough for four 1" thick steaks. Broil them 4" from the heat. The time will depend on their thickness and the degree of doneness you like. (Also see box, page 88.) All recipes serve 4.

The Basic Steps:	Sprinkle both sides with salt and pepper. Then coat as follows:	Broil both sides, turning once, until done to taste. Baste if required. Top and finish as directed.
Greek Style *White feta melts into chunks of tomatoes and black olives.*	Whisk together 2 tablespoons olive oil; 1 garlic clove, crushed; 1 tablespoon lemon juice; salt and pepper.	**Topping:** 4 ounces feta cheese; 4 quartered cherry tomatoes; and 4 halved pitted black olives. Return to broiler until cheese melts.
Pesto and Pine Nut *A fresh basil flavor.*	Spread with pesto (purchased or your own, see page 18), using ½ tablespoon on each side.	**Topping:** 2 tablespoons chopped parsley and 2 tablespoons pine nuts. Return to broiler until nuts brown.
Hoisin *Has a sweet and pungent taste.*	¼ to ⅓ cup hoisin sauce.	Baste frequently with hoisin. **Topping:** 1 tablespoon minced green onion.
Persillade *Tops steak with garlicky crumbs, crunchy and browned.*	Rub meat with salt and pepper.	**Topping:** a mixture of 2 tablespoons melted butter; ½ teaspoon minced garlic; ¼ cup toasted fresh bread crumbs; ¼ cup Parmesan cheese; 3 tablespoons chopped parsley. Return to broiler until golden.

Chinese Beef and Onions

This is a mixture of thinly sliced beef and onions in just enough savory soy-sherry sauce to hold them together. It doubles and triples beautifully, and can be made ahead, so it's a good choice for a big party.

Prep Time: 10 minutes
Cooking Time: 8 to 10 minutes

4 teaspoons cornstarch
4 tablespoons soy sauce, divided
4 teaspoons dry sherry, divided
1 pound top round beefsteak or chuck,
*   very thinly sliced*
6 tablespoons cooking oil, divided
3 cups thinly sliced onions
½ teaspoon sugar

In a medium mixing bowl, combine cornstarch, 2 tablespoons of the soy sauce and 2 teaspoons of the sherry. Add the sliced beef and mix until thoroughly coated. Set aside while you prepare the onions.

In a 10" skillet, heat 2 tablespoons of the oil. Add the onions and sauté just until limp; don't let them color. Add the sugar and the remaining soy sauce and sherry. Cook and stir for about 30 seconds. Remove the onions to a plate or dish.

Put the remaining oil in the skillet. Add the beef and sauté over medium-high heat until browned. Stir in the onions and cook until well heated.

Yield: 4 servings.

The Clever Chef: If the meat is partially frozen it will be easy to slice thin.

The Adventurous Chef: To make Beef and Onions à la Steak Diane, for the soy sauce and sherry substitute 2 teaspoons Dijon mustard, 2 teaspoons port wine, ½ teaspoon Worcestershire sauce and salt to taste. When you combine the meat and onions, add 2 tablespoons lemon juice and ¼ cup minced parsley.

Cranberry ❧ Iced Tea ❧

This is a refreshing summer drink.

2 family-size or 6 regular-size tea bags
1 teaspoon whole cloves
2 cinnamon sticks, 2½" long
2 cups sugar
2 cups cranberry juice cocktail
1 cup orange juice
¼ cup lemon juice

In a 1-quart pan or bowl place the tea bags, cloves and cinnamon sticks. Pour 1 quart boiling water over. Cover and steep for 5 minutes. Strain the mixture into a 4-quart container. Stir in sugar and cranberry, orange and lemon juices. Add 2 quarts water. Serve over ice.

Yield: 4 quarts.

Beef Stroganoff

Everyone was serving this party dish in the 60s. Today it's more of a novelty but guests still love these tender beef strips bathed in sour cream and mushrooms. This freezes very well.

Prep Time: 15 minutes
Cooking Time: 30 minutes

1½ pounds beef round steak or tenders
    (see box p. 88)
1 tablespoon oil
2 tablespoons butter, divided
1 large onion, chopped fine
8 ounces mushrooms, sliced
½ teaspoon meat glaze such as Bovril
½ teaspoon tomato paste
2 tablespoons flour
1 cup chicken broth
1 cup sour cream
2 teaspoons finely chopped fresh dill or
    1 teaspoon dried (optional)
salt and pepper to taste

Cut beef into fingers ½" thick and 2" long. Heat the oil and 1 tablespoon of the butter in a large skillet. Add the meat and brown quickly. Remove from the pan to a plate.

Add the remaining butter to the skillet. Add onions and mushrooms and cook over medium heat until the onion is soft but not brown.

Off the heat, stir in the meat glaze, tomato paste and flour. Add the broth and stir over medium heat until the sauce comes to a boil. Season with salt and pepper.

Return the meat to the skillet, cover and simmer for 20 minutes.

Whisk in the sour cream a little at a time. Reheat if necessary but don't let it boil. Sprinkle the top with dill.

Yield: 4 servings.

Make-Ahead
❧ Trick ❧

When you make a sauced meat dish for company, put the sauce—without the meat—in a double boiler over hot, not boiling, water. This way it will hold for an hour or more. At serving time, add the meat and heat thoroughly. This way the meat won't overcook while it waits.

Beef Stir-Fries You May Not Have Tried

All recipes are for 1 pound boneless beef cut into thin strips or 1" cubes. Remember to salt. Use about 1 teaspoon unless the ingredients include soy sauce. You can also make these recipes with 1 pound of boneless, skinless chicken breast, turkey breast, pork, lamb, or raw whole shrimp, shelled and deveined.

The Basic Steps:	Mix and reserve for use in Column 4:	Heat 2 tablespoons oil in wok or skillet. Add beef. Stir-fry over high heat for 2 minutes. Salt and pepper. Then add:	Stir in the sauce from column 1 and add it along with the items below. Cook and stir until thickened. Check seasonings.
Fajita *All the fajita flavors along with corn and black beans.*	Mix 1 package fajita seasoning mix; ½ cup water and 2 tablespoons oil with meat. Let stand 15 minutes. Drain meat in sieve and discard marinade.	1 bell pepper in squares; 1 small zucchini sliced diagonally; ½ small onion in thin wedges. Stir fry 2-3 minutes.	⅔ cup salsa; 1 teaspoon chili powder; ½ cup whole kernel corn; ½ cup canned black beans rinsed and drained. Heat through. Serve with warm flour tortillas and shredded cheese.
Italian *Goes on spaghetti with lots of cheese.*	2 teaspoons cornstarch; ¼ cup Marsala; 1 can (14.5 ounces) Italian-style stewed tomatoes with juice; 1 cup Italian-style tomato sauce.	1 large zucchini in thin, 2" strips; 3 cloves garlic, minced. Stir fry 3-4 minutes.	Cook and stir 1 minute or until thickened. Serve over pasta with lots of Parmesan.
Sprouts *Deliciously fresh and crunchy with traditional Chinese flavors.*	Toss beef with this first: 2 tablespoons soy sauce; 1 tablespoon cornstarch; 1 teaspoon sugar; ½ teaspoon ground ginger. Mix in a bowl: 1 tablespoon cornstarch; 2 tablespoons water.	1 onion, sliced thin; 4 ribs celery, sliced diagonally; 1 pound bean sprouts (6-7 cups). Stir fry just until sprouts wilt.	Stir fry until thickened. Garnish with fresh coriander leaves.

The Basic Steps:	Mix and reserve for use in Column 4:	Heat 2 tablespoons oil in wok or skillet. Add beef. Stir-fry over high heat for 2 minutes. Salt and pepper. Then add:	Stir in the sauce from column 1 and add it along with the items below. Cook and stir until thickened. Check seasonings.
Far-East Peanut *Has the irresistable Thai and Indonesian combination of peanuts, salt, sweet and hot.*	3 tablespoons soy sauce; 2 to 3 tablespoons brown sugar; 2 tablespoons creamy peanut butter; 1 teaspoon lemon juice; ½ teasooon garlic powder; ¼ teaspoon dried crushed red pepper; ¼ teaspoon black pepper.	1 sweet red pepper in strips and 4 green onions in 1" pieces. Stir-fry 2 minutes.	Mix well. Lower heat to medium low, cover and cook 3 minutes. Serve with rice.

✌ Ice Cream Soufflé with Strawberry Sauce ✌

A creamy, puffy soufflé, crunchy with bits of macaroon. If it freezes solid, serve the sauce hot for a magical contrast. If there's less time, the ice cream will be soft-set and mingle with the berries and sauce.

1 pint vanilla ice cream, softened
4 amaretti, crumbled (see note)
¼ teaspoon almond extract
½ cup whipping cream, whipped
1 pint fresh strawberries, washed, hulled, and halved
2 tablespoons sugar
2 tablespoons chopped toasted almonds
2 teaspoons powdered sugar

Put the ice cream in a bowl. Add the amaretti and almond extract. Gently fold in the whipped cream and pour into a pretty glass serving dish. Cover with plastic and freeze.

In a small saucepan simmer the strawberries and sugar until the berries are soft but not mushy.

To serve, remove the dessert from the freezer. If it is frozen hard, leave at room temperature for 5 to 10 minutes. Sprinkle with toasted almonds and powdered sugar. Serve the strawberry sauce separately, heated if the soufflé is firm.

Yield: 4 servings.

The Clever Chef: Amaretti are dry Italian macaroons that come in tins. If you can't find them, substitute any macaroon.

Russian Shepherd's Pie

The creamy Swiss and cottage cheese topping of this herb-scented meat pie is reminiscent of Voreniki, which are exquisite little Russian cream cheese dumplings.

Prep Time: 20 minutes
Cooking Time: 25 minutes

Crust:

2 cups biscuit mix
1 egg, slightly beaten
¼ cup milk

Filling:

1 ½ pounds lean ground beef
½ cup chopped onion
½ teaspoon salt
½ teaspoon Italian herbs
¼ teaspoon freshly ground black pepper
1 clove garlic, minced

Topping:

1 egg, slightly beaten
2 cups creamed cottage cheese
½ cup shredded Swiss cheese

Preheat oven to 375°.

In a medium bowl combine biscuit mix, egg and milk. Form the dough into a ball. Pat it out ½" thick and line a 10" pie plate with it.

Heat a 10" skillet over medium heat. Add the beef, onion, salt, Italian herbs, pepper and garlic. Cook until the beef is browned. Drain off any excess fat. Put the mixture into the pie shell.

In a small bowl, mix the egg and cottage cheese. Spoon this over the meat mixture. Bake for 15 minutes. Top with the shredded cheese and bake for 10 minutes more.

Yield: 6 servings.

Chinese Pot Sticker Filling

Make the pie with a Chinese pot sticker filling.

1 pound ground beef
2 cups finely chopped cabbage
1 teaspoon salt
2 cloves garlic, minced
½ teaspoon ground ginger
a large pinch of five-spice powder
2 teaspoons soy sauce
a grind or two of pepper

Sauté everything as in the recipe above.

Meatballs in Marinara Sauce

These meatballs are deliciously moist and tender, perfect for pasta, good on their own. Remember them when you need a hot hors d'oeuvre. Guests devour them.

Prep Time: 10 minutes
Cooking Time: 25 minutes

*1½ pounds ground beef, pork or veal,
   or a combination*
¼ cup chopped parsley
1 clove garlic, chopped fine
¼ cup grated Parmesan cheese
½ cup soft bread crumbs
1 egg, slightly beaten
1 teaspoon salt
1 tablespoon olive oil
*2 cups marinara (tomato) sauce, your
   own or purchased*
*cooked spaghetti or other pasta as an
   accompaniment*
pepper to taste

In a large bowl combine meat, parsley, garlic, Parmesan, bread crumbs, egg and salt and pepper to taste.

Divide the mixture into 16 equal pieces and shape each into a ball. In a skillet large enough to hold the meatballs in one layer without touching, heat the oil over medium heat. Cook meatballs until nicely browned on all sides.

Add the marinara sauce and simmer gently for 15 to 20 minutes. If necessary, transfer to a large saucepan. Serve meatballs and sauce over pasta.

Yield: 6 servings.

Savory
❧ Butterflakes ❧

These are a lovely bread to go with a salad luncheon.

Preheat oven to 425°. Partly separate the leaves of brown-and-serve butterflake rolls. Spread the leaves with either: a mixture of equal parts mayonnaise and Parmesan cheese, or mayonnaise flavored with a little garlic salt or curry powder. Place on baking sheet and bake for 4 or 5 minutes.

Pita Devils

These snappy pita pockets make a good supper dish. They are also ideal for Sunday game watchers because knives and forks aren't needed. A big, crisp salad or raw vegetable sticks are all that's needed to make a full meal.

Prep Time: 5 minutes
Cooking Time: 10 minutes

6 6" pita breads
1 tablespoon oil
1 pound lean ground beef
1 tablespoon Worcestershire sauce
1 tablespoon Dijon mustard
1 tablespoon prepared horseradish
2 tablespoons capers
2 teaspoons cornstarch
2 tablespoons water
¼ cup beef broth
grated cheese as a garnish (optional)
pickles as an accompaniment

Wrap the pita bread in foil and heat it in a 350° oven.

In a wok or large skillet, heat the oil over high heat. Add the beef and cook and stir until it is no longer pink. Stir in the Worcestershire sauce, mustard, horseradish and capers. In a small dish mix the cornstarch with the water. Add this along with the beef broth and stir and cook until thickened.

Cut pitas in half and fill with the deviled meat. Top with grated cheese if you like. Serve hot with lots of pickles.

Yield: 6 servings.

❧ *Joan's Onion Cheese Polenta* ❧

From my cooking confrère who knows good eating and food.

½ cup chopped onion
2 tablespoons butter
5 cups cold water
1½ cups cornmeal
1¼ cups half-and-half
½ cup Parmesan cheese
¾ cup grated mozzarella cheese

In a medium saucepan sauté the onions in the butter until soft. Add 3½ cups of the water and bring to a boil. Put the cornmeal in a medium bowl and stir in the remaining water. Add this to the boiling mixture, give it a quick stir, cover and let it cook undisturbed over low heat for 10 minutes or until thickened and creamy. Add more liquid if necessary to make it drop from the spoon in soft plops. Stir in half-and-half and Parmesan cheese. Pour into a greased shallow ovenproof dish, sprinkle with mozzarella and run under the broiler just long enough to melt the cheese.

Yield: 4 servings.

Greek Meatballs

A huge dose of garlic, parsley, and oregano makes these meatballs seductive. The texture is different from regular meatballs due to a quick buzz in the processor. Don't use extra lean beef—it won't taste as good. Remember, the excess fat cooks out.

Prep Time: 15 minutes
Cooking Time: 8 minutes

2 cloves garlic
1 medium onion, cut into chunks
1 pound ground beef or lamb
1 cup parsley leaves, firmly packed
1 teaspoon salt
1 teaspoon dried oregano

Put the metal blade in the food processor, turn on the motor and drop the garlic through the tube. Then, with the motor still running, drop in the chunks of onion. When the onion is minced quite fine, stop the motor. Add the meat, and process until the meat is almost a paste. Add parsley, salt and oregano.

Form small balls and fry, or form sausage shapes about 4 or 5 inches long around skewers, pressing the meat on firmly, and broil or grill, turning often, for 5 to 8 minutes. Don't overcook or they'll be dry.

Serve the meatballs with Tahini Sauce and lemon wedges or stuffed in pitas with Cucumber Yogurt Sauce, shredded lettuce and chopped tomatoes.

Yield: 4 servings.

Tahini Sauce

½ cup tahini
⅓ cup lemon juice
1 clove garlic, crushed
salt and pepper to taste
chopped parsley as a garnish

Place the tahini in a small bowl. With a large spoon, gradually work in the lemon juice, beating hard. Beat in the garlic, salt and pepper, and enough water (up to ½ cup) to make a pouring consistency like that of heavy cream. Sprinkle generously with chopped parsley.

Yield: About ¾ cup.

The Clever Chef: Tahini is a Middle Eastern sesame seed paste. You'll find it in the international or health foods section of the grocery store.

Cucumber Yogurt Sauce

2 cups plain yogurt
½ medium onion, chopped
½ medium cucumber, peeled, seeded and diced
2 to 3 teaspoons olive oil
1 tablespoon white vinegar
1 teaspoon fresh mint leaves or ½ teaspoon dried
salt and pepper to taste

In a small bowl mix the yogurt, onion, cucumber, olive oil, vinegar and mint. Season to taste with salt and pepper.

Yield: About 2½ cups.

Fun Things to Do with Rice

Here are some ideas for making rice more interesting. Follow the table suggestions, then come up with your own ideas.

The Basic Steps:	Melt 1 tablespoon butter in medium saucepan. Add 1 cup rice and items below. Sauté 2 to 3 minutes.	Add 1½ cups water or broth plus the following ingredients. Bring to a boil, lower heat, cover and cook for 20 minutes.	Fluff with a fork and add any of the items below.
Royal Saffron *Fantastic with lamb.*	1 cup chopped onion; 1 small bell pepper, chopped.	⅔ cup frozen peas; 3 tablespoons sherry; pinch saffron threads or ¼ teaspoon turmeric.	3 tablespoons Parmesan cheese; 2 slices bacon fried crisp and crumbled; black pepper.
Cheddar *Delicious with grilled meats.*	1 teaspoon minced garlic; ½ cup chopped green onions (green and white parts).	1 bay leaf.	1 cup grated Cheddar; ¼ cup chopped parsley.
Anna's Italian *Try this with Italian sausage and peppers.*	⅔ cup chopped onion.	2 tablespoons white wine; 2 tablespoons tomato purée; optional pinch saffron.	Sprinkle with parsley.
Pecan *The basil makes this special.*	⅓ cup chopped onion	⅔ cup finely chopped pecans; 3 tablespoons chopped parsley; ¼ teaspoon ground ginger; ¼ teaspoon dried basil.	Garnish with fresh basil leaves.
Mexican Pilaf *Better than anything you'll get at your local Tex-Mex restaurant.*	Sauté rice until golden. Stir in 3 medium tomatoes, chopped; 3 medium green peppers, chopped; 1 large clove garlic, minced. Sauté 5 minutes.	1 teaspoon ground cumin; ¼ teaspoon salt; a little black pepper.	Sprinkle with parsley or cilantro.

Individual Barbecued Meat Loaves

These little loaves of beef, turkey and liverwurst bake in a barbecue sauce so they come out moist and nippy. Serve them with mashed potatoes to which you've added some chives and a little Parmesan.

Prep Time: 15 minutes
Cooking Time: 35 minutes

⅓ cup fresh breadcrumbs
½ cup red wine
1 small clove garlic, minced
1 pound ground beef
½ pound ground turkey
½ pound liverwurst
2 tablespoons finely chopped onion
2 tablespoons finely chopped celery
2 tablespoons parsley
2 tablespoons finely chopped green pepper
1¼ teaspoons salt
¼ teaspoon freshly ground pepper
½ teaspoon paprika
1½ cups barbecue sauce, purchased or
   homemade

Preheat the oven to 375°.

In a small bowl mix the crumbs, wine and garlic. Set aside.

In a large bowl mix ground beef, ground turkey, liverwurst, onion, celery, parsley, green pepper, salt, pepper and paprika. Add the crumb mixture and mix well. Shape 6 meat loaves, making them about 2" thick.

Place the loaves in a shallow pan. Pour the barbecue sauce over and bake for 35 minutes. Baste the loaves with the sauce 2 or 3 times.

Yield: 6 servings.

The Adventurous Chef: For a party or picnic, serve these loaves in a pastry crust. After the loaves have baked, cool them to lukewarm. While they cool, preheat the oven to 425° and make up a package of pie crust mix or roll out two 9" prepared crusts. Roll the dough quite thin. Cut 6 squares, each large enough to enclose a loaf. Wrap each loaf neatly and seal all edges well. Bake for 10 minutes. Remove from the oven and brush each with a little melted butter (about 2 tablespoons total), then return to the oven for 10 minutes. Serve hot or cold with barbecue sauce.

🏵 Barbecue Sauce 🏵

Use this sauce for any baked or grilled meat or poultry.

1 cup catsup
½ cup vinegar
¼ cup Worcestershire sauce
2 teaspoons prepared mustard
1 teaspoon chili powder
1 teaspoon salt
1 clove garlic, mashed

Mix all ingredients.

Yield: About 1¾ cups.

Charlie's Meatballs in Mushroom Sauce

The mushroom soup base is utterly transformed by the flavors it gains from the cooking meatballs. It may seem fiddly to plop all those little balls into the skillet, but once that's done you're home free. The dish cooks while you boil the rice and toss a salad.

Prep Time: 15 minutes
Cooking Time: 20 minutes

2 slices white bread, pulled into crumbs

1¼ cups milk, divided

2 eggs

1 teaspoon salt

½ teaspoon freshly ground black pepper

¼ teaspoon allspice

1 medium onion, chopped fine

1 pound lean ground beef

2 tablespoons cooking oil

1 can (10½ ounces) condensed cream of mushroom soup

cooked rice as an accompaniment

Put the crumbs in a large mixing bowl with ¼ cup of the milk and let them soak for a couple of minutes. Add the eggs, seasonings and onion. Mix well. Add the beef.

Heat the oil in a large skillet. Form 1" meatballs, drop them into the pan and brown. (Do this in batches if necessary.)

Combine the soup and remaining milk and pour this over the meatballs. With a wooden spoon stir and scrape the bottom of the skillet to bring up all the browned pan juices and mix them into the sauce. Cover and simmer gently for 15 to 20 minutes. Serve over rice.

Yield: 4 servings.

❧ Herb Toasts ❧

These are delicious with soups.

½ cup butter

1 teaspoon chopped parsley

¼ teaspoon dried oregano

¼ teaspoon dried thyme

¼ teaspoon black pepper

¼ teaspoon minced garlic

¼ teaspoon salt

¼ teaspoon minced shallot or onion

6 slices day-old bread

Preheat oven to 350°. In a small skillet melt the butter along with the parsley, oregano, thyme, black pepper, garlic, salt and shallot. Trim crusts from the bread and cut it into fingers. Dip them into the herb butter to coat both sides. Place on a baking sheet and bake until brown, 15 to 20 minutes, turning once. These are good hot, warm or at room temperature

Yield: About 24 toast fingers.

Taco in a Casserole

This is an easy meal in so many ways: it's quickly prepared, needs just 15 minutes in the oven, and provides main dish, salad and bread in one dish. How can you lose? P.S. It tastes awfully good.

Prep Time: 20 minutes
Cooking Time: 15 minutes

1 pound lean ground beef

½ cup chopped onion

1 cup tomato sauce

1 cup cooked red kidney beans, drained and rinsed

1 teaspoon chili powder, or more to taste

¾ teaspoon salt

¼ teaspoon freshly ground black pepper

6 crisp taco shells

1 cup shredded Cheddar cheese or Monterey Jack with jalapeños

1 to 2 cups iceberg lettuce, chopped coarsely

1 tomato, peeled, seeded and chopped coarsely

sour cream and taco sauce as garnishes

Preheat the oven to 350°. In a 10" skillet, brown the beef and onion. When the meat is no longer pink, stir in tomato sauce, beans, chili powder, salt and pepper.

Pile the meat mixture in a 9" pie plate. Break the taco shells into quarters and poke the pieces around the edge. Crumble the remaining quarters and set aside for later. Put the cheese on top of the meat. Bake for 15 minutes.

Remove the casserole from the oven, sprinkle the crumbled taco shells over the cheese, and bake for 5 minutes longer. Before serving, top the casserole with lettuce and tomatoes. At table pass sour cream and taco sauce.

Yield: 4 servings.

❧ Mexican Biscuits ❧

1 can (7 ounces) large refrigerated buttermilk biscuits

¾ cup chunky salsa

¾ cup Monterey Jack or mozzarella cheese, shredded

¼ cup chopped green pepper

⅓ cup sliced black olives

Preheat the oven to 400°. Cut each biscuit into 6 pieces. In a large bowl toss biscuit pieces with salsa to coat well. Spoon biscuit mixture into a lightly greased 9" round baking dish or pie plate. Top with cheese, green pepper and ripe olives. Bake for 25 minutes or until center is well set. Let stand 15 minutes before cutting.

Yield: 8 servings.

Steaks with Shiitake Madeira Sauce

S teaks in a creamy sauce perfumed with woodsy mushrooms and the faint sweetness of Madeira.

Prep Time: 10 minutes
Cooking Time: 15 minutes

½ pounds fresh shiitake mushrooms

1 tablespoon olive oil

2 cloves garlic, minced, divided

1 teaspoon dried thyme

½ teaspoon freshly ground pepper

4 tenderloin steaks or chuck tenders (see box p. 88)

2 teaspoons butter

2 shallots, finely chopped

1 cup Madeira wine

½ cup condensed beef broth

¼ cup whipping cream

salt and pepper to taste

Remove and discard the mushroom stems. Cut the caps into thin slices and put them in a small bowl. In another small bowl mix the olive oil, half the minced garlic, thyme and pepper. Coat the steaks with this mixture.

Heat a large non-stick skillet over medium-high heat until very hot. Add the steaks. Cook the steaks, turning them once, for a total of 10 to 15 minutes, or until done to taste. Remove from the skillet to a plate and keep warm. Salt and pepper them.

Pour off any fat from the skillet. Add butter and when it has melted add the shallots and remaining garlic. Stir to coat them with butter and cook, stirring, for 1 minute. Add the Madeira. Raise the heat and bring the mixture to a boil. Simmer over medium-high heat until the liquid is reduced to half a cup, 5 to 10 minutes.

Add broth and mushrooms. Cook, stirring occasionally, for 3 minutes or until the mushrooms are tender. Stir in the cream and any juices that have accumulated around the meat. Cook until the cream bubbles up and thickens slightly. Pour over the steaks.

Yield: 4 servings.

The Adventurous Cook: Substitute any mushrooms for the shiitake. Portobellos would be wonderful, oyster would be exotic. You could even use plain-Jane white ones, which may not be fashionable, but are good nonetheless.

Sesame Bagel Toasts

Preheat the broiler. Cut bagels in half horizontally. Place them cut-side-down under the broiler and toast lightly. Turn them over and spread the cut side with butter and sprinkle with sesame seeds. Return to the broiler and broil until the seeds are toasted.

Black Beans and Steak

You heap this slightly soupy combination of rare steak cubes, garlicky black beans and black eyed peas on corn tortillas and nestle in sprigs of cilantro, spring onion, salsa and cheese. If that doesn't make your mouth water, you need education.

Prep Time: 15 minutes
Cooking Time: 20 minutes

1 cup chopped onion
½ cup chopped green pepper
2 tablespoons oil, divided
1 tablespoon flour
6 garlic cloves, minced
½ teaspoon salt
½ teaspoon paprika
¼ teaspoon cumin
¼ teaspoon dried oregano
⅛ teaspoon red pepper flakes, or to taste
2½ tablespoons tomato paste
1 can (15 ounces) black beans, drained and rinsed
½ cup canned black-eyed peas, drained and rinsed
¾ pound sirloin steak, ½" to 1" thick
salt and pepper to taste
corn tortillas as an accompaniment
chopped green onions, fresh cilantro sprigs, salsa, shredded Cheddar and Monterey Jack cheese as garnishes

In a 10" skillet sauté onion and green pepper in 1 tablespoon of the oil until tender, 5 to 6 minutes. Stir in the flour, garlic, salt, paprika, cumin, oregano and red pepper flakes and cook 1 minute. Add 1½ cups water, tomato paste, beans and black-eyed peas. Bring to a boil. Lower heat and simmer uncovered for 15 minutes, stirring occasionally.

Heat the remaining tablespoon of oil in a medium skillet until very hot. Add the steak and brown each side, adding salt and pepper after each side browns. Lower heat to medium and continue to cook until the steak is medium rare with a dark pink center, or to your liking.

Remove steak to a plate or cutting board and let it rest for 5 minutes to allow the juices to be absorbed back into the center of the meat. Cut into ½" pieces. Stir the steak and any accumulated juices into the hot bean mixture. Heat briefly if necessary. Serve with tortillas and garnishes.

Yield: 4 servings.

Quick Beef Burgundy

This is not the slow-simmered dish with salt pork and carrots, but a sophisticated sauté of sirloin in a rich wine sauce that tastes classy and makes you think about lighting a couple of candles.

Prep Time: 10 minutes
Cooking Time: 25 minutes

5 tablespoons soft butter, divided

1 tablespoon minced shallot

¾ cup burgundy or other robust red wine

½ cup water

1 can (10 ½ ounces) condensed beef broth

1 small bay leaf

¼ teaspoon dried thyme

1 large clove garlic, pressed

2 teaspoons red currant jelly

4 tablespoons flour, divided

2 tablespoons vegetable oil

1½ pounds top sirloin, fillet steak, or chuck steak tenders, cut into ¾" cubes (see box p. 88)

freshly ground black pepper to taste

parsley as a garnish

In a 10" skillet heat 1 tablespoon of the butter and sauté the shallots until just heated and coated. Add wine, water, broth, bay leaf, thyme, garlic and black pepper. Cook rapidly over high heat, stirring, 5 to 10 minutes or until the sauce is reduced to 2 cups. (This equals 2 hours of long, slow simmering and mellows the wine). Stir in the currant jelly.

In a small bowl, make a paste with 2 tablespoons of the butter and 2 tablespoons of the flour. Off the heat, drop the paste in little blobs into the hot wine mixture and whisk madly. Return the pan to the heat and bring to a boil. Cook and stir until it thickens, which it will almost immediately. Remove the bay leaf and keep the sauce warm.

Toss the meat with the remaining 2 tablespoons of flour. Heat the remaining 2 tablespoons of butter and the oil in a large skillet over high heat. When the butter stops foaming add the beef and brown it quickly. You want it browned and crusty on the outside but still rare inside. Stir the meat gently into the wine sauce and sprinkle with parsley.

Yield: 4 servings.

The Adventurous Chef: I had beef burgundy done this way once in Germany. Stir-fry mushrooms, carrots and snow peas and fold them into the finished dish. Bake four 6" squares of frozen puff pastry and split them horizontally. Place the bottom pieces on individual plates. Ladle a fourth of the beef burgundy mixture onto each and top each with pastry. Add a jaunty sprig of watercress to each plate. If that doesn't impress your guests, they're not worth another invitation.

Fun with Napkin Folding

It doesn't take much time to fold napkins into pretty shapes and make your table come alive. I'm not proposing fancy napkin artistry that requires starched cloth dinner napkins. We Speedy Chefs have other things to do with our time. But that doesn't mean we have to forego a gracious table. Here are elegant napkin folds that work with soft, permanent press napkins or good-quality, dinner size paper ones.

Napkin Ring Thing

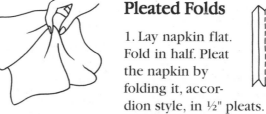

1. Grasp the center of the napkin.

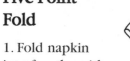

2. Pull it through the napkin ring and fluff the top.

Five-Point Fold

1. Fold napkin into fourths with open points at bottom. Bring the first point up to within 1" of the top.

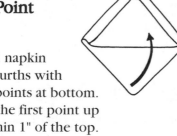

2. Repeat with remaining three points, leaving 1" between each point. Tuck left and right sides underneath.

Pleated Folds

1. Lay napkin flat. Fold in half. Pleat the napkin by folding it, accordion style, in ½" pleats.

2. Pull pleated napkin through the ring and spread the pleats.

Pleated Folds II

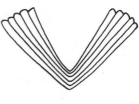

1. Lay napkin flat. Pleat the napkin by folding it, accordion style, in ½" pleats.

2. Carefully fold pleated napkin in half and poke the folded end into a napkin ring. Fan out the pleats.

Easy Sukiyaki

Don't look at all those things to be sliced and minced and chopped and decide it's too much bother. That's the only real work involved in this light, utterly delicious Japanese dish.

Prep Time: 20 minutes
Cooking Time: 7 minutes

1 pound boneless, trimmed beef rib eye or sirloin, thinly sliced

2 tablespoons minced fresh ginger

2 medium onions

8 large mushrooms

2 cups thinly sliced celery

8 green onions cut in 3" lengths

½ pound spinach, stems trimmed, rinsed and drained

½ cup canned condensed consommé

¼ cup dry sherry

¼ cup soy sauce

1 tablespoon sugar

2 tablespoons salad oil

boiled rice as an accompaniment

Place the beef and ginger in a small bowl. Slice the onions and mushrooms thinly and place them in another bowl with the celery. Place the green onions with the prepared spinach. In a bowl mix the consommé, sherry, soy sauce and sugar.

In a wok or 12" skillet heat the oil until very hot. Add beef and ginger and stir-fry until the beef loses its pinkness, about 2 minutes. With a slotted spoon, transfer beef to a bowl. Add the sliced onions, mushrooms and celery to the pan and stir fry for 2 minutes. Add the green onions and spinach and stir until the spinach wilts, about 1 minute. Add the cooking sauce and beef. Stir until it boils. Serve in bowls with the rice.

Yield: 4 servings.

No-Bake Fudge Brownies

When the hankering for chocolate becomes irresistible, here's an instant cure. These brownies are rich, chewy, chocolatey—and the raw dough is safe to eat!

1 package (12 ounces) semisweet chocolate chips

1 cup plus 2 teaspoons evaporated milk, divided

3 cups vanilla wafer crumbs

2 cups miniature marshmallows

1 cup chopped pecans

1 cup sifted powdered sugar

½ teaspoon salt

Combine chocolate chips and 1 cup evaporated milk in a heavy saucepan. Cook over low heat, stirring occasionally, until morsels melt. In a large bowl combine vanilla wafer crumbs, marshmallows, pecans, powdered sugar and salt. Mix well. Set aside ½ cup of the chocolate mixture. Stir the rest into the crumbs. Press this evenly in a well-greased 9" square pan. Combine the reserved chocolate mixture with 2 teaspoons of evaporated milk and spread evenly over the brownies. Chill. Cut into squares.

Yield: 3 dozen.

Try Some of the New Mushrooms

	Mushroom	Uses
Chanterelle	Golden-hued, vase-shaped with delicate flavor and texture. Harvested wild seasonally. Available dried. Very expensive.	Risottos, pasta sauces, salads.
Crimini	Hearty, darker-colored relative of the white button mushroom but with a more intense, earthier flavor. Cultivated. Inexpensive.	All uses.
Enoki	These are fragile, tiny white, long-stemmed mushrooms shaped like nails. Delicate flavor. Relatively inexpensive.	Salads or garnish. If you use them in a cooked dish, add at the end.
Morel	Brown, cone-shaped and sort of sponge-textured. Hearty flavor. Most often found dried. Expensive. Tend to have grit in all their little holes, so clean carefully. If you plan to use the soaking water from dried ones, strain through a coffee filter.	Delicious in sauces.
Oyster	Oyster-shaped cap, hence the name. Can be anywhere from white to dark. Cultivated. Relatively inexpensive. Firm-textured when cooked.	Sauces. If you use them for salads, sauté first.
Porcini (Italian) Cepe (French)	Looks like the fairy-tale toadstool. Brown. Wild only. Usually found dried. Very expensive but a little goes a long way.	Sauces, risottos—many sorts of dishes. Wonderful in pasta sauces.
Portobello	A member of the button mushroom/crimini family. Huge caps, generally at least 4" wide. Rich, meaty flavor; chewy texture. Relatively inexpensive.	Delicious grilled, fried or roasted. Use wherever button or crimini mushrooms are called for.
Shiitake (or Black Forest)	Umbrella shape. Tan to dark cap, tough brown stem (discard before cooking). Cultivated. Dried or fresh. Woodsy flavor. Expensive.	Use whenever you need mushrooms. Versatile like portobello, crimini and button.

Sunflower Nacho Pizza

When you just want to put on your slippers and robe and eat something fun, here's a way to turn an unassuming can of chili into a very pretty dish. The tortillas make a petaled edge and peppers and onions peek out jauntily from the golden center.

Prep Time: 10 minutes
Cooking Time: 25 minutes

12 corn tortillas

*1 can (15 to 20 ounces) chili, with or
    without beans*

1 medium green pepper, cut into strips

1 small onion, sliced

*8 ounces jalapeño cheese spread, cubed, or
    grated Cheddar*

*sour cream and salsa as accompaniments
    (optional)*

Preheat the oven to 400°. Spread the tortillas in one layer on a big baking sheet and bake until crisp but not brown (3 to 5 minutes). Lower oven heat to 350°.

Lightly grease a 14" round pizza pan. Cover bottom and edges with overlapping layers of tortillas. The edge will look like a giant flower. Spread the chili on evenly. Top with green pepper and onion. Bake for 20 minutes. Top with cheese and bake 5 minutes longer. Cut into wedges using a pizza cutter. Serve as is or with sour cream and salsa.

Yield: 6 servings.

The Adventurous Chef: Use the topping on regular pizza dough. Use chili without beans and sprinkle with ½ cup sliced pimento-stuffed olives and 2 4-ounce packages of shredded Cheddar cheese (2 cups). Top the baked pizza with 1 cup finely shredded lettuce.

✿ Chili Pie ✿

My friend Charlotte grew up on this and even though she is now a worldly business-woman, she still eats it with relish.

1 package (4 ounces) corn chips
1 can (15 to 20 ounces) chili without beans
½ cup chopped onion
1 cup grated American cheese

Preheat the oven to 350°. Place a layer of tortilla chips in the bottom of a greased 8" casserole or pie plate. Make a layer of half the chili, half the onion and half the cheese. Add the remaining chili and onion but hold off on the cheese. Bake uncovered at 350° for 25 minutes. Top with the remaining cheese and bake 5 minutes more or until the cheese has melted.

Yield: 4 servings.

Tamale Casserole

S ome nights you're tired of thinking cholesterol and "strive for 5" and ordering the kids to eat their peas or else. You want something fun and off the shelf. Go ahead, enjoy this zesty, dietetically incorrect casserole. Once in a while won't do any harm, no one will rush in and take away your gourmet badge.

Prep Time: 10 minutes
Cooking Time: 25 minutes

1 can (13 ounces) tamales
1 can (15 ounces) chili with beans
1 ½ cups shredded Cheddar cheese
2 cups crushed corn chips

Preheat the oven to 350°. Remove the tamales from the can. Save the liquid but discard any solid fat. Remove the paper from the tamales and cut them in half crosswise.

Lightly grease a shallow, 6-cup ovenproof dish. Place the tamales in the dish and spoon the liquid over them. Top with the chili, the cheese and finally, the corn chips.

Bake for 20 to 25 minutes or until heated and bubbly.

Yield: 6 servings

The Adventurous Chef: Mix into the chili a small can of whole kernel corn and ½ cup sliced black olives and spoon it on the bottom of the casserole. Top with the tamales and their sauce, then the cheese. Don't add corn chips. Bake as above.

Fresh Strawberries ❧ Spanish Style ❧

What could be simpler? You assemble the ingredients. Guests dip their berries into whatever they fancy. It's easy, delightful and so delicious.

1 cup sour cream
1 teaspoon grated lemon peel
½ cup powdered sugar plus more
*   as a garnish*
2 tablespoons Grand Marnier
1 quart strawberries with stems, washed
½ cup orange juice

Blend together the sour cream, lemon peel, ½ cup powdered sugar and Grand Marnier. Spoon into a small serving bowl, cover and chill. To serve, heap the berries in a pretty serving bowl. Set out a bowl of powdered sugar and a bowl of grand Marnier sauce. Diners dip their berries into whatever suits them.

Yield: 6 servings.

Chili Avocado Tostada

E asy does it with this one. Perfect for evenings when you don't feel gourmet or sophisticated or even grill-and-salad ordinary. Kick off your shoes and have a hot tostada oozing with chili, avocado, tomato, cheese and a cool splash of sour cream.

Prep Time: 8 minutes
Cooking Time: 20 minutes

4 flour tortillas

1 can (15 ounces) chili with beans

1 cup chunky salsa

2 avocados, sliced

1 onion, chopped

2 medium tomatoes, chopped

8 ounces Monterey Jack cheese, grated (2 cups)

sour cream and black olives as garnishes

Preheat the oven to 350°. Place the tortillas on a baking sheet and rub them with oil. Bake them for 5 minutes or until crisp.

Divide the chili among the tortillas. Return them to the oven for 20 minutes. Remove. Layer the tortillas with salsa, avocados, onion, tomatoes and cheese. Top each with a dollop of sour cream and a sprinkle of olives.

Yield: 4 servings.

❧ Lite Refried Beans ❧

As well as a full-flavored vegetable, this makes a super dip. Try it topped with grated cheese, although of course, at that point it is no longer lite.

4 ounces bacon, coarsely chopped (about 5 or 6 slices)
2 medium onions, chopped
2 cloves garlic, minced
2 cans (15 ounces each) navy beans or black beans, drained and rinsed
½ to 1 cup chicken broth
1 tablespoon white vinegar, approximately
salt and pepper to taste
red pepper flakes (optional)

Put the bacon in a cold 10" non-stick skillet. Cook and stir over medium heat until the bacon begins to brown, about 4 minutes. Discard all but 1 tablespoon of the drippings. Add the onions and garlic. Cook, stirring often, until the onions are soft and bacon is browned, 5 to 7 minutes. Add the beans along with ½ cup broth and the vinegar. With a fork or the back of a spoon, coarsely mash the beans. Taste and correct the seasoning with extra salt, pepper, pepper flakes or vinegar. The beans should be moist and the texture of soft mashed potatoes. If the mixture seems dry and stiff, add up to ½ cup more broth a little at a time until you get the right consistency.

Yield: 4 or more servings.

Try Pork Tonight

Today's lean pork is the darling of the quick cook. This pork has to be cooked fast or it will be dry and tough and an insult to your sauce and heated plates. Three to four minutes per side in a very hot pan leaves the average chop brown outside and succulent beneath. Like chicken, pork's mildness gets on cheerily with almost any flavor combination you introduce it to. If pork is in the fridge tonight you have all sorts of exciting possibilities for dinner. It is a lovely replacement for chicken breast in this book's recipes. If you liked a chicken recipe, fix it with pork next time. You can do a world of mixing and matching in the kitchen so do what you want, have fun, and win a little glory at your table. As I say in all the chapter introductions, seek out the recipes in the tables. The noodle broccoli stir-fry is super. Ham and sausage are two more friends of the speedy gourmet because both start with the rich flavors that usually come only after long cooking. Add some robust ingredients like peppers, onions and beans and you've got long-cook eating in short-cook time.

"Pork has to be cooked fast or it will be dry and tough and an insult to your sauce and heated plates."

Pork with Dried Mushrooms, Onions and Cinnamon

P ork cutlets are bathed in the flavors that suit them so well: the sweetness of melted onions, garlic and cinnamon, and the deep, smoky richness of dried mushrooms. Light, a little different and delicious.

Prep Time: 5 minutes
Soaking Time: 30 minutes
Cooking Time: 18 minutes

½ cup dried mushrooms, any type
2 tablespoon oil, divided
4 boneless pork loin chops
½ cup dry white wine
½ cup chicken broth
2 cups onion, chopped fine
1 clove garlic, minced
½ teaspoon cinnamon
salt and pepper to taste

❧ A Pork Pointer ❧

Today's pork is very lean and dries out easily in cooking. It's perfectly safe, and generally tastier, to eat it when it is still a little pink. Parasites are all but a thing of the past, and in any case are killed at 130°, which is well below the 160° needed for minimum doneness.

Soak the dried mushrooms in warm water for 30 minutes. Then rinse them several times (they can be very sandy) and dry thoroughly with paper towels. Heat a dry skillet over medium heat, add the mushrooms and cook for 2 to 5 minutes, watching carefully and turning a few times, to evaporate excess water.

While the mushrooms soak, heat a skillet over medium-high heat, add 1 tablespoon of the oil and brown pork cutlets on both sides. Salt and pepper them and remove to a plate. Pour the wine and broth into the hot skillet, scrape up all the browned drippings, and pour over the pork.

Place skillet over medium heat and add the remaining tablespoon of oil. Add onions and fry until they soften and turn transparent, 3 to 5 minutes. Add the mushrooms and cook for another 3 minutes. Add garlic, cinnamon, salt and pepper. Top with the pork and its cooking juices. Cover. Simmer gently for 5 minutes or until the pork is just done.

Yield: 4 servings.

Venetian Sausage Bowls

This rich, herby mix of meats in crunchy, hollowed-out rolls is a good choice when you invite folks over to watch the Super Bowl. Serve it with a crisp salad and cold beer.

Prep Time: 20 minutes
Cooking Time: 20 minutes

4 to 6 round hard rolls or submarine rolls
¾ pound ground beef
8 ounces Polish sausage, cut into ½" pieces
8 ounces brown and serve sausages, cut into 1" pieces
1 large onion, sliced
1 jar (15 ounces) spaghetti sauce
1 teaspoon Dijon style mustard
chili powder, mixed Italian herb seasoning, garlic powder to taste
6 ounces grated Cheddar cheese

Preheat oven to 350°.

To make the bread bowls, cut into the top of each roll with a sharp knife, cutting down around the edge to leave a ¾" wall.

Pull out the insides with your fingers. Brush the cut surfaces of each bowl with a teaspoon of olive oil and sprinkle a tablespoon of Parmesan cheese in each. Place on a cookie sheet along with the lids and bake for 15 minutes or until the cheese is melted.

While the bowls bake, brown the ground beef, sausages and onion in a large skillet. Drain off excess fat. Add the spaghetti sauce and mustard. Bring to a boil and simmer for 10 minutes, stirring occasionally. Sample the mixture and add chili powder, Italian herb seasoning and garlic powder to taste.

Fill the bread bowls with the meat mixture. Top with equal portions of cheese and return to the oven for a few minutes to melt the cheese. Serve immediately.

Yield: 4 to 6 servings.

The Adventurous Chef: Instead of Polish sausage, use frankfurters in 1" pieces, or a mix of both. Stir in the frankfurters after the ground beef and other sausages have browned. ◆ You will think of a hundred uses for this savory mixture. Stuff it into warmed pita halves, or let diners do it themselves, adding cheese and shredded lettuce. Ladle it over polenta or corn bread. Wrap it in flour tortillas.

❧ Pork Cassoulet ❧

Make the Quick Cassoulet on p. 154 with navy beans, substituting cubed ham or knackwurst for the lamb.

Pork Loin Chops with Cheese, Tomatoes and Tarragon

You'll love these pork chops sauced with fresh tomato, tarragon and gooey, barely melted cheese on a bed of pasta. Broccoli is good with this. Round out the meal with some crunchy French bread.

Prep Time: 10 minutes
Cooking Time: 15 minutes

3 ounces Monterey Jack cheese

3 tablespoons olive oil

4 boneless pork loin chops, about 4 ounces each

¾ pound ripe tomatoes, peeled and seeded and finely chopped

1½ teaspoons fresh tarragon or ½ teaspoon dried

salt and pepper to taste

cooked spaghettini as an accompaniment

Cut the cheese into ¼" slices and then into ⅛" strips.

Heat the oil in a medium skillet over medium heat. Add the pork and sauté for 2 minutes on each side. Sprinkle with salt and pepper. Add the tomatoes and tarragon. Simmer for 6 to 8 minutes or until most of the water has cooked out of the tomatoes and the sauce is slightly thickened. Turn the chops once or twice during cooking.

Scatter the cheese strips over the top and cook only until the cheese starts to melt. Serve each chop on a bed of cooked pasta and ladle the sauce over all.

Yield: 4 servings.

The Right Pan for Sautéing

Choose the right size pan—one that insures that the bottom is fully covered by the food being cooked. If you sauté 2 chops in a pan designed for 4 or 6, the pan bottom will overheat and the sauce or fat in the unused area will burn.

Thai Style Grilled Pork

Americans have fallen in love with the complex flavors of Thai food: spicy-sweet, hot-sour, peppery-cool. These pork chops will convince you that the Thai know what they are doing.

Prep Time: 10 minutes
Marinating Time: 30 minutes
Cooking Time: 12 minutes plus time to heat the grill

½ cup canned, unsweetened coconut milk

3 tablespoons soy sauce, divided

2 cloves garlic, minced

1¼ teaspoons ground coriander, divided

¼ teaspoon freshly ground black pepper

⅛ teaspoon Chinese chili-garlic paste

4 boneless pork loin chops

2 teaspoons lime juice

⅛ teaspoon red pepper flakes

1 teaspoon sugar

1 tablespoon dry-roasted peanuts, chopped

In a large plastic zip lock bag, combine the coconut milk, 2 tablespoons of the soy sauce, the garlic, 1 teaspoon of the coriander, the pepper and the chili paste. Close the bag and squeeze the ingredients around until they are well mixed. Slash the fat at the edges of the pork chops so they won't curl and add them to the bag. Close it and squeeze until the pork is completely coated. Leave at room temperature for 30 minutes, turning the bag several times.

Prepare the grill. Remove meat from marinade and drain; discard marinade. Place the pork on a lightly greased grill 4 to 6 inches above medium coals (or place under the broiler, about 4 inches from the heat.) Cook, turning often, until the pork is browned and offers only slight resistance when you press it lightly, 10 to 12 minutes.

In a small pan or microwave-safe bowl mix the lime juice, the remaining tablespoon of soy sauce, the remaining ¼ teaspoon of coriander, red pepper flakes, sugar and peanuts. Heat quickly. Place the meat on serving plates and spoon a little sauce over each portion.

Yield: 4 servings.

The Unhurried Chef: The pork benefits nicely from the short marinade, but it will have even more zest after 6 hours in the refrigerator.

Jazzed-Up ❧ Bread Sticks ❧

6 frankfurter rolls
soft butter
any of these: minced parsley, chives, poppy
    seeds, caraway seeds, Parmesan cheese

Preheat the oven to 425°. Cut the rolls in half lengthwise. Cut each piece in half lengthwise again to make sticks. Spread butter on all sides. Roll in any of the above seasonings. Bake at 425° for 5 to 10 minutes.

Yield: 24 sticks.

Pork Chops with Reuben Sauce

Here's a pork chop bathed in all the good stuff of a Reuben sandwich: a smooth, sweet-tart sauce and a blanket of gooey cheese. Unlike the sandwich, however, this isn't rich. So you can enjoy your Reuben and have a dab of dessert too.

Prep Time: 8 minutes
Cooking Time: 15 minutes

3 tablespoons butter
3 tablespoons flour
1½ cups skim milk
1½ teaspoons vinegar
1½ teaspoons Dijon mustard
6 tablespoons chili sauce
2 teaspoons vegetable oil
4 pork chops, about ½" thick
4 thick slices Swiss cheese, cut to fit the chops
salt to taste

In a small saucepan melt the butter. Stir in the flour and cook, stirring, for 1 minute. Add the milk and whisk and cook until smooth. Stir in the vinegar, mustard and chili sauce.

Heat the oil in a 10" skillet over medium-high heat. Brown the pork chops on both sides, about 2 minutes per side. Salt and pepper them. Pour off any excess fat. Lay a slice of cheese on each chop and pour the sauce over. Cover the pan and cook gently for 3 to 4 minutes, or until the sauce is heated through and the cheese has melted.

Yield: 4 servings.

The Adventurous Chef: Drain a 1-pound can of sauerkraut and pat half a cup on each chop before you add the cheese.

✄ Elephant Stew ✄

This is really silly, but there are nights when it is just the thing you need to keep you from taking a hard day's events too seriously.

1 elephant, medium size
2 rabbits (optional)
salt and pepper to taste
brown gravy, quite a lot

Cut the elephant into bite-size pieces. This will take about 2 months. Reserve the trunk as you will need something to store the pieces in.

Put the elephant pieces in a very large pot. Add enough brown gravy to cover. Cook over a kerosene fire for about 4 weeks at 467°.

This will serve about 3,800 people. If more are expected, add the 2 rabbits, but do this only if necessary as most people do not like to find a hare in their stew.

Now, don't you feel better?

Pork Chops with Horseradish

S weet onions, pungent horseradish and tangy vinegar make a perfect marriage with the gentle pork.

Prep Time: 10 minutes
Cooking Time: 30 minutes

2 tablespoons oil, divided
4 pork chops
4 medium onions, thinly sliced
⅔ cup chicken broth
⅓ cup white wine vinegar
1 bay leaf
salt and pepper to taste
3 tablespoons bottled horseradish

Heat 1 tablespoon of the oil in a large skillet over medium high heat. Brown the pork chops on each side and remove to a plate.

Add the remaining oil to the skillet and sauté the onions over medium heat, stirring, until they are soft but not brown. Add the chicken broth, vinegar, bay leaf, salt and pepper and simmer uncovered for 10 minutes. Return the chops to the pan and simmer 10 minutes more. Remove from heat, stir in the horseradish and serve.

Yield: 4 servings.

The Adventurous Chef: This recipe is very good using leftover pork. Brown the pork quickly, and proceed as in the recipe.

Poppy Seed ❧ Cheese Loaf ❧

1 loaf (1 pound) French or Italian bread
½ cup soft butter
1 medium onion, minced
¼ cup Dijon style mustard
2 tablespoons poppy seeds
8 ounces Swiss cheese in 1½" square slices

Preheat oven to 375°. Cut the loaf into 1" slices, cutting almost but not all the way through. Mix butter with onion, mustard and poppy seeds and spread on one side of each slice. Insert cheese slices between bread slices. Spread remaining butter mixture over the top of the loaf. Bake for 20 minutes or until light golden brown and cheese has melted.

Yield: 8 to 10 servings.

Pork Tenderloin with Honey Mustard Glaze

Easy and special. The honey mustard is perfect with the sweetness of pork.

Prep Time: 5 minutes
Cooking Time: 30 minutes

1 pork tenderloin, about 1 pound
1 to 2 tablespoons Dijon mustard
2 teaspoons honey

Preheat oven to 375°.

Mix mustard and honey. Coat the tenderloin thickly on all sides with the mixture. Place the meat in a shallow roasting pan and roast at 375°, basting occasionally, for 20 to 30 minutes or until a meat thermometer registers 160°. Slice thin and serve hot.

Yield: 4 servings.

Quick Toppings for Vegetables

Plain vegetables are fine, but not every night. Here are some ideas for putting oomph into the veggies. Just scan the list until something tempts you.

- **Mix equal amounts of melted butter and dry bread crumbs**—good on most anything.

- **Cook bacon crisp** in the microwave and crumble. Good with almost every vegetable except beets.

- **Thin slices of white onion** are good with carrots, peas or beans.

- **Sauté onions and mushrooms** (use canned mushrooms if you don't have fresh), and mix with any vegetable. Mixed onions and mushrooms also make a good vegetable on their own—scrumptious with grilled or sautéed beef or lamb.

- **Toasted almonds, hazelnuts or macadamia nuts** are good with Brussels sprouts, spinach or broccoli.

- **Grated Parmesan cheese** is good on any baked or broiled vegetable like zucchini, mushrooms or tomatoes.

Fun with Couscous

In case you're curious, couscous is made from the same grainy semolina flour as pasta. The grains are rolled, dampened and coated with finer wheat flour so they cook up separate and fluffy. Use this soft, tender grain as you would rice. You've probably eaten couscous salad (it soaks up dressing deliciously), but have you tried it hot with milk and raisins or dates for a morning cereal? Or sweetened and mixed with fruit and a bit of spice for dessert? Try it. You may love it or hate it, but you'll have broken the old routine.

The Basic Steps:	**Sauté the following in butter or oil for 1 to 2 minutes:**	**Add 2 cups boiling stock, 1 cup couscous and the items below. Simmer 3 minutes. Remove from heat, cover and let sit for 15 minutes.**	**Fluff couscous with a fork. Then blend in the following:**
Pilaf *Delicious with lamb or chicken. Try it as a stuffing.*	In 1 tablespoon butter, sauté 1 small onion, chopped; 1" piece cinnamon stick; 2 whole cloves.	Nothing added.	2 tablespoons each walnuts; golden raisins; currants and onion, chopped and sautéed in 1 tablespoon butter.
Curry *Serve with grilled meat or poultry.*	In 3 tablespoons butter, sauté ¼ cup chopped onion and 5 cloves garlic, minced.	1½ tablespoons ground cumin; 1½ teaspoons curry powder; ¾ teaspoon salt.	Nothing added.
Orange Pistachio *Lovely with pork or chicken.*	No sauté.	Finely grated zest of 1 orange; 2 tablespoons butter; ¼ teaspoon salt.	½ cup shelled, roasted pistachios, chopped coarse; 1¼ teaspoons orange flower water (optional but fun if you have it).

Mustard Pork Chops in a Cheese Blanket

Pork chops coated with tangy mustard and melting Swiss cheese are a breeze to prepare and fit for the most elegant dinner or a family treat.

Prep Time: 10 minutes
Cooking Time: 15 minutes

4 pork chops, about ½" thick
1 teaspoon olive oil
4 teaspoons butter
¾ teaspoon salt
freshly ground black pepper
4 teaspoons Dijon mustard
1 cup grated Swiss Cheese
⅓ cup vermouth

Slash the fat around the edges of the chops so they remain flat. In a large, heavy skillet that can go in the oven, heat the oil and butter over medium heat. Add the chops and brown them for 4 minutes on each side. Sprinkle with salt and pepper. Pour off the fat, cover the skillet and cook over medium low heat for 5 minutes. Turn the chops, cover again and cook for 5 minutes more.

Preheat the broiler. Place the chops on the broiler pan. Spread ½ teaspoon of mustard on each and sprinkle them with half the cheese. Broil 6 inches from heat until the cheese melts, 1 to 2 minutes. Turn the chops, spread with the remaining mustard, top with the remaining cheese, and broil again long enough to melt the cheese. Place the chops on a warm platter.

Reheat the juices that remain in the skillet. Add vermouth and scrape up all the brown bits. Boil until the liquid is slightly syrupy. Pour a little sauce over each chop.

Yield: 4 servings.

Blue Cheese ❧ Sourdough Toasts ❧

2 tablespoons butter
2 tablespoons crumbled blue cheese
8 slices of sourdough or French bread

In a small saucepan melt butter and blue cheese over low heat and stir to mix. Brush the mixture on both sides of the slices. Toast in the toaster oven or under the broiler for 10 to 15 minutes, or until lightly browned.

Yield: 4 servings.

Pork Chops with Spinach

These chops nestle under a silken purée of spinach, garlic and thyme which marries perfectly with the pork's slightly bland sweetness. Fix rice or buttered noodles and a salad with a fruit accent and you've got a feast.

Prep Time: 10 minutes
Cooking Time: 20 to 25 minutes

4 pork chops
flour
2 tablespoons olive oil
1 tablespoon plus 1 teaspoon butter,
*   divided*
1 clove garlic, minced
2 tablespoons minced parsley
½ cup chopped onion
½ cup dry white wine, divided
¼ teaspoon thyme
½ teaspoon Dijon mustard
2 packages (10 ounces) spinach, thawed
¼ cup grated Parmesan cheese
salt to taste

Salt the chops and rub with flour. Heat the oil in a large skillet and brown the chops on each side. Remove to a plate.

To any drippings in the skillet add 1 teaspoon butter, garlic, parsley and onion. Cook and stir over medium heat until the onion softens but doesn't brown, 3 to 4 minutes. Add ¼ cup of the wine, thyme, mustard, salt and spinach. Cover and cook for 5 minutes. Drain off any excess liquid. Stir in 1 tablespoon butter.

Purée the spinach mixture in the processor or blender. Taste and add salt if needed. Return the pork chops to the skillet along with any accumulated juices and top each with an equal amount of the spinach mixture. Add remaining wine. Over high heat, bring liquid to a boil. Cover and cook over medium-low heat for 5 to 8 minutes, depending on the thickness of the chops.

Remove to a serving platter or individual plates. If the liquid in the pan is thin, boil it down over high heat until syrupy. Pour over the chops.

Yield: 4 servings.

The Skinny Chef: Eliminate the butter. It will still taste good.

❧ Cheddar Buns ❧

A yummy use for extra hot dog buns. Once you try these you'll buy buns just for this purpose.

Cut 5 diagonal slices down from the top of each bun, not quite through to the bottom. Into each slit insert a piece of cheddar cut to fit and a thin slice of onion. Bake on a baking sheet in a 425° oven for 10 minutes or until the cheese melts.

Riviera Pork Chops

This is a nice dish for summer—pretty with the red tomatoes and green peppers. Serve with pasta or rice.

Prep Time: 12 minutes
Cooking Time: 20 minutes

2 tablespoons olive oil

4 pork chops

1 large clove garlic, crushed

1 green pepper, diced

½ pound mushrooms, sliced

2 tomatoes, peeled, seeded and cut into thin strips

½ teaspoon dried oregano

3 tablespoons dry white wine or vermouth

salt and pepper to taste

Heat the oil in a large skillet over medium heat. Add pork chops and brown on each side. Salt and pepper them. Transfer the chops to a plate.

To the oil left in the pan add the garlic, green pepper and mushrooms. Raise the heat to medium high and cook and stir until mushrooms are lightly browned. Return the chops to the pan along with any accumulated juices. Add the tomatoes, oregano and wine. Season the vegetables with salt and pepper. Cover. Simmer 3 to 5 minutes or until the pork is done and the liquid has thickened slightly. Don't overcook. Serve with the vegetable garnish.

Yield: 4 servings.

❧ Baby Carrots with Orange and Bourbon ❧

You need baby carrots, or at least the youngest ones you can find, because they are sweetest and cook quickest.

¾ pound peeled baby carrots

⅔ cup orange juice

2 tablespoons butter

2 tablespoons brown sugar

1¼ teaspoons cornstarch

1 teaspoon grated orange rind

2 tablespoons bourbon

⅛ teaspoon salt

Place carrots in a saucepan with the orange juice. Cook, covered, for 12 to 15 minutes or until tender. Pour the juice off into a little pan, leaving the carrots in their pan. To the juice add the butter, brown sugar, cornstarch, orange rind, bourbon and salt. Cook and stir over medium heat until the butter melts and the sauce thickens. Pour the sauce over the carrots.

Yield: 4 servings.

The Clever Chef: If you don't use baby carrots, add an extra 5 minutes to the cooking time.

Pork Chops with Garlic and Parsley

This recipe comes from a friend who has to live on a salt-free diet, a rough thing for a gourmet. Interestingly enough, the restrictions have made him a genius at seasoning, as this superb recipe demonstrates. Of course, I add salt when I make it.

Prep Time: 10 minutes
Marinating Time: 15 minutes
Cooking Time: 10 minutes plus time to heat the grill

½ cup parsley, chopped
1 clove garlic
4 tablespoons olive oil
1 ½ tablespoons lemon juice
4 pork chops
salt and pepper to taste

Chop the parsley and garlic in the food processor or a mini chopper, then, with the motor running, dribble in the olive oil and lemon juice. Or, mash the parsley and garlic to a paste in a mortar and work in the olive oil and lemon juice. Add salt and pepper to taste. Cover the pork chops all over with this mixture, rubbing it in well. Marinate at room temperature for 15 minutes.

Prepare the grill or broiler. Grill, broil or fry the chops until done to taste.

Yield: 4 servings.

The Unhurried Chef: Give the chops a longer marinade. Put them in the fridge for 1 to 2 hours or even overnight.

The Adventurous Chef: This marinade is delicious with lamb chops and chicken.

Toasted Onion ❧ Puff Bread ❧

This is wonderful with a salad meal.

1 loaf (1 pound) French or Italian bread
½ cup grated onion
½ cup grated Parmesan cheese
1 cup mayonnaise.

Preheat broiler. Cut the loaf in half lengthwise. In a small bowl mix the onion, Parmesan cheese and mayonnaise. Spread the cut sides with the mixture. Broil for 2 minutes or until golden brown and puffed.

Yield: 8 to 10 servings.

Pork Chops with Mustard and Sauerkraut

This is probably the best sauerkraut you will ever eat. It is slightly sweet and smoothed with cream. A wonderful autumn dinner. Mashed potatoes would be good with this.

Prep Time: 10 minutes
Cooking Time: 30 minutes

3 teaspoons Dijon mustard

¾ cup heavy cream (or light cream or half-and-half)

2 tablespoons brown sugar

3 cups sauerkraut, rinsed and squeezed dry

4 loin pork chops, 1" thick, trimmed of fat

4 tablespoons flour, seasoned with salt and pepper

2 tablespoons vegetable oil

salt and pepper to taste

Preheat the oven to 375°.

In a bowl mix the mustard, cream and brown sugar. Stir in the sauerkraut and salt and pepper to taste. Place the sauerkraut in a baking dish large enough to hold the chops in one layer without a lot of extra space.

Coat the chops with seasoned flour. Heat the oil in a 12" skillet over medium heat. When the oil is hot, brown the chops for 2 to 3 minutes per side or until they have a nice golden crust. Season with salt and pepper and lay them on the sauerkraut. Bake uncovered at 375° for 20 minutes. Don't overcook. Serve the chops with the sauerkraut on the side.

Yield: 4 servings.

❧ Some Quick Vegetable Ideas ❧

Corn Casserole: Pour a can of cream-style corn into a buttered casserole. Top with buttered crumbs and bake at 350° for 10 to 15 minutes or until heated through and golden on top.

Peas and Onions: Cook a 1-pound can of peas or cook a 10-ounce package frozen peas as directed on the package. Add a jar of cocktail onions (drained) and 2 tablespoons butter or ¼ cup sour cream (don't let it boil). Add salt and pepper to taste and heat through.

Green Beans and Mushrooms: Cook a 10-ounce box of frozen green beans. Add a drained 4-ounce can of sliced mushrooms. Heat with 2 tablespoons of butter or ¼ cup sour cream, as for Peas and Onions, and season to taste.

Vegetables au Gratin: This is especially good with cauliflower, broccoli, or Brussels sprouts. Cook them a little less than crisp-tender, place in a greased casserole and pour cheese sauce over all. Top with buttered crumbs and bake at 350° for 15 minutes.

Look What You Can Do With Broiled Pork Chops!

Coat Them And Top Them With Something Delicious

The toppings are enough for 4 pork chops. Grill or broil them 4" from heat 5 to 7 minutes per side. The time will depend on the thickness of the chops. Don't overcook. Pork is so lean that it can't take long cooking. Cut into one to check. When the wet pinkness disappears it's done.

The Basic Steps:	Sprinkle both sides with salt and pepper. Then coat as follows:	Broil both sides. Turn once. Mix topping and finish as follows:
Honey Mustard *A delicious sweet-pungent mixture.*	Mix 2 tablespoons mild honey, 2 teaspoons whole-grain mustard and ½ teaspoon rosemary. Spread on both sides. Place on broiler rack and let sit 15-30 minutes. Save any unused mixture.	After turning, spread with remaining honey mustard mixture.
Saté Style *Topped with peanut butter, soy and sugar.*	Mix 4 tablespoons crunchy peanut butter; 1 red chili pepper; seeded and finely chopped (optional); 2 teaspoons lemon juice; 1 tablespoon soy sauce and 1 teaspoon sugar. Spread over chops.	Garnish with sliced chilies if you like.
Orange Coriander *Fragrant with delicately flavored melted butter.*	Mix ¼ cup soft butter; 1 tablespoon grated orange rind; 2 teaspoons orange juice; 1 tablespoon chopped coriander leaves; 1 teaspoon coriander seeds and ½ teaspoon salt. Spread on both sides of chops. Save remaining butter.	Salt the chops when you turn them. Before serving, top each chop with ¼ of the remaining butter mixture.
Apple Sage Stuffing *Has a crisp buttery top of stuffing with crisp apple and sage.*	No Coating.	In a small skillet in 2 tablespoons butter sauté 1 chopped onion 1 minute. Add ¾ cup soft bread crumbs; ⅔ cup chopped apple; ½ teaspoon sage and 1 teaspoon grated lemon rind. Cook 3 to 4 minutes. Add 1 or 2 tablespoons water to bind. Broil until golden.

Ellen's Stuffed Pork Chops with Peanut Sauce

My artist friend, Ellen, appears in all my books because she is endlessly creative. This combination of an apple-nut stuffing and Indonesian peanut sauce is a winner.

Prep Time: 15 minutes
Cooking Time: 17 minutes

½ cup water

1 tablespoon butter

½ cup chicken-flavored stuffing mix

1½ tablespoons cooking oil, divided

¼ cup finely diced apple

¼ cup canned chestnuts (not water chestnuts) or unsalted cashews or pecans

4 double-thick pork chops

2 tablespoons creamy peanut butter

1 tablespoon or more orange juice

¼ teaspoon crushed garlic

2 teaspoons soy sauce

salt and pepper to taste

✣ Stuffing Trick ✣

I like to make extra stuffing and stir it into cooked rice to accompany this dish. If you want to try it, make a double recipe of the stuffing. Cook 1 cup of raw rice the usual way. When it is done, fluff it with a fork, fold in the extra stuffing and heat briefly to rewarm.

In a medium saucepan bring the water and butter to a boil. Add stuffing mix, cover, remove from heat and let stand for 5 minutes.

In a skillet heat ½ tablespoon of the oil. Add the apple and cook and stir over medium heat for 1 to 2 minutes or until slightly softened. Add the apple to the stuffing along with the chestnuts.

Cut a deep pocket in the side of each chop and slash the fat on the chops so they won't curl. Sprinkle salt and pepper inside the pockets and fill each one with stuffing. Season the outside lightly with salt and pepper. In a 10" skillet heat 1 tablespoon oil. Add the chops. Turn the heat to low and sauté covered for 7 minutes. Turn the chops, cover, and cook for 5 minutes.

In a small dish mix the peanut butter, orange juice, garlic and soy sauce. When the chops are done, uncover the pan and spread sauce on each chop. Cover and cook for 5 minutes more.

Remove the chops to warm plates. If the sauce in the pan is thin, turn the heat to high and boil rapidly until sauce makes big bubbles and is syrupy. Pour over the chops and serve.

Yield: 4 servings.

Spicy Pork and Tofu

This recipe dates from my Chinese cooking classes back in the 70s. Meaty pork contrasted with silky-soft tofu in an aromatic, sweet-hot sauce.

Prep Time: 15 minutes
Cooking Time: 8 to 10 minutes

½ pound lean fresh pork, finely ground
2 tablespoons soy sauce
2 tablespoons dry sherry
1 teaspoon sugar
1 tablespoon cornstarch
1 tablespoon water
¼ cup oil
10 ounces tofu, in ½" slices
2 tablespoons brown bean sauce
hot red pepper flakes to taste
2 teaspoons minced fresh ginger
1 teaspoon minced garlic
4 minced green onions, white part only
½ cup chicken broth
1½ teaspoons salt
1 tablespoon Oriental sesame oil
cooked rice as an accompaniment

In a medium bowl mix the pork, soy sauce, sherry and sugar. In a small bowl mix the cornstarch with 1 tablespoon of water.

Place a wok or skillet over high heat. Add the oil and when it is very hot, add the pork mixture. Stir-fry 2 to 3 minutes. Add the tofu, bean sauce, hot pepper, ginger, garlic, green onions, chicken broth and salt. Stir-fry for 2 to 3 minutes. Stir up the cornstarch paste and add. Cook and stir until thickened and clear. Add the sesame oil. Serve hot with rice.

Yield: 4 servings.

The Clever Chef: Brown bean sauce and sesame oil are available in Oriental markets and in the Oriental section of many supermarkets.

❧ When You Don't Have Fresh Salad Greens ❧

These cooked vegetables make a lovely salad tossed with vinaigrette (see box p. 199): green beans, asparagus, hearts of palm, artichoke hearts, beets or beans (garbanzos, kidney, black), beets.

These cooked vegetables combine well with mayonnaise: mixed vegetables (canned or frozen), peas, potatoes.

Try the following ideas for thawed frozen peas: Mix 2 cups peas with ½ cup sour cream, 2 tablespoons chopped chives, 2 teaspoons dried dill weed and salt and pepper to taste.

Mix 1½ cups peas with ½ cup sliced celery, ¼ cup sliced radishes, ¼ cup sliced green onions, ½ cup sour cream, 1 tablespoon lemon juice, ¼ teaspoon Dijon mustard and salt and pepper to taste.

Mix 2 cups peas with ½ cup salted peanuts and ½ cup mayonnaise.

Yield: All recipes make 4 servings.

Pork Stir-Fries You May Not Have Tried

All these wonderful, quick recipes use 1 pound of boneless pork cut into thin strips or 1" cubes. Remember to salt. Unless the ingredients include soy sauce, use about 1 teaspoonful. You can also make these recipes using boneless, skinless chicken or turkey breast, lamb, beef or raw whole shrimp, shelled and deveined. Use the same amounts.

The Basic Steps:	Mix and reserve for use in Column 4:	Heat 2 tablespoons oil in wok or skillet. Add pork, salt and pepper. Stir-fry over high heat for 2 minutes. Add the following:	Stir the sauce from column 1 and add it along with the items below. Cook and stir until thickened. Check seasonings.
Zucchini and Pepper *There are lots of vegetables in this Italian-style stir-fry.*	¼ cup chicken broth; ⅛ teaspoon pepper; hot red pepper flakes to taste; 1 teaspoon corn-starch.	2 cloves garlic, minced; 1½ cups green pepper; 1 medium onion; 2 cups zucchini, all thinly sliced; 1½ tea-spoons Italian herbs; salt and pepper. Stir-fry 4-5 minutes.	When thickened stir in ¼ cup grated Parmesan cheese. Serve with more cheese.
Mushroom and Snow Pea *A more traditional stir-fry.*	¾ cup chicken broth; ¼ cup soy sauce; and 3 teaspoons cornstarch.	2 cups diced celery; 6 ounces snow peas; 6 large mushrooms, sliced; and 5 green onions, sliced. Stir-fry 3-4 minutes or until crisp-tender.	Stir in ¾ cup slivered almonds that have been quickly toasted in a dry skillet over medium-high heat.
Noodle Broccoli *With curly Oriental noodles.*	1⅔ cups water; 3 tablespoons soy sauce and 2 table-spoon sherry.	1 cup bell pepper in ¾" squares; 2 cups broccoli florets; ⅔ cup green onions in 1" pieces. Stir-fry 2-3 minutes.	6 ounces ramen noodles (soup pack-age is fine). Stir-fry 3-4 minutes or until noodles are soft and liquid absorbed.
Sesame Cauliflower Broccoli *A lovely mix of tastes and colors.*	Mix 2 tablespoons cornstarch and 2 tablespoons soy sauce with pork.	2 tablespoons sesame seeds. Stir-fry 1 min. Add 1 cup broccoli and 1 cup cauliflower in ½" cubes. Stir-fry 3-4 minutes.	Nothing added.

Pork Chops with Tomatoes, Capers and Olives

The sauce for these succulent chops is thick, chunky and ample. You'll scrape up every little nugget. Delicious with rice or pasta tossed with cheese.

Prep Time: 10 minutes
Cooking Time: 20 minutes

4 loin pork chops, 1" thick

1 tablespoon oil

⅔ cup finely chopped shallots

½ cup dry white wine or vermouth

2 cans (14 to 16 ounces each) plum tomatoes, drained and chopped

1½ teaspoons dried basil

¼ teaspoon dried thyme

12 pitted black olives, quartered (Mediterranean are best)

2 tablespoons drained capers

2 tablespoons butter

½ teaspoon sugar

¼ cup chopped parsley

salt and pepper to taste

Pat the chops dry and season with salt and pepper. In a medium skillet heat the oil over medium high until very hot. Brown the chops and remove to a plate. Add the shallots to the skillet and cook over medium-high heat, stirring, until they are soft. Add the wine, tomatoes, basil and thyme. Break up the tomatoes.

Simmer, stirring occasionally, for 5 minutes. Add the olives, capers, butter, sugar, and salt and pepper to taste. Mix well then return the chops along with any accumulated juices. Cover and simmer for 5 minutes or until the pork is no longer pink. Don't overcook. Place the chops on a heated platter, spoon the sauce around them and sprinkle with parsley.

Yield: 4 servings.

❧ Cheese Puffies ☙

1 package (7 ounces) refrigerated biscuits
1 egg
2 tablespoons light cream
⅛ teaspoon dry mustard
¼ teaspoon salt
½ cup grated cheese (any type)

Preheat the oven to 450°. Oil an 8" pie plate. Arrange the biscuits in a circle, overlapping, leaving the center area open. In a small bowl beat the egg with the cream, mustard, salt and cheese. Pour this over the biscuits. Bake for 15 minutes. Serve warm. To serve, tear apart with a fork.

Yield: 4 servings.

Ginger Pork

Crispy-edged, marinated pork strips with a heady, pungent-sweet ginger soy sauce. Serve with pasta and a spinach salad, and imagine yourself in a little three-star bistro.

Prep Time: 10 minutes
Marinating Time: 15 minutes
Cooking Time: 10 minutes

1 pound ½" thick boneless pork loin cut
   into ½" strips

1 teaspoon dry sherry

½ cup chopped onion

¼ cup soy sauce

5 teaspoons white vinegar

½ teaspoon mild honey

4 teaspoons sugar

4 teaspoons peeled, grated ginger

½ teaspoon cornstarch

3 tablespoons chopped green onion, green
   part only

¼ cup flour seasoned with salt and pepper

¼ cup vegetable oil

freshly ground black pepper to taste

In a bowl mix the pork, sherry, onion and pepper to taste. Let stand for 15 minutes.

In a blender place soy sauce, vinegar, honey, sugar, ginger and cornstarch. Purée. Pour into a small saucepan and bring to a boil over medium-high heat, stirring. Stir in the green onion.

Lift the pork from the marinade and dredge it in the flour. If some onion clings to the pork, so much the better.

In a medium skillet heat the oil over medium-high heat until hot but not smoking. Stir-fry the pork for 4 to 5 minutes or until all pinkness has gone. Drain on paper towels. Serve with the ginger-soy sauce.

Yield: 4 servings.

❦ Fun Things to Do with Quick Pasta ❦

For a fast side dish for four, cook 8 ounces of angel hair, capellini, fine egg noodles or tiny shells—any of these should cook in 3 to 4 minutes. Then pick one of the ideas below.

Toss buttered pasta or noodles with: ½ teaspoon caraway or poppy seeds or ¼ teaspoon nutmeg ♦ ⅔ cup whipping cream ♦ ⅔ cup heavy cream and ¾ cup Swiss cheese ♦ 1 to 2 tablespoons

any fresh, chopped herbs, especially parsley, basil and dill ♦ 2 tablespoons parsley, 2 tablespoons Parmesan cheese and ⅛ teaspoon garlic powder, heating briefly to melt the cheese.

Top buttered pasta or noodles with: Soft breadcrumbs browned in butter ♦ ¼ cup Parmesan cheese, dots of butter (brown under the broiler).

Apricot Raspberry Stuffed Pork Chops

The apricot stuffing is heavenly, the sauce tart-sweet, the end result wonderful.

Prep Time: 15 minutes
Cooking Time: 16 minutes

¼ cup raspberry vinegar
¼ cup orange juice
3 tablespoons mustard
1 teaspoon honey
1 teaspoon dried tarragon
4 boneless pork loin chops, 1" thick
½ cup dried apricots, sliced
¼ cup seedless raspberry preserves
1 tablespoon olive oil

In a small bowl combine vinegar, orange juice, mustard, honey and tarragon. Set aside.

Cut a deep pocket in the side of each pork chop. In a small bowl mix the apricots and preserves. Put an equal amount of fruit mixture in the pocket of each chop.

In a heavy skillet, heat oil over medium-high heat. Brown the chops on one side for 2 to 3 minutes. Turn. Add the vinegar mixture and lower the heat. Cover and simmer gently for 8 to 10 minutes or until done.

Yield: 4 servings.

❧ Things to Add to Your Green Salads ❧

Crisp Accents: Croutons, nuts, jicama, real bacon bits, water chestnuts, diced fennel or celery.

Soft Accents: Tomato, mushrooms, avocados. Hard-cooked eggs, sliced, diced or riced.

Cooked Vegetables: Potatoes, garbanzos, beets, artichokes (marinated or not), water chestnuts, bamboo shoots, marinated mushrooms.

Fruits: Oranges, tangerines, grapefruit, apple, grapes, papaya, pineapple. Use these with discretion.

Fresh Herbs: Tarragon, chives, parsley, chervil, basil (perfect with tomatoes), dill (wonderful with tomatoes or cucumbers). Most of these, except for parsley, are also good dried.

Cheese: Swiss, feta, blue, Roquefort. Mozzarella is made for tomatoes and basil.

Nuts and Seeds: Walnuts, peanuts, macadamias, toasted almonds, cashews, pine nuts, sunflower seeds. I like to sauté nuts with an herb like rosemary.

Ham Slices in Port and Cream

The sweetness of onion and carrot caramelized in butter and the mellow richness of port melt into the cream that coats the smoky ham slices. This is a sauce to roll luxuriously over your tongue.

Prep Time: 15 minutes
Cooking Time: 25 minutes

1 tablespoon butter
1 tablespoon oil
1 medium onion, finely chopped
1 medium carrot, finely chopped
2 ribs celery, finely chopped
1 cup white port wine, divided
1 pound cooked ham, sliced ¼" to ⅓" thick
1 cup whipping cream
salt, cayenne pepper and paprika to taste

In a large skillet, heat the butter and oil. Add the onion, carrot and celery and cook and stir over medium heat for 5 minutes. Add ¼ cup of the port. Raise the heat to high and cook until the sauce is thick and syrupy, 4 to 5 minutes. Lay the ham on the sauce. Add the remaining port. Reduce heat to medium low and simmer covered for 15 minutes.

Remove the ham to a heated platter and keep it warm. Raise the heat to medium high and boil uncovered until the liquid has reduced by half. Lower heat, stir in the cream and cook and stir for 5 minutes or until slightly thickened. Don't let it come to a boil. Season to taste with salt, pepper and paprika. Pour sauce over ham slices.

Yield: Serves 4.

The Skinny Chef: Instead of whipping cream use light cream, half-and-half or milk mixed with 1 tablespoon of flour and cooked until thickened.

❧ Carrots with Fresh Green Grapes ❧

I bet you never thought of this combination: the sweetness of carrots balanced by the juicy tartness of grapes. The speed trick is shredding the carrots so they cook more quickly.

4 cups very coarsely shredded carrots
2 tablespoons butter, cut into pieces
¼ teaspoon anise seed
½ teaspoon salt
½ teaspoon sugar
2 tablespoons water
1 cup seedless green grapes

Combine carrots, butter, anise seed, salt, sugar and water in a 1-quart saucepan. Cover and cook for 5 to 10 minutes or until carrots are tender. Stir in grapes and continue to cook until the grapes are heated through. Serve hot and buttery.

Yield: 4 servings.

Ham and Cheese Curry

This is a wonderful way to serve that chunk of ham in the fridge. The curry sauce is just right with the salty, smoky ham, and the accompaniments give it a sparkle. Serve with a green salad and crusty bread.

Prep Time: 15 to 20 minutes, depending on accompaniments
Cooking Time: 10 minutes

2 tablespoons butter

2 tablespoons flour

½ teaspoon salt

½ teaspoon pepper

½ teaspoon paprika

1 to 2 tablespoons curry powder

1 cup milk

2 medium onions, grated

½ cup sharp Cheddar cheese, grated

¼ cup sherry or vermouth

2 cups ham in 1" cubes

boiled rice, plus little dishes of raisins, almonds, chutney, crumbled bacon, fresh pineapple cubes, avocado cubes and so forth as accompaniments

Melt the butter in a medium saucepan, stir in the flour and let it bubble for a couple of minutes. Add salt, pepper, paprika and curry powder. Cook and stir for 30 seconds. Add milk and cook and stir until thickened. Add the grated onions, Cheddar cheese, wine and ham. Cook and stir until thoroughly heated. Serve with rice and accompaniments.

Yield: 4 servings.

The Vegetarian Chef: Replace ham with cooked brocolli or cauliflower.

Hot Herb Loaf

½ cup softened butter
1 teaspoon dried tarragon
1 teaspoon dried basil
1 teaspoon dried oregano
1 loaf (1 pound) French or Italian bread

Preheat oven to 350°.

In a small bowl, mix butter and herbs. Cut the loaf in half horizontally and spread the cut sides with herb butter.

Press the halves together firmly. Heat in a 350° oven for 20 minutes. To serve, cut the loaf into 2" slices.

Yield: 6 to 8 servings.

Ham, Tomato and Cheese Tart

This is so pretty with its garnish of tomato slices and parsley. It's just the thing to serve when you have a group to lunch.

Prep Time: 20 minutes
Cooking Time: 25 to 30 minutes

1 cup finely chopped cooked ham
1 baked 9" pie shell
2 medium tomatoes, sliced
3 tablespoons minced onion
½ teaspoon dried oregano
¼ cup mayonnaise
4 ounces Cheddar cheese, grated
4 ounces Monterey Jack cheese, grated
⅛ teaspoon garlic powder
1 thinly sliced tomato and
    2 tablespoons minced parsley for garnish
salt and pepper to taste

Preheat oven to 350°. Place the ham in the pie shell and cover with the tomatoes. Sprinkle with onion, oregano, salt and pepper. Bake for 20 minutes.

In a small bowl mix mayonnaise, cheeses and garlic powder. When the 20-minute baking time is up, remove the flan from the oven and spread with the cheese mixture. Return it to the oven and bake until the cheese melts and puffs, 5 to 10 minutes. Garnish with tomato slices and parsley.

Yield: 6 to 8 servings.

No-Bake Chocolate Cherry Clusters

Here's the solution when the school has asked you to send cookies. They're a good Christmas cookie too.

1 cup sugar
1 square (1 ounce) unsweetened chocolate
¼ cup milk
1 tablespoon butter
¼ cup smooth peanut butter
1 cup quick-cooking oatmeal
2 tablespoons flaked coconut or chopped nuts
2 tablespoons chopped maraschino cherries

In a saucepan mix the sugar, chocolate, milk and butter. Heat over medium-low heat, stirring constantly, until the chocolate melts. Boil for 1 minute, stirring occasionally. Remove from the heat and blend in the peanut butter. Mix well. Add the oats, coconut and cherries. Mix thoroughly. Drop by teaspoonfuls onto wax paper and cool.

Yield: 4 dozen.

Red Beans and Rice

Homey comfort food. Good on a winter evening or when you get a longing for the simple life.

Prep Time: 10 minutes
Cooking Time: 25 minutes

1 pound smoked or Polish sausage, in ½" slices

1 medium onion, chopped

1 green pepper, chopped

1 clove garlic, pressed

2 cans (15 ounces each) kidney beans, drained and rinsed

1 can (14 to 16 ounces) chopped stewed tomatoes with their liquid

½ teaspoon dried oregano

½ teaspoon pepper

dried hot red pepper flakes (optional)

cooked rice as an accompaniment

In a large saucepan, cook the sausage over low heat for 5 to 8 minutes. Add the onion, green pepper and garlic and sauté until tender, about 5 minutes. Drain off fat if necessary. Add beans, tomatoes and seasonings, and simmer uncovered for 20 minutes. Serve over rice.

Yield: 4 to 6 servings.

The Adventurous Chef: Mash part of the beans against the side of the pan and then stir to mix them in. This gives a nice change of texture.

The Vegetarian Chef: Omit the sausage.

Fruit Romanoff

This was the specialty of an Austrian friend who gave lovely parties. The thick, heavenly liqueur-flavored sauce settles down through the berries so that each bite is blissfully cream-laden. You can use strawberries, raspberries, peaches—as you like it.

1 cup whipping cream

3 tablespoons kirsch, Grand Marnier or framboise liqueur

2 tablespoons powdered sugar

½ cup toasted, slivered almonds (optional)

1 pint vanilla ice cream, slightly softened

2 to 3 cups raspberries or strawberries

In a medium bowl whip the cream until stiff. Beat in liqueur and sugar. Fold in almonds. Put the softened ice cream in a large bowl and fold in the whipped cream mixture. Cover and put in the freezer until dessert time—an hour will make it barely firm, which is what you want. To serve, spoon berries into individual dishes and top with a spoonful of the sauce.

Yield: 6 servings.

Galloping Horses

This Oriental dish of hot spicy pork cubes ladled over chilled lettuce and orange sections is so beautiful you know it's good before you taste it. Serve it with Lemon Chive Pasta (see p. 78) or couscous mixed with minced green onion.

Prep Time: 15 minutes
Cooking Time: 8 to 10 minutes

Boston, romaine or leaf lettuce
2 cans mandarin oranges, drained
2 tablespoons oil
2 cloves garlic, minced
1 pound pork, in ¼" dice (2 cups)
¼ cup finely chopped peanuts
2 tablespoons sugar
2 tablespoons soy sauce
2 tablespoons water
salt and cayenne to taste

Arrange a bed of lettuce leaves on a platter or on 4 individual plates. Top with the oranges and chill while you prepare the pork.

In a wok or medium skillet heat the oil. Add the garlic and pork and stir fry until the pork is browned, 2 to 3 minutes. Add the peanuts, sugar, soy sauce, water and salt and cayenne to taste. Stir-fry over high heat until it is well mixed and the sauce is syrupy. Don't overcook the pork. Pour pork and its sauce over the chilled salads and serve at once so diners can appreciate the contrast of hot and cold.

Yield: 4 servings.

❧ Easy Dobos Torte ❧

A pound cake, some chocolate chips and sour cream, and voilà—a delectable, multi-layered, fudge-filled cake. Make it in minutes, enjoy it at leisure.

12 ounces chocolate chips
1 cup sour cream
½ teaspoon vanilla
⅛ teaspoon salt
1 frozen pound cake, thawed

Melt the chocolate in a double boiler or over low heat—or in your microwave. Let it cool to lukewarm. Place the sour cream in a medium bowl and fold in the melted chocolate, vanilla and salt. Cut a frozen pound cake into 4 horizontal layers. Fill and frost the top and sides with the chocolate mixture.

Yield: 8 to 10 servings.

Lesco

This hearty Eastern European stew of sweet peppers, onions, tomatoes and spicy Polish sausage makes a wonderful casual meal. Serve it in wide soup plates with lots of French bread to soak up the sauce.

Prep Time: 15 minutes
Cooking Time: 20 minutes

2 medium onions, sliced top to bottom

2 medium green peppers, in 1" squares

2 tablespoons butter

2 teaspoons paprika

1 pound Polish sausage, skinned and sliced into 2" diagonal sections

4 medium tomatoes, cut into eighths

1 cup beer

⅛ teaspoon pepper

salt to taste

parsley as a garnish

In a heavy casserole sauté the onions and peppers in butter until the vegetables are limp. Stir in paprika. Add the sausages, tomatoes, beer and pepper. Cover. Simmer for 15 minutes, stirring occasionally. Taste and correct the seasoning. Sprinkle lightly with parsley.

Yield: 4 servings.

The Vegetarian Chef: Omit the sausage.

❧ Fresh Pineapple Flambé ❧

A ripe pineapple shell is filled with succulent fruits and set aflame at the table. You want drama? Here's your dish.

1 medium ripe pineapple

½ cup slivered toasted almonds

¾ cup flaked, sweetened coconut

½ cup sugar

½ cup apricot jam

2 to 3 tablespoons dark rum

Preheat the oven to 350°. Cut the pineapple in half lengthwise and remove the fruit. Discard the core and dice the fruit. Place it in a large saucepan along with the almonds, coconut, sugar and jam. Heat over medium heat, mixing gently, until the sugar and jam melt and the fruit is just heated through. Don't let it cook.

While the fruit heats, place the pineapple shells on a cookie sheet in a 350° oven to warm through, about 15 minutes.

To serve, heap the fruit in the pineapple shells. Heat the rum in a small pan, set it afire carefully, and spoon it flaming over the fruit. It's fun to show off and do this at the table. Spoon the fruit into dessert bowls.

Yield: 6 or more servings.

Try Lamb Tonight

Middle Easterners, who eat so well, consider lamb their staple meat so you will find a lot of recipes from that area in this chapter. Turkish Wedding Lamb is a celebration for the palate. The pita pockets, filled with lamb, herbs and feta are divine, and the hearty quick cassoulet is a must on a cold winter night when you've put on your warm slippers and a fire is snapping on the hearth. When you've gone through the good things in this chapter, look through the rest of the book for inspirations. The topping for Greek Style beef steaks in the Grilled Beef chart is delicious on lamb loin or shoulder chops and you shouldn't miss it. Lamb also makes luscious, unexpected stir-fries. Look through the stir-fry charts in the Poultry, Pork and Beef chapters for ideas. Two absolute favorites with lamb are the Far-East Peanut in the Beef Stir-Fries and the Indian Curry in the Chicken Stir-Fries. Note that the Lamb and Eggplant Skillet in this chapter is really a stir-fried moussaka. You can also make it with beef.

"The hearty quick cassoulet is a must on a cold winter night when you've put on your warm slippers and a fire is snapping on the hearth."

Wedding Lamb

My friend Mary, who grew up in Turkey, gave me a longer-cooking version of this. She says this combination of lamb, cinnamon, clove and dill is a typical wedding dish. Serve with rice and a salad of green and red peppers and tomatoes.

Prep Time: 10 minutes
Cooking Time: 20 minutes

1 pound boneless lamb steak cut from the shoulder or leg
1 tablespoon vegetable oil
¼ teaspoon cayenne pepper
1 teaspoon ground cinnamon
1½ teaspoons dill seed
¼ teaspoon ground clove
6 green onions, in ½" slices
½ cup water
½ cup yogurt
salt and pepper to taste

Cut lamb into bite-size pieces. Heat the oil in a medium skillet over medium-high heat. Add the lamb and give it a stir. Sprinkle with cayenne, cinnamon, dill seed, clove, and salt and pepper to taste. Cook and stir until the meat browns slightly. Add green onions. Continue to fry for 2 or 3 minutes, stirring occasionally. When onions have softened, add water, cover and cook over medium heat for 8 to 10 minutes or until meat is tender. Stir yogurt into the sauce or serve it on the side.

Yield: 4 servings.

The Adventurous Chef: The Turks serve this dish on a bed of fried onions.

Avocado Orange Salad

1 avocado
2 cups shredded lettuce
½ cup canned mandarin oranges, drained
¼ cup plain yogurt
2 teaspoons honey
⅛ teaspoon ground coriander

Peel the avocado and cut it in half lengthwise. Remove the seed. Slice each half into 8 long pieces. Place lettuce on 4 salad plates. Arrange 4 avocado slices on each, with 2 orange slices between each 2 avocado slices. In a small bowl mix the yogurt, honey and coriander. Pour it diagonally across the fruit.

Yield: 4 servings.

Lamb in a Jacket

Succulent lamb is topped with a savory herb mixture, melting feta and tomato, all baked in individual wrappers. The aroma that greets you when you open your package is mouth-watering.

Prep Time: 20 minutes
Cooking Time: 35 minutes

2 tablespoons butter

1 small onion, chopped fine

1 clove garlic, crushed

1 cup firmly packed parsley leaves, minced fine

2 tablespoons dry white wine

1½ teaspoons dried oregano, divided

1 pound boned leg of lamb

1 tablespoon olive oil

3 ounces feta cheese, crumbled (¾ cup)

4 slices of red-ripe tomato

salt and pepper to taste

Melt the butter in a small pan. Add the onion and garlic and sauté over medium heat, stirring, for 3 minutes. Add parsley, wine and ½ teaspoon of the oregano. Cover and simmer for 3 minutes.

Preheat the oven to 375°. Trim lamb of fat and cut the meat into 4 long pieces of equal size. Heat olive oil in a large skillet over medium-high heat. Add the lamb, remaining teaspoon of oregano, and salt and pepper. Sauté over medium heat for 3 minutes on each side.

Cover each piece of meat with an equal portion of the parsley mixture and top with crumbled feta. Place a tomato slice on each and salt and pepper lightly. Place each fillet on a piece of aluminum foil and fold to seal tightly. Place the packets on a baking sheet and bake for 25 minutes.

To serve, place a hot packet on each plate. Diners open their packets and slip out the meat and juices onto their plates. Have a plate available for the crumpled foil.

Yield: 4 servings.

Quick Cheese Loaf

2 packages (6 ounces each) refrigerated flaky biscuits
¼ cup butter, melted
1¼ cups grated Parmesan cheese

Preheat the oven to 350°. Separate each biscuit into 2 rounds with a serrated knife. Dip each in butter to coat all sides, then coat with cheese. Stand the biscuits on their sides in two long rows in a greased 8 ½" x 4 ½" x 3" loaf pan. Sprinkle the top with more cheese. Bake for 20 to 25 minutes or until golden.

Yield: 8 to 10 servings.

Greek Islands Stew

Cinnamon and rosemary perfume this lovely stew. Try serving it with rice or a small pasta tossed with butter and feta.

Prep Time: 20 minutes
Cooking Time: 35 minutes

2 tablespoons olive oil
1 pound lamb shoulder chops
1 onion, chopped
1 clove garlic, minced
1 cup canned whole tomatoes, drained
½ cup tomato sauce
¼ cup white wine
1 bay leaf
1" stick cinnamon
2 cloves
¼ teaspoon rosemary
salt and pepper to taste
cooked rice or pasta as an
*   accompaniment*

In a large, heavy skillet heat oil and brown lamb chops. Salt and pepper them. Add to the skillet the onions and garlic and continue to cook over medium heat until the onions are softened, 3 to 4 minutes. Add tomatoes, tomato sauce, white wine, bay leaf, cinnamon stick, cloves and rosemary. Make sure everything is well combined. Cover, reduce heat, and simmer for 25 minutes.

Serve the chops on rice or pasta with the sauce poured over.

Yield: 4 servings.

❧ Russian Salad ❧

1 cup cut green beans, canned or cooked
1 cup diced carrots, canned or cooked
1 cup green peas, cooked
1 cup diced canned beets
1 cup diced canned small potatoes
3 green onions, thinly sliced
⅓ cup vinaigrette (see p. 199)
mayonnaise
salt and pepper to taste
salad greens as an accompaniment

Combine all vegetables and vinaigrette dressing. Toss lightly to mix and marinate as long as you can. An hour is ideal, but 30 minutes will do.

Before serving add enough mayonnaise to bind the vegetables together. Season with salt and pepper. Serve on a bed of soft lettuce leaves.

Yield: 4 to 6 servings.

Look What You Can Do With Risotto!

Risotto is the creamy Italian rice dish that runs the gamut from "simple white" (butter and cheese), to saffron, herb, seafood, meat or poultry versions. The rice grains don't fluff as when steamed or boiled, but form a savory mass which mounds softly on spoon or fork. It's easy to make and a joy to eat. Don't avoid it because you think you will have to stand there and stir. It's only a matter of 15 minutes or so and in that time you are making the whole meal except for, perhaps, the salad to accompany it. This is the dish to make when you want to ponder the day's events in peace. Consider it therapy.

Simple White Risotto

3½ to 4 cups chicken broth
2 tablespoons butter, divided
¼ cup chopped onion
1 cup rice, arborio or long grain
¼ cup grated Parmesan cheese
2 tablespoons cream (optional)

In a saucepan bring the broth to a simmer and keep warm over low heat.

In a 2 to 3-quart pan or a 10-inch skillet over medium heat, melt 1 tablespoon of the butter. Add the onion. Cook, stirring, until soft, 3-5 minutes. Add the rice. Stir and cook until it is opaque and coated with butter, 2 more minutes.

Add ½ cup of broth. Cook and stir until it is absorbed, 2 or 3 minutes. It's fun to watch the rice thicken and the liquid vanish. Continue adding broth in half-cup amounts and cooking and stirring until the rice is tender but still offers a little resistance to your teeth. Stir constantly if you like (Marcella Hazan does) or stir now and then (as Jim Beard did).

Usually the rice needs 3⅓ cups of broth. On rare occasions it takes more, so with 4 cups you are prepared.

Remove the pan from the heat. Stir in the cheese and, if you like, the remaining tablespoon of butter or the optional cream. Serve in soup plates or bowls.

Yield: 4 servings

Risotto Variations:

Saffron (Milanese): Add a large pinch of saffron when you heat the broth.

Shellfish: Cook a chopped garlic clove with the onion. Heat 2 cups any cooked shellfish in 2 tablespoons butter. Mix into cooked risotto and omit the cheese.

Chicken: Add 1½ cup raw chicken breast meat cut into 2" x ¼" strips to the risotto about 10 minutes before it is finished (figure 15-20 minutes total cooking time).

Asparagus: Snap off the tough ends of ½ pound asparagus. Cut spears into ½" lengths, drop into boiling water and cook 3 minutes. Drain. Add to rice with the last addition of broth.

Green Bean or Pea: Stir 1½ cups green beans, cut into pieces and cooked crisp-tender, or 2 cups cooked peas into the finished risotto.

Dessert Idea: Fruit and Sour Cream

This is an easy yet sophisticated combination of fruit (fresh, frozen or canned, hot or cold), liqueur, sour cream and toppings. Whip the sour cream to lighten it and sweeten with a little sugar if you like. Make individual servings or let diners assemble their own: first the fruit, then a splash of liqueur (optional), top with whipped sour cream and add a garnish.

Fruit	Liqueur	Garnish
Apricot halves	Apricot brandy	Almonds and grated chocolate
Figs	Orange liqueur or rum	Grated or slivered orange rind
Black cherries	Kirsch or Cherry Heering	Cinnamon sugar
Seedless green grapes	None	Brown sugar
Pears	Brandy	Grated chocolate
Pineapple	Rum	Coconut and mint leaves
Melon balls	None	Minced chutney and walnuts
Strawberries	Orange liqueur or kirsch	Grated orange rind and chocolate
Raspberries	Framboise	Almonds or grated chocolate
Sliced peaches	Amaretto	Almonds

Armenian Lamb Pilaf

A zesty pilaf is folded into a mixture of lamb, green peppers, raisins and pine nuts, with a hint of cinnamon and mint. This is not to be missed.

Prep Time: 15 minutes
Cooking Time: 30 to 35 minutes

4 tablespoons olive oil, divided

1 cup uncooked rice

2 tablespoons minced green onion

1½ cups chicken broth

1 pound lamb, ½" slices, cut in 2" pieces

1 large red onion, chopped

1 green pepper, seeded and cut in strips

1 clove garlic, minced

½ cup pine nuts

½ cup raisins

⅛ teaspoon cinnamon

¼ teaspoon allspice

*1 tablespoon chopped fresh mint leaves or
    1 teaspoon dried*

plain yogurt, as an accompaniment

In a heavy, deep saucepan heat 2 tablespoons of the oil. Add rice and stir over low heat until the grains are coated with oil. Don't let them brown. Add the green onion and cook and stir until softened. Pour chicken broth over the rice, raise the heat to high, and bring to a boil. Cover and cook over low heat for 20 minutes.

While the rice cooks, heat the remaining 2 tablespoons oil in a heavy skillet. Brown the lamb quickly on all sides over high heat, 2 to 3 minutes. Lower the heat to medium. Add the onion, green pepper and garlic. Cook and stir over medium heat until soft but not browned. Add the pine nuts, raisins, cinnamon, allspice and 2 tablespoons of water. Cover skillet and cook over low heat for 10 minutes. Stir in the mint.

When the rice is cooked, stir it into the meat and vegetable mixture. Serve with a bowl of yogurt to spoon over individual portions.

Yield: 4 servings.

❧ Cutting Boards ❧

Most of us think the wooden block in the counter is for chopping. I certainly did until a professional chef pointed out that cutting boards must be portable. You carry a small chopping board right to the pot, pan or bowl. Buy one anywhere from 8" x 14" (chopped bits can fall off the edges of these) to 10" x 17" (can hold all the bouncing bits, but hard to fit in the dishwasher). A board with a handle is nifty because you can hold it in one hand while the other scrapes things off. Polyethelene is the best material. If the board slides around when you use it, put a damp cloth or paper towel underneath.

Lamb Chops with Mushrooms and Carrots

This is super-quick because it uses canned vegetables, although you can use fresh mushrooms if you have the time. The canned carrots actually enhance the flavors because they are already soft and ready to soak up all the wonderful flavors of butter, garlic, wine and tomato.

Prep Time: 5 minutes
Cooking Time: 15 minutes

4 lamb chops, shoulder or loin

3 tablespoons butter

2 sliced onions

1 teaspoon minced garlic

1 can (1 pound) diced carrots, drained

2 cans (4 ounces each) mushrooms with their liquid

2 teaspoons tomato paste

¼ cup dry red wine

salt and pepper to taste

Rub each chop with salt and pepper. Broil the chops 4" from the heat for 4 to 5 minutes per side, or until done to your taste.

In a medium skillet heat the butter. Add onion and garlic and cook, stirring, until softened, about 5 minutes. Add the drained carrots and the mushrooms with their liquid. Cover and simmer for 5 minutes. Add the tomato paste and wine. Simmer uncovered for 5 minutes longer. Serve the sauce over the chops.

Yield: 4 servings.

☙ Lemon Butterflakes ❧

These are lovely with salad.

3 tablespoons soft butter

1 teaspoon lemon juice

1½ teaspoons grated lemon rind

1 package brown-and-serve butterflake rolls

Preheat oven to 375°. In a small bowl mix butter, lemon juice and lemon rind. Partially separate the leaves of the rolls and spread with the butter mixture. Wrap in foil and bake on baking sheet for 10 to 15 minutes or until heated through.

Yield: 4 to 6 servings.

Grilled Rosemary Lamb Chops

Rosemary and lamb were made for each other. With the addition of butter and lemon, you have something very tasty.

Prep Time: 5 minutes
Cooking Time: 10 to 15 minutes

¼ cup butter, melted

3 tablespoons lemon juice

4 cloves garlic, minced

1 teaspoon fresh rosemary or
    ½ teaspoon dried

4 lamb rib chops, 1" thick

fresh rosemary sprigs as a garnish

In a small pan melt the butter. Add the lemon juice, garlic and rosemary. Prepare grill or broiler. Place the chops 4 to 6 inches from the heat and cook, turning once, until done to your taste. Baste often with the rosemary butter.

When serving, pour any remaining basting sauce over the chops. Garnish with fresh sprigs of rosemary.

Yield: 4 servings.

The Adventurous Chef: If you broil the chops, pour the remaining basting mixture into the broiler pan. Stir it into the juices, scraping up any browned bits. It makes a wonderful sauce.

Fun Dessert Coffees III

A Scandinavian Trick: Throw a few cardamom pods in with the ground coffee before brewing.

A Persian Trick: Break a few cinnamon sticks onto the grounds before brewing.

Orange Spice: Add to dry coffee grounds 1 strip orange rind, 1 strip lemon rind and 10 whole cloves. Serve brown sugar with the coffee.

Black and White: Pour espresso or extra strong coffee over ice and top with a scoop of vanilla ice cream.

Mocha: For every 2 cups of coffee, put one tablespoon cocoa on the dry ground coffee.

Look What You Can Do with Broiled Lamb Chops!

Coat Them And Top Them With Something Fun

The toppings are enough for 4 thick lamb chops. Broil them 4" from heat. Cook 4 to 7 minutes per side. Cooking time will depend on thickness of chops. Don't overcook.

The Basic Steps:	Sprinkle both sides with salt and pepper. Then coat as follows:	Broil both sides, turning once, till done to taste. Baste if required. Mix topping and finish as follows:
Mustard Garlic *A delicious coating of the flavors that best suit lamb.*	No coating.	**Topping:** Mix 2 tablespoons Dijon mustard; 1½ teaspoons olive oil; 1½ teaspoons soy sauce; 1 small clove garlic, minced; ½ teaspoon rosemary and a pinch of ginger. Return to broiler until top is bubbly.
Peach and Spice *Spiced preserves caramelize the chops.*	Coat with salt, pepper and oil.	**Topping:** Mix ¼ cup peach jam; ¼ teaspoon ground cumin; ⅛ teaspoon cinnamon and a fat pinch of cloves. Return to broiler until glaze caramelizes.
Rosemary Parsley *A crunchy topping of buttery crumbs, rosemary and garlic.*	Coat with salt, pepper and oil.	**Topping:** Mix ½ cup fresh white breadcrumbs; 1 pressed clove garlic; ¼ cup parsley; 2 tablespoons olive oil; ½ teaspoon salt and ¼ teaspoon rosemary. Return to broiler until golden.
Mint Butter *Bathed in a delicious herb butter.*	Mix ¼ cup butter; 1 teaspoon grated lemon rind; 1 teaspoon lemon juice; 1½ tablespoons fresh mint or 1½ teaspoons dried and ¼ teaspoon salt. Spread both sides with half the mixture. Chill remaining butter.	Turn once. Salt when you turn. To serve, top each chop with ¼ of remaining butter mixture.

From top to bottom, clockwise: Betsy's Special Tart, page 28; Galloping Horses, page 136; and Lemon Chive Pasta, page 78.

From top to bottom, clockwise: Ham, Tomato and Cheese Tart, page 134; Italian Seafood Stew, page 42; Fettuccine with Peas and Ham, page 10.

Greek Pita Pockets

These delicious hot pockets are loaded with lamb, feta, garlic and mint. They make a delightful spring or summer meal. Serve them with a tossed salad and Armenian pilaf.

Prep Time: 10 minutes
Cooking Time: 15 minutes

1 tablespoon olive oil

⅔ cup chopped green onion (4 to 5, using about half the green tops)

1 pound lean ground lamb or beef

1½ tablespoons chopped fresh mint or 1 teaspoon dried

dash of cinnamon

2 medium zucchini, cut into ⅛" rounds

12 cherry tomatoes, quartered

¼ cup chopped parsley

6 ounces feta cheese, cut into small pieces

sprinkle of cayenne pepper

sprinkle of garlic powder

4 6" pita breads

salt and pepper to taste

Heat oil in a 10" skillet over medium heat and sauté the green onion for 3 or 4 minutes until it softens. Don't let it brown. Stir in lamb, mint and cinnamon. Sauté gently until the meat loses its pinkness.

Preheat oven to 375°. Put the zucchini in a small saucepan with ½" water and simmer for 2 to 3 minutes, until just tender. Drain and set aside. When the lamb is ready, drain off the fat. Add the tomatoes and parsley and cook and stir over medium heat for 1 to 2 minutes. Stir in half of the feta, add the zucchini, cayenne, garlic powder and salt and pepper to taste. Remove from heat.

Slit the pitas halfway around the edge. Add the remaining feta to the lamb mixture and fill each pita equally. Lay them on a baking sheet and heat for 5 minutes in the oven. Serve hot and eat with a knife and fork.

Yield: 4 servings.

❧ Armenian Pilaf ❧

1 tablespoon oil
¼ cup fine egg noodles
1 cup rice
1 teaspoon finely chopped garlic
1½ cups chicken broth
2 tablespoons butter
¼ cup finely chopped parsley
salt and pepper to taste

In a medium saucepan heat the oil. Add the dry noodles. Cook, stirring, until they brown delicately. Stir in the rice and garlic. Add broth, butter and salt and pepper to taste. Cover and cook over low heat for 18 minutes. Stir in the parsley.

Yield: 4 servings.

Lamb Chops with Tomato and Cheese Pasta

The Greeks braise lamb shanks in tomato sauce and finish by cooking orzo, a small oval shaped pasta, in the resulting rich, garlicky tomato sauce. This version, made with quicker-cooking chops, is more delicate but retains the superb blend of flavors.

Prep Time: 5 minutes
Cooking Time: 15 minutes

8 loin lamb chops or 4 shoulder chops
1 teaspoon salt
2 teaspoons dried oregano, crushed
½ teaspoon coarsely ground black pepper
1½ tablespoons flour
1 tablespoon oil
1 clove garlic, crushed in the garlic press
1 can (14 to 16 ounces) stewed tomatoes
1½ cups tomato juice
2 tablespoons chopped parsley
2 cups small pasta shells or orzo
½ cup grated Parmesan cheese

Trim extra fat from the lamb chops. On a sheet of wax paper mix salt, oregano, pepper and flour. Coat the chops on both sides.

In a 10" skillet over medium-high heat, heat the oil and cook lamb chops 4 to 5 minutes on each side for medium-rare (less time if chops are thinner than 1"). Cook longer if you want them done more. Turn once. Remove chops to a platter and keep warm.

Discard all but 1 tablespoon of fat from the skillet. Over medium heat cook the garlic for a few seconds, stirring constantly. Add the tomatoes, tomato juice and parsley. Scrape up all the brown bits left from the chops. Bring to a boil over high heat. Add the pasta, cover, turn the heat to medium high and cook for 3 to 5 minutes or until just tender. Stir now and then and if the mixture looks dry, add a little water. Stir in the Parmesan cheese. Serve the pasta and lamb chops separately.

Yield: 4 servings.

Lamb and Eggplant Skillet

This is the combination that makes moussaka so good: eggplant, onions, tomato and cheese melting on top. Serve it with a side dish of yogurt.

Prep Time: 12 minutes
Cooking Time: 15 minutes

2 tablespoons olive oil, divided

1 pound lean ground lamb or beef

1 teaspoon garlic powder, plus extra for vegetables

1 teaspoon dried oregano, plus extra for vegetables

¾ teaspoon salt

¼ teaspoon pepper

1 small eggplant (about 8 ounces), cut into ¼" rounds

1 medium onion, thinly sliced

¾ cup tomato purée

¼ cup sour cream

2 ounces mozzarella or Muenster cheese, grated

lots of chopped parsley as a garnish

yogurt as an accompaniment

In a large, deep skillet over high heat, heat 1 tablespoon of the oil until it is very hot but not smoking. Add the meat, garlic powder, oregano, salt and pepper. Cook and stir, breaking up the meat with a wooden spoon, until all the pink is gone. Remove it to a bowl.

Pour the excess fat out of the pan. Heat the remaining tablespoon of oil in the skillet. Add the eggplant and onion. Shake on a little garlic powder and oregano and fry over medium heat, stirring often, for 3 to 4 minutes. Add the lamb, ½ cup water, tomato purée and sour cream. Mix well. Lower the heat, cover and cook for 12 to 15 minutes, or until eggplant and onions are soft. Sprinkle with cheese.

Top with parsley and serve with yogurt.

Yield: 4 servings.

The Skinny Chef: You can substitute low-fat sour cream.

The Adventurous Chef: Add some mint to the yogurt or try the Cucumber Garlic Sauce on p. 209.

Hoisin Lamb in a Pocket

Hoisin sauce and cilantro are perfect partners for lamb, and these tasty sandwiches make a delicious supper. A dish of eggplant would be very good with this.

Prep Time: 10 minutes
Cooking Time: 15 minutes

¾ pound ground lean lamb
1 medium onion, minced
3 cloves garlic, minced
¼ cup dry sherry
¼ cup chicken broth
1 teaspoon cornstarch
¼ cup minced fresh cilantro leaves
2 tablespoons hoisin sauce
4 6" pita breads
3 cups finely shredded Chinese cabbage
hot garlic oil as an accompaniment

Heat a 10" skillet over medium high heat. Add the lamb, onion and garlic and cook and stir until the meat is well browned, 10 to 12 minutes. In a small bowl mix the sherry, broth and cornstarch and add it to the meat along with the cilantro and hoisin sauce. Stir until the sauce boils.

Cut pita breads in half and fill the pockets with equal amounts of cabbage. Top each with lamb mixture and serve while the lamb is hot. You may want a few shakes of hot garlic oil, so put the bottle within reach.

Yield: 4 servings.

❧ Five-Minute Cheesecakes ❧

These are quick, cute, and yummy. Freeze them unbaked and you'll always have a little treat up your sleeve.

slices of soft white bread
whipped cream cheese
cinnamon sugar
melted butter

Preheat the oven to 350°. Cut the crusts from the bread and flatten the slices with a rolling pin. Spread slices with an ⅛" layer of cream cheese. Cut each slice into 3 equal strips and fold the strips into thirds to make little pack-

ets. Brush the packets all over with melted butter, then roll them in cinnamon sugar. Bake the cheesecakes on a lightly greased cookie sheet for 5 minutes. Serve warm or at room temperature.

The Clever Chef: To make cinnamon sugar, mix 1 part cinnamon to 4 parts granulated sugar.

Lamb with Yogurt Mint Sauce

This couldn't be simpler or taste more spring-like. It's delicious with bulgur wheat or rice and a crispy green salad.

Prep Time: 5 minutes
Cooking Time: 14 minutes

⅔ *cup plain yogurt*
¼ *cup firmly packed fresh mint leaves*
2 tablespoons sugar
4 lamb chops, about 1" thick (1 pound total)
salt to taste

In the blender or food processor blend yogurt, mint and sugar until smooth. Pour into a serving bowl.

Spray the broiler rack with non-stick cooking spray. Place the lamb on the rack and broil 3" from the heat for 12 to 14 minutes or until done to taste. Turn the chops after 6 minutes. Serve with the yogurt sauce.

Yield: 4 servings.

❧ Lemon Raspberry Napoleons ❧

This is utterly, shamefully, seductively delicious. The pastry layers shatter in your teeth, the lemon cream is dense and rich and the raspberry purée adds the perfect note of tartness. Would you believe you can make it in a few minutes?

1 can (14 ounces) sweetened condensed milk
1 package (8 ounces) cream cheese, softened
¼ *cup lemon juice*
½ *teaspoon vanilla extract*
1 teaspoon grated lemon rind
2 cups fresh or frozen whole raspberries
¼ *cup powdered sugar*
1 sheet frozen puff pastry, thawed, from a 17½ ounce package

In a small mixer bowl beat the condensed milk, cream cheese, lemon juice, vanilla and lemon rind with a mixer until smooth. Place in the refrigerator until needed. Purée raspberries and powdered sugar in the food processor. Push the purée through a strainer and discard the solids. Set aside.

Preheat the oven to 400°. Unfold the puff pastry sheets and cut nine 3" rounds. Place them on an ungreased baking sheet. Prick the entire surfaces with a fork, to prevent the top from ballooning. Bake for 10 minutes or until lightly browned. Cool on a wire rack.

To serve, split each pastry round into two discs. Spoon equal portions of raspberry sauce on each of 6 dessert plates, saving a little to drizzle over the tops of the desserts. Top each with a pastry round. Divide half of the lemon filling among the pastry rounds. Add second rounds and the remaining filling. Top each with a third round and drizzle with purée. Serve immediately while pastry is still crisp.

Yield: 6 servings.

Quick Cassoulet

This richly seasoned dish of beans, lamb, sausage and garlic is perfect for a cold winter night. Made with a can of pork and beans, it is slightly sweet and smoky; with navy beans it resembles the famous French cassoulet. Both versions are delicious.

Prep Time: 8 minutes

Cooking Time: 25 minutes

2 tablespoons olive oil

4 lamb shoulder chops, about 1½ pounds total

2 onions, chopped

1 can (1 pound) baked beans, or navy or big lima beans, drained

2 cups canned tomatoes, drained and cut up

8 ounces Polish sausage

2 tablespoons flour

2 cloves garlic, crushed

½ teaspoon thyme

1 bay leaf

salt and pepper to taste

In a large, heavy saucepan, heat the oil. Add the chops and brown them on both sides. Add the onions and sauté for 2 to 3 minutes or until softened. Stir in the beans, tomatoes, sausage, flour, garlic, thyme, bay leaf and salt and pepper to taste. Bring the mixture to a boil, stirring. Reduce the heat to low. Cover and simmer for 20 to 25 minutes. Remove the bay leaf and serve. The beans will be slightly soupy and wonderful.

Yield: 4 servings.

❧ Creamed Spinach ❧

You should be warned that this will upstage anything you serve it with. People have been known to attack it with spoons and ignore the other things on the plate.

2 packages (10 ounces) frozen chopped spinach

2 tablespoons butter

1 package (3 ounces) cream cheese, diced

½ teaspoon salt, or to taste

½ teaspoon Worcestershire sauce

Put the frozen spinach in a medium skillet with ¼ cup of water. Cover and cook over medium heat. As the spinach begins to thaw, break it up with a fork. Cook gently until thawed and cooked. Turn into a sieve and press out all the liquid. If you want to take the time, put the spinach on a board and give it a few chops.

In the same skillet, melt the butter over medium heat. Add the spinach, cream cheese, salt and Worcestershire. Cook and stir until the cheese melts and everything is well mixed, about 5 minutes.

Yield: 4 to 6 servings.

Mongolian Lamb with Green Onions

The people of Northern China eat a lot of lamb, a fact we tend not to think of. This combination of lamb and spring onions is light, savory and quick. You'll make it often.

Prep Time: 10 minutes
Cooking Time: 6 minutes

½ teaspoon five-spice powder

1 egg white

2 cloves garlic, slivered

1 teaspoon minced ginger root

3 teaspoons cornstarch, divided

5 teaspoons soy sauce, divided

*1 pound boneless lamb from the leg or
    shoulder, cut into strips*

6 tablespoons sherry

2 tablespoons water

10 green onions

2 tablespoons oil

In a medium bowl mix the five-spice powder, egg white, garlic, ginger, 1 teaspoon of the cornstarch and 1 teaspoon of the soy sauce. Add the lamb and mix to coat well. In a small bowl mix the remaining 2 teaspoons of cornstarch, 4 teaspoons soy sauce, sherry and water.

Cut the white part of the green onions in half crosswise. Cut the green tops in sections about 1½" long.

In a wok or large skillet heat the oil over high heat until very hot. Add the lamb and stir fry until it browns lightly. Return the lamb to the bowl.

Add the cornstarch mixture to the wok along with the white part of the onion. Cook and stir until the mixture thickens. Return meat to the wok along with the green onion tops. Stir until the sauce simmers and the lamb is thoroughly heated.

Yield: 4 servings.

The Clever Chef: You'll find Five-Spice Powder, (a mixture of black pepper, star anise, fennel, cinnamon and clove) in the Oriental section of the grocery store.

Herb Buttered ❧ French Bread ❧

1 loaf (1 pound) French bread
½ cup butter
1 tablespoon fresh parsley, chopped
1 tablespoon fresh chives, snipped
*1 tablespoon fresh basil, chopped, or
    ½ teaspoon dried*

Preheat the oven to 350 °. Cut the loaf into 1" slices, almost but not quite through to the crust. Combine butter, parsley, chives and basil. Spread on cut sides. Wrap the loaf in foil and bake for 10 to 15 minutes.

Yield: 8 to 10 servings.

Try a Meatless Meal Tonight

Whether you're in the mood for spicy, soothing, delicate, or robust, you'll find what you want in this array of luscious dishes. The fat, lacy Japanese Pancakes are a treat; the Spaghetti Squash with Chili Cream is worthy of your most show-off dinner party. I love to serve Curried Potatoes with their pungent chutney at summer lunches along with a cold lentil salad. Take note of the soufflé at the end of the chapter. It's made with a cream soup instead of white sauce. It's dead easy and swoops up quivering, golden and yummy. If you are a vegetarian or tend in that direction, look at the list of meatless dishes in the Hidden Treasures section at the front of the book for other recipes which adapt deliciously.

"I love to serve the curried potatoes with their pungent chutney at summer lunches with a cold lentil salad."

Curried Potatoes

This recipe from my Indian friends makes a delightful meatless dinner. Scoop up some spicy potatoes in a thin bread wrapper and top with a dollop of cool, garlicky chutney. Heavenly!

Prep Time: 5 minutes
Cooking Time: 28 minutes

2 pounds boiling potatoes, peeled
¼ cup vegetable oil
½ teaspoon fennel seeds
½ teaspoon cumin seeds
½ teaspoon mustard seeds
10 fenugreek seeds
2 tablespoons ground cumin
½ teaspoons salt
1 teaspoon cayenne pepper, or to taste
¼ teaspoon turmeric
1½ cups peas, cooked or thawed frozen
minced cilantro as a garnish
lavash (see note) or flour tortillas and
   Coriander Chutney (see box) as
   accompaniments

Cook potatoes in boiling water until tender, about 20 minutes. Cut them into ½" dice. Heat the oil in a large skillet over medium-high heat. Add the fennel, cumin, mustard and fenugreek seeds. As soon as the mustard seeds start to pop (after about 20 seconds) remove the pan from the heat and stir in the ground cumin, salt, cayenne and turmeric. Add the potatoes and peas. Stir and cook over medium-low heat until the potatoes are well colored, about 8 minutes. Top with minced cilantro.

Serve with lavash and Coriander Chutney.

Yield: 4 servings.

The Clever Chef: Lavash is paper thin Middle Eastern bread. Fenugreek seeds are found in stores that sell Indian and Asian ingredients.

❧ Coriander Chutney ❧

⅓ cup fresh coriander leaves, lightly packed
2 cloves garlic
½ teaspoon ground ginger
pinch cayenne pepper
1 teaspoon lemon pulp
1 teaspoon brown sugar
salt to taste
1 cup (approximately) yogurt, divided

Place coriander leaves, garlic, ginger, cayenne, lemon pulp and brown sugar in the blender or food processor. If you use the blender, add 2 or 3 tablespoons of yogurt to help it work. Blend smooth. Scrape into a small bowl and stir in enough more yogurt, ⅔ to ¾ cup, to give it the consistency of thick cream.

The Clever Chef: Lemon pulp is the juicy flesh without the membrane.

Spaghetti Squash with Chili Cream

This sauce is thick, creamy and as hot as you want it. It provides a luscious contrast to the slightly crunchy spaghetti squash strands.

Prep Time: 8 minutes
Cooking time: 20 minutes

1 spaghetti squash (about 3 pounds)
1 tablespoon vegetable oil
1 large green pepper, chopped fine
1 large onion, chopped fine
2 medium cloves garlic, minced
1 can (4 ounces) green chilies, hot or mild
1 cup canned sliced stewed tomatoes with
   juice
4 ounces light cream cheese or Neufchatel
1 tablespoon butter
grated Parmesan cheese as an
   accompaniment

Split the spaghetti squash lengthwise and scoop out the seeds and fibers. Place it cut-side down in a pot containing 2" of water, cover and boil gently for 20 minutes or until tender. You can also steam the squash whole for 25 to 30 minutes, then split and remove seeds and fibers.

Heat the oil over medium heat in a medium skillet and sauté pepper, onion and garlic until tender, 7 to 10 minutes. Add the chilies and tomatoes, and stir over low heat, breaking up the tomatoes as you stir. Cut the cream cheese into lumps and add, stirring and mashing until sauce is creamy. Keep warm.

Drain the cooked squash, and as soon as it is cool enough to handle, scrape a spoon lengthwise down the halves to remove the spaghetti strands. Toss the squash with the butter and serve with the chili cream. Pass Parmesan at the table.

Yield: 4 servings.

Seeding Canned Tomatoes

I have a thing about tomato seeds—I don't like them in my food. Maybe it's because they look messy and get in your teeth. When I use canned tomatoes I put a sieve over the saucepan. I open each tomato with my fingers, poke the seeds out into the sieve along with the juice, and drop the tomato into the other ingredients. It takes only a minute and for me, at any rate, it makes a difference.

Bagna Cauda

This recipe, inspired by Elisabeth Rosin, is the way to work blissfully through all those wonderful holiday leftovers: relish tray vegetables, cooked Brussels sprouts, chunks of roasted birds, French bread. Spear something on your fork and dip it into this heavenly hot cream, hauntingly flavored with garlic, a hint of anchovy and crunchy pecans. Of course, you don't need to wait for the holidays to eat this.

Prep Time: 8 minutes
Cooking Time: 20 minutes

Sauce:

4 anchovy fillets
2 cups heavy cream
½ teaspoon chicken bouillon granules
4 teaspoons minced or pressed garlic
½ cup pecans, chopped the size of peppercorns

Dippers:

assorted cooked vegetables
celery stalks
Belgian endive, split lengthwise
tomato quarters or cherry tomatoes
radishes
green onions
mushrooms
broccoli
cauliflower
green peppers
carrots, zucchini or fennel
slices or cubes of Italian or French bread, pita wedges, bagel chunks
cubes of any mild, firm cheese
boiled, peeled shrimp
cubes of cooked turkey, chicken, roast beef or ham

In a small dish, mash the anchovies to a paste with the back of a spoon.

In a chafing dish or small, heavy pan, place the cream, bouillon granules, garlic and mashed anchovies. Bring to a boil over medium heat. Simmer gently until it thickens, 10 to 15 minutes. Stir in the pecans.

Serve hot in a chafing dish or over a warmer and provide forks for spearing.

Yield: 4 to 6 servings.

The Social Chef: Bagna Cauda is traditionally served in a chafing dish with the dippers arranged on a platter. If you want to avoid drips and be more elegant, give each diner an individual dish of sauce. This is the ultimate hors d'oeuvre. Remember it for your next party.

Fun with Polenta

Polenta is Italian, the gourmet's cornmeal mush. We'll forget about molding and slicing, which take more time than you have, and instead stir in something wonderful and serve it soft like mashed potatoes, which is a very Italian way to enjoy it. Here is a super easy way to make polenta. No stirring, no constant attention.

Polenta

5 cups cold water, milk or half water/half chicken broth, divided

1 teaspoon salt (omit if using salted broth)

1½ cups yellow cornmeal

In a heavy saucepan bring 3⅓ cups of the liquid to a boil. Put the cornmeal in a medium bowl and stir in the remaining liquid. Add this to the boiling liquid, give it a quick stir, cover and let it cook undisturbed over low heat for 10 minutes or until thickened and creamy. Add more liquid if necessary to make it drop from the spoon in nice soft plops.

Yield: 4 servings.

Polenta Stir-ins:

Classic Butter and Parmesan*:* Stir in 4 tablespoon butter and 6 tablespoons Parmesan cheese.

Garlic Polenta: Sauté 2 cloves of minced garlic gently in 3 tablespoons butter until it turns pale gold. Stir into hot polenta along with 3 tablespoons whipping cream. Lovely.

Pecan Polenta: Add ⅔ cup toasted, chopped pecans and ⅓ cup finely chopped parsley.

Cheese Polenta: Add ¾ cup Parmesan or mozzarella cheese or ⅓ cup Gorgonzola. Add 2 or 3 tablespoons of whipping cream if you want.

Herb Polenta: Add 1½ teaspoons dried rosemary, sage, or Italian seasoning.

Polenta Toppings:

Cream: Mix 1 package (3 ounces) cream cheese with ⅓ cup sour cream and place it in a small serving dish. Diners make a well in their steaming polenta and spoon in a dollop of the mixture.

Sausage: Sauté 12 ounces of sliced Italian sausage over medium heat until brown. Add 2 sliced bell peppers and 1 sliced onion. Cook until soft. Drain off the fat. Add 3 cups chopped, canned Italian tomatoes with their liquid. Heat well. Mound cooked polenta on a platter, spoon on the topping, sprinkle with lots of Parmesan cheese and enjoy.

Mushroom: Fry 8 ounces of mushrooms with 2 cloves minced garlic. Spoon the mixture over the polenta.

Fun With Garnishes

I t only takes a minute and very little concentration to make a dish look pretty. You want to dine, not eat, and pretty food feeds the soul as well as the stomach. A friend of mine who is a cycling enthusiast comes back from weekend rides, mud-splattered and tired. She likes to invite fellow bikers in for a quick dinner. "I garnish the food," she says proudly, "and they're impressed!" She turns out a tomato rose in minutes, and so can you. Or an onion brush or a lemon basket in which to pop sprigs of herbs or tartar sauce for the oven-fried fish. Your diners will be enchanted.

Tomato Rose

1. With a sharp paring knife, peel the tomato in one long strip.

2. Gently coil the peel around itself to form a flower.

Lemon Basket

1. With a felt-tip pen, draw a handle and basket rim on a lemon. Cut as shown. Remove the two top pieces and scoop out the inside.

2. Fill the basket with herbs, a tiny bouquet of flowers or a sauce.

Green Onion Whisk

1. Cut off white bulb and some of the green end of a green onion, leaving a 4" piece. Start in the middle and make thin cuts with a knife toward the green end.

2. Place the whisk in ice water until the fronds curl. **Variation:** Make whisks with 6" celery pieces.

Chili Pepper Flower

1. Cut tip off pepper. With a knife, cut toward the tip end, to make petals ⅛" wide at widest point.

2. Place the flower in ice water until petals curl. The longer it soaks, the curlier the petals will be.

Two Bean Chili

This chili cooks up thick and savory with no single flavor dominating. It's delicious with rice or flour tortillas.

Prep Time: 6 minutes
Cooking Time: 26 minutes

1 ½ cups chopped onion
1 ½ cups chopped green pepper
1 ½ tablespoons olive oil
1 ½ tablespoons flour
6 cloves garlic, minced
¾ teaspoon paprika
½ teaspoon ground cumin
¼ teaspoon dried oregano
¼ teaspoon cayenne pepper, or more to taste
2 ½ tablespoons tomato paste
1 can (15 ounces) black beans, drained and rinsed
1 cup canned butter beans, drained and rinsed
salt to taste
chopped green onion, cilantro, salsa and sour cream as garnishes

In a 10" skillet, sauté the onion and green pepper in oil until tender, 5 to 10 minutes.

Stir in flour, garlic, paprika, cumin, oregano, cayenne and salt and cook for 1 minute. Add 1¾ cups water, tomato paste and beans. Bring to a boil. Simmer 15 minutes uncovered. Serve with garnishes.

Yield: 4 servings.

The Adventurous Chef: Add fried slices of chorizo or any garlic sausage to the finished chili. It makes a nice change.

❧ Quick Cornbread ❧

With a box of cornbread mix on hand, you can have cornbread double quick by baking it in the waffle iron! Stir together equal parts mix and milk and use about 1 cup of batter per waffle. Presto and voilà.

Pilaf with Broccoli and Cashews

This ingredient list looks long, but note that there's very little chopping. Most of the ingredients are ready to add and the dish goes together rapidly. If you haven't had this combination before, you're in for a treat. Even broccoli haters adore it.

Prep Time: 10 minutes
Cooking Time: 25 minutes

Pilaf:

2 tablespoons vegetable oil

2" cinnamon stick, broken into 3 or 4 pieces

6 whole cloves

14 whole peppercorns

5 cardamom pods, seeds only

1¼ teaspoons grated ginger root

1¼ teaspoons salt

1⅓ cups rice

1 small bay leaf

Broccoli:

4 stalks broccoli, florets only

2 tablespoons vegetable oil

½ teaspoon ground coriander

¼ teaspoon ground cumin

1 medium onion, thinly sliced

¼ teaspoon salt, or to taste

⅛ teaspoon pepper

⅔ cup unsalted roasted cashew nuts

In a heavy 3-quart pot heat the oil over medium heat and add the cinnamon stick, cloves, peppercorns, and cardamom seeds. Fry the spices until they are fragrant, 1 to 2 minutes.

Add the ginger and salt, stir, and add the rice and bay leaf. Stir in 2 cups of water. Raise the heat to high. When the water boils, turn the heat to low, cover tightly, and cook for 20 minutes.

While the pilaf cooks make the broccoli garnish. Cut the broccoli florets into ¼" thick diagonal slices. Heat the oil in a 10" skillet and fry the coriander and cumin for a few seconds. Add the onions and cook over low heat until they soften and turn pale brown, about 10 minutes. Add the broccoli and stir-fry until it turns bright green. Add ⅔ cup of water and salt and pepper. Cover partially and cook over medium-high heat for 2 to 3 minutes. The broccoli should be crisp-tender and there should be about ⅓ cup of water left in the pan.

Mix the cooked rice into the broccoli. Cover and cook over very low heat for 3 to 4 minutes. Spoon the pilaf into a serving dish and garnish with the cashew nuts.

Yield: 4 servings.

Meatless Stir-Fries You May Not Have Tried

Of course you can add meat, poultry or seafood to any of the recipes in the table. Use 1 pound, thinly sliced or 1" cubes. All recipes serve 4.

The Basic Steps:	Heat 2 tablespoons of oil in a wok or skillet. Add:	Add these and cook as directed.
Cheese Chick Pea *A robust dish with a wonderful flavor from lemon, horseradish and mustard.*	2 cups sliced mushrooms; 1¼ cups coarsely shredded carrot; ¼ cup thinly sliced green onions and 2 cloves garlic, chopped fine. Stir-fry 1-2 minutes or until crisp-tender.	In a bowl mix 2 tablespoons lemon juice; 2 teaspoons prepared horseradish; 2 teaspoons mustard; ½ teaspoon salt; ½ teaspoon pepper and 2 cans (1 pound each) chick peas drained and rinsed. Add and cook uncovered until heated, stirring often. Sprinkle with 1 cup shredded Monterey Jack cheese. Cover until cheese melts.
Black Bean and Vegetable *Fennel creates a subtle anise flavor.*	1 medium red onion sliced thin; 1½ cups red bell pepper in squares and 1 small fennel bulb, sliced crosswise. Stir-fry 2-3 minutes or until crisp-tender.	2 teaspoons dried oregano; 2 cans (1 pound each) black beans drained and rinsed; 2 tablespoons water and salt and cayenne to taste. Cook over medium-low heat for 5 minutes. Good with yogurt or sour cream.
Vegetable Cashew *Crisp vegetables mingle with the soft sweetness of cashews.*	Stir-fry 3 tablespoons cashew halves until they start to darken. Remove. Add ¼ cup water chestnuts; 1 pound vegetables from the salad bar (broccoli and cauliflower florets; sliced carrots; green pepper; etc.) or frozen stir-fry mix.	In a bowl mix 4 teaspoons cornstarch; ¾ cup chicken broth; ½ teaspoon garlic powder; ⅛ teaspoon ground ginger; 4 teaspoons soy sauce. Add. When thickened add cashews. Good with yogurt.
Red Pepper Broccoli with Yogurt Peanut Sauce *The Yogurt Peanut Sauce is a show stopper.*	1 cup chopped onion; 2 teaspoons finely chopped fresh ginger and 4 cloves minced garlic. Stir-fry for 2 minutes.	Add 6 cups small broccoli florets and stems cut into ¼" slices; 1 cup red bell pepper in strips, and ¼ cup soy sauce. Stir-fry 3 minutes or until broccoli is bright green. Serve with **Peanut Sauce:** Mix 1 cup plain yogurt; 6 tablespoons creamy peanut butter; 2 teaspoons sugar; 2 teaspoons soy sauce; salt and hot red pepper flakes to taste.

Indian Lentils (Dal)

I got this delicately spiced curry from an Indian friend who was a terrific hostess in our Kathmandu days. Saraswati made hers with mung beans or green lentils, which take about 40 minutes to cook. Red lentils cook in less than half that time.

Prep Time: 10 minutes
Cooking Time: 18 minutes

1 cup red lentils
½ teaspoon ground turmeric
¼ cup butter
¼ cup finely chopped onion
3 large cloves garlic, minced
2" stick cinnamon
1 tablespoon grated fresh ginger
1 large tomato, chopped
1 teaspoon salt
1 to 5 tablespoons fresh lemon juice
1 teaspoon dried red pepper flakes
½ teaspoon crushed, toasted fenugreek seeds (see note)
steamed rice and yogurt as accompaniments

Place the lentils in a medium saucepan with enough water to cover them by 1½", about 4 cups. Add the turmeric, cover and bring to a boil. Reduce the heat and simmer for 15 minutes or until tender.

Melt the butter in a medium saucepan over medium heat. Add onion and garlic and cook until softened, stirring frequently, about 5 minutes. Add the cinnamon and ginger and cook and stir for 2 minutes.

When the lentils have cooked, add them to the onion mixture along with the tomato, salt, 1 tablespoon of lemon juice, red pepper flakes and fenugreek. Heat through. Taste for salt and add enough lemon juice to spark the flavor, up to 4 more tablespoons. Serve accompanied by steamed rice and yogurt.

Yield: 4 servings.

The Clever Chef: To toast fenugreek seeds, stir them in a heavy skillet over medium heat for 5 minutes. Crush either in a mortar or with the back of a spoon against your cutting board.

The Healthy Cook: My friend Meryl delights health-conscious guests with this dish, using canola oil and omitting the salt, which is not missed because of the lovely spicing. She accompanies it with orange slices and chutney.

English Crisps

Spread English muffin halves with butter. Sprinkle with: (1) caraway, sesame or poppy seeds, (2) grated cheese or (3) any herbs, snipped fresh ones or dried. Toast in a toaster oven or under the broiler.

Soft Tacos with Cheese and Beans

These are so good. You bite into a warm flour tortilla, just on the edge of crisping, and an ooze of mashed, garlicky beans and soft, gooey white cheese melts on your tongue. If you added a glob of salsa, a plop of sour cream, you will know true bliss.

Prep Time: 10 minutes
Cooking Time: 10 minutes

1 cup canned kidney beans, drained
1 clove garlic, finely chopped
4 8" flour tortillas
1 cup ricotta cheese
¼ cup grated Parmesan cheese
¼ cup chopped green onion, including the green top
1 tablespoon chopped fresh cilantro leaves
salsa and sour cream as accompaniments

Preheat the oven to 350°. Mash the beans with the garlic and add a little water if the mixture seems very dry. Place the tortillas on an ungreased baking sheet and spread about ¼ cup of bean mixture on half of each, covering to within ½ inch of the edge.

In a small bowl mix the ricotta, Parmesan, green onions and cilantro. Spread an equal amount on each tortilla. Fold the tortillas over the filling and bake for 10 minutes or until they begin to freckle and the filling is hot and gooey.

Serve with bowls of salsa and sour cream.

Yield: 4 servings.

❧ Cherry Crunch ❧

In our years abroad when John phoned that he had visitors at the Embassy and was bringing them to lunch, this was one of my favorite quick desserts. Guests loved it. The slightly crunchy top has a glorious buttery flavor.

1 can (21 ounces) cherry pie filling
½ package (18.25-ounce size) yellow cake mix (see note)
½ cup soft butter

Preheat the oven to 400°. Grease an 8" or 9" square pan. Pour the pie filling into it. In a bowl, using your fingers or a pastry blender, mix the cake mix with the soft butter. Put the mixture on top of the pie filling. Bake uncovered until very brown and crusty, 30 to 45 minutes.

Serve warm with whipped cream or ice cream.

Yield: 6 or more servings.

The Clever Chef: Half a package of cake mix is about 2 cups plus 6 tablespoons.

Japanese Pancakes

These fat, slightly shaggy pillows make a delicious light lunch or supper; just the right amount of crunch and slightly sweet. Leftovers are still good the next day.

Prep Time: 15 minutes
Cooking Time: 20 minutes

small cabbage
¾ cup coarsely grated carrot
½ cup coarsely chopped yellow onion
⅓ cup celery in ⅛" slices
⅔ cup flour
2 teaspoons brown sugar (packed)
¾ teaspoon salt
½ teaspoon baking powder
1 cup half-and-half or evaporated milk
1 egg, slightly beaten
¼ teaspoon cumin seeds
¼ cup oil, divided
hoisin sauce, hot pepper oil and chutney
as accompaniments

How's That Again?

I am assured by a friend that an old book of English phrases for Russian tourists to the United States instructed them to order thusly in American restaurants: "Please give me curds, sower cream, fried chicks, pulled bread and one jelly fish."

Cut the cabbage into quarters. Remove the cores. Halve each quarter lengthwise and cut across it in ⅛" slices until you have enough to fill 3 cups. Place sliced cabbage in a large bowl. Add carrot, onion and celery.

In a medium bowl mix the flour, sugar, salt and baking powder. Add the half-and-half a third at a time, stirring well after each addition. Stir in the egg and cumin seeds. Mix the batter with the vegetables.

In a large, heavy non-stick skillet heat 2 tablespoons of oil. For each pancake, drop a heaping tablespoon of the pancake mixture into the oil. When you dip out the mixture, make sure you get some batter with each spoonful of vegetables. You will get about 4 cakes in the pan, about half the recipe. Fry over medium to medium-low heat until golden, about 4 to 5 minutes. Turn and cook the second side the same way. Remove to paper towels. Add another 2 tablespoons of oil and fry the rest.

Serve the pancakes hot, warm, or at room temperature with hoisin sauce, chutney and/or Chinese hot oil.

Yield: 4 servings.

The Clever Chef: An easy way to make these is to fry them in an electric skillet set at 325°.

The Speedy Chef: Use packaged cole slaw mix for the cabbage and carrot (about 6 cups).

Huevos Rancheros

S ome nights you don't want a big meal; you want something easy with lots of flavor that doesn't try too hard. This is the dish: fried eggs on a corn tortilla covered with tomato sauce and melted Cheddar.

Prep Time: 5 minutes
Cooking Time: 15 minutes

1 medium onion, chopped

1 large clove garlic

1 can (14 to 16 ounces) whole tomatoes, drained and chopped

2 tablespoons chopped green chilies

2 tablespoons oil, divided

½ teaspoon salt

8 corn tortillas

8 eggs

1½ cups Muenster or Monterey Jack cheese, grated

sliced avocado, as a garnish

1 can plain or refried beans, optional

Parmesan ❧ Hard Rolls ❧

2 crusty Kaiser (hard) rolls
2 tablespoons melted butter
8 teaspoons grated Parmesan cheese

Preheat broiler. Split each roll in half horizontally. Brush cut sides with equal amounts of melted butter. Sprinkle each with 2 teaspoons Parmesan. Place on baking sheet, cut sides up. Place under broiler several inches from source of heat and broil until golden brown on top (2 to 3 minutes).

Yield: 4 servings.

In the blender or food processor place the onion and garlic. Give it two pulses. Add the tomatoes and pulse 5 to 10 times to make a lumpy, coarse purée. Add the chilies and pulse 2 or 3 times. In a 1-quart saucepan heat the oil. When it is hot add the tomato mixture and the salt. Bring to a boil, lower the heat, and simmer uncovered for 10 minutes. Stir once or twice.

In a 10" skillet, heat the remaining oil and fry the eggs either sunny-side-up or over easy. While the eggs fry, preheat the broiler. Place the tortillas on a baking sheet and heat briefly under the broiler. Place a fried egg on each tortilla, spoon on some tomato sauce and cover each with 3 to 4 tablespoons of cheese. Place under the broiler until the cheese melts. Garnish with avocado slices if you wish.

Yield: 4 servings.

The Speedy Chef: Substitute bottled salsa (red or green) for the tomato sauce. You'll need about ¼ cup per egg.

The Adventurous Chef: If your diners have a lean and hungry look, add a can of plain or refried beans. Place beans on each plate along with the eggs, sprinkle with cheese and run the whole thing under the broiler to melt. This makes a wonderful brunch dish.

Fun with Pizza

Now that you can buy refrigerated crusts or the packaged Boboli crusts, pizza becomes fast food. Ever made a white pizza? I show you several of them. Try an ethnic topping—I've given you a couple to get your ideas going—or look to your cupboard and refrigerator for inspiration. You'll be amazed at the delicious combos you can come up with. Remember, tomato sauce is not obligatory. Neither is cheese! Just give your topping a nice drizzle of olive oil. With the chart and the ideas that follow you can do something different and fun. A green salad is all you need to accompany your pizza. Why not open a bottle of Chianti to wish it well?

How to Build a Pizza

1. Preheat oven to 425°.

2. Unroll packaged, refrigerated pizza crust and press out on a baking sheet or pizza pan. Or use a Boboli-type crust.

3. Brush crust with 1 tablespoon olive oil then spread with tomato sauce (purchased or your own). You'll need ¼ to ½ cup. Spread the sauce with the back of a spoon.

4. Think up a topping to suit your whim or what you have in fridge and cupboard. Or use some of the ideas below.

5. Sprinkle with 1 cup cheese—mozzarella is the usual, but no one says it's the only pizza cheese. Use whatever you like. Sprinkle on an herb, dried or fresh.

6. Drizzle with 1 tablespoon olive oil and bake for 10 to 12 minutes.

Tomato Sauce Pizzas

Margherita: Just tomato sauce, mozzarella and oregano.

Pepperoni, Green Pepper and Olive: 2 to 3 ounces pepperoni, sliced thin; 1 green pepper, sautéed in 2 tablespoons oil or left unsautéed for crispness—you choose; halved pitted black olives.

Capricciosa: Ham, mushrooms, artichoke hearts, olives, cheese and a sprinkle of rosemary.

Sausage: 8 ounces bulk pork sausage, sautéed and drained; 2 tomatoes, peeled, seeded, cut in small pieces. Basil and oregano over the cheese. (Fresh basil is best. Dried oregano is fine.)

Meatlover's: 8 ounces ground pork sausage, cooked and drained; 8 slices bacon, cooked and crumbled; 2 ounces sliced pepperoni. Instead of mozzarella, try a package of shredded 4-cheese mixture.

Sailor's: ½ can (7 ounces) tuna, drained; ½ can (5½ ounces) sliced black olives; ½ cup thinly sliced mushrooms; 1 jar (6 ounces) marinated artichoke hearts, drained. After baking, top with 2-ounce can rolled anchovies and a sprinkle of parsley.

Casalinga: 2 to 3 ounces cooked ham strips; thin bottled roasted red pepper strips; halved anchovy fillets; halved, pitted black olives. Sprinkle oregano over the cheese.

Unorthodox Pizzas

Greek: On top of the mozzarella place 6 ounces of raw shrimp, cleaned and halved lengthwise; ¼ cup Kalamata olives; ¾ cup crumbled feta cheese and a dash of rosemary.

Riviera: No tomato sauce. After brushing with olive oil, sprinkle with ¾ cup diced mild goat cheese; 1 diced tomato, drained; ¼ cup thinly sliced red onion; 1 ounce prosciutto (cut slices in thirds); 1 teaspoon dried Italian herbs. Top with ½ cup Fontina cheese. Drizzle on the olive oil and savor.

Southwest: Over the tomato sauce use Monterey Jack cheese. Then add thinly sliced onion rings, red or green bell peppers and chopped jalapeno peppers. Sprinkle with 2 tablespoons fresh coriander leaves, 2 tablespoons Parmesan and olive oil.

Pesto-Tomato: Substitute prepared pesto for tomato sauce. Top with slices of Italian tomatoes, mozzarella and Parmesan cheeses.

Tex-Mex: Substitute salsa for tomato sauce. Sprinkle with green onions and black olives. Use Monterey Jack cheese.

Roasted Pepper: No tomato sauce. Top with bottled roasted red pepper strips and thinly sliced red onions. Sprinkle with finely minced garlic. Use mozzarella cheese.

Fresh Tomato: 1 to 2 medium tomatoes, seeded and thinly sliced; 4 ounces crumbled feta cheese; 1 teaspoon dried basil; ¼ cup black olives; 1 teaspoon dried rosemary, crushed.

✄ Quick and Easy Pizza Sauce ✄

1 can (14 to 16 ounces) chopped tomatoes, undrained
1 cup tomato purée
1 large clove garlic, pressed
½ teaspoon dried oregano
¼ teaspoon salt, or to taste
⅛ teaspoon freshly ground black pepper

Combine tomatoes, tomato purée, garlic, oregano, salt and pepper in a medium saucepan. Bring to a boil, lower heat, and simmer uncovered for 5 minutes, stirring often.

Yield: 5 cups.

White Pizzas

White: Make a paste of ¾ pound grated mozzarella, 4 chopped anchovies (optional) and 3 tablespoons olive oil (you can use less) and spread it on the crust. Top with ½ cup snipped fresh basil leaves and 1 tablespoon Parmesan. Lovely!

Elegant White: The crust turns slightly chewy with this winner. We love it for a simple meal with a salad. Drizzle the crust with 2 to 3 tablespoons olive oil and sprinkle with 3 tablespoons Parmesan. That's it!

Chicken or Tuna: Top the oiled dough with thin slices of cooked or canned chicken or turkey, or drained, chunked tuna fish; sliced tomatoes; and thinly sliced onions. Use any cheese.

Show-Off: This is a version of the luxurious pizza served at Spago in San Francisco. Spread your dough with oil and bake it for 10 minutes or until golden. Cut the pizza in quarters. Spread each quarter with about 1½ tablespoons sour cream, top with a slice of smoked salmon (about 1 ounce), and in the center put a spoonful of caviar. Spago uses golden caviar, but you don't have to get that fancy.

White Anchovy: A 2-ounce can anchovies, rinsed and dried; ¼ cup sliced black olives; mozzarella; and a sprinkle of grated Parmesan (about ¼ cup).

✣ Bake Pizza in a Skillet ✣

Why always do things the same way? This is different and will chase away the boredom.

Use a 10-ounce refrigerated pizza crust. In a 12" skillet heat 1 tablespoon vegetable oil over medium-low heat. Unroll the dough and press into the skillet. Cover and cook for 5 to 6 minutes, or until the bottom is lightly browned. Take it from the heat. Brush the crust with a little olive oil. Then layer on ¾ cup tomato sauce, whatever toppings you choose, and 1 cup grated cheese and a sprinkle of dried herbs. (If you use fresh herbs, put them on after cooking). Cover and cook over medium low for 3 to 5 minutes more or until the crust is golden and the cheese melted.

Omelet Blintz

Some nights you feel like putting on your robe and slippers and curling up with an omelet. This one is filled with cottage cheese, which turns soft and creamy when it is heated. Serve it with crisp bacon, sliced tomatoes and English muffins.

Prep Time: 3 minutes
Cooking Time: 8 minutes

1 cup large-curd cottage cheese
6 eggs
⅓ cup milk
½ teaspoon salt
pepper to taste
2 tablespoons butter
1 to 2 tablespoons chopped green onion
crisp bacon slices and sliced tomatoes
*   as a garnish*

Put the cottage cheese in a bowl and let it come to room temperature.

In a medium bowl beat the eggs slightly to combine yolks and whites. Beat in the milk, salt and pepper.

Heat the butter in a 10" skillet. When it is very hot and the butter has stopped foaming, pour in the egg mixture. Turn the heat to medium high. As the edge sets, run a spatula around to lift it and allow uncooked egg to flow beneath. When the omelet is just cooked and the top has barely lost its shine, spoon cottage cheese down the center. Sprinkle with onion. Fold both edges toward the center, over the filling. Slide the omelet out onto a warm platter.

Garnish with bacon and tomato slices.

Yield: 4 servings.

❧ Mexican Mocha ☙

Make brunch, lunch or supper a glamorous occasion by serving this slightly thickened, chocolate-coffee concoction. Guests lap it up. So does family.

2 ounces unsweetened chocolate
2 tablespoons hot water
⅔ cup sugar
1 tablespoon cornstarch
2 teaspoons ground cinnamon
½ teaspoon salt
2 cups strong brewed coffee
3 cups milk
1 teaspoon vanilla

Heat chocolate and water in the top of a double boiler over hot, not boiling water until the chocolate melts. Stir in sugar, cornstarch, cinnamon and salt to mix thoroughly. Then stir in coffee until smooth. Cook over medium heat for 5 minutes. Stir in milk and vanilla. Before serving, whiz it to a creamy froth in the blender.

Yield: About 6 coffee cupfuls.

Spicy Tofu Pockets

Silky tofu and gooey Cheddar with olives, onions, chilies and tomatoes, stuffed into pita pockets or rolled up in flour tortillas—either way, a delicious lunch or supper dish.

Prep Time: 15 minutes
Cooking Time: 12 minutes

¼ cup olive oil

⅔ cup finely chopped green onion

8 ounces soft tofu, drained and diced

2 cloves garlic, mashed

2 tomatoes, peeled, seeded and finely chopped

3 tablespoons chopped black olives

2 tablespoons canned chopped mild green chilies

½ teaspoon chili powder

½ teaspoon salt

¼ teaspoon ground cumin

2 tablespoons wine vinegar, red or white

1½ cups grated Cheddar cheese

4 6" pita breads or 8" flour tortillas

Heat the oil in a large skillet over medium heat. Add green onion and sauté until softened, about 3 minutes. Add the tofu and garlic and cook for 3 to 4 minutes, stirring constantly.

Reduce the heat. Add the tomatoes, olives, chilies, seasonings, and vinegar. Continue to cook, stirring frequently, until the mixture is heated through.

Remove from heat and blend in the cheese. Stir until melted. Stuff the hot filling into warmed pita halves or roll up in flour tortillas.

Yield: 4 servings.

❧ Herbed Cream Cheese Sorcery ❧

- Spoon herbed cream cheese into a baked potato for a light meal.

- Spread herbed cream cheese on plum tomato halves or spoon into raw mushroom caps and serve cold. Or, bake the plum tomato halves or mushroom caps at 350° for 12 to 15 minutes or until bubbly.

- Mix 1⅓ cups of herbed cream cheese with ¾ cup milk. Toss with 1 pound of hot pasta until the cheese melts and turns into a sauce.

- Spread herbed cream cheese on boneless, skinned chicken breasts and bake at 425° for 15 to 20 minutes.

Cheese Soufflé

This is the trick of the week: a soufflé made with a base of cream soup rather than white sauce. It goes together in minutes and the result is pure magic. It soars out of the dish, golden topped, trembly light, and melt-in-the-mouth delicious.

Prep Time: 15 minutes
Cooking Time: 30 minutes

1 can (10½ ounces) condensed cream of mushroom soup
½ cup half-and-half or light cream
1 cup cheese, grated
4 eggs plus 1 egg white
⅛ teaspoon cream of tartar

Preheat the oven to 375°. In a heavy saucepan place soup, half-and-half and cheese. Heat and stir until the cheese melts.

Separate the eggs, dropping the 4 yolks into a small dish and placing the 5 egg whites in a large bowl.

Cool the soup mixture slightly. Stir in the yolks one by one. Put the pan in the refrigerator to cool. Add cream of tartar to the egg whites and beat until stiff.

Generously spray a 10" pie plate with cooking spray.

Remove the soup mixture from the refrigerator and whisk in a little egg white to lighten it. Fold the soup mixture into the egg whites. Pour into the prepared dish and bake at 375° for 30 minutes.

Yield: 4 servings.

The Adventurous Chef: Add 1 cup of chopped cooked chicken, ham, tuna, broccoli, or spinach with the cheese. ♦ Use cream of celery, asparagus, or chicken soup. ♦ We like to eat strawberry jam with cheese soufflé. It sounds odd, but the combination is delicious.

A Luscious Roquefort Dressing

3 tablespoons Roquefort or mild blue cheese
2 tablespoons Dijon mustard
2 tablespoons wine vinegar
1½ cups sour cream
salt and freshly ground pepper to taste
optional additions: a few drops of Worcestershire, hot pepper sauce, minced parsley or chives

With a fork mash the cheese with the mustard, vinegar and sour cream until smooth. Season to taste with salt and pepper. Add any optional additions you like.

Yield: About 2 cups.

Kidney Beans in Sour Cream

The sour cream and onions give these beans a smooth sweetness that is very satisfying. This is a dish that keeps you eating just one more bite.

Prep Time: 5 minutes
Cooking Time: 30 minutes

4 medium onions, thickly sliced
3 tablespoons butter
2 cans (15 ounces each) red kidney beans, drained
1 cup sour cream
salt and pepper to taste

Preheat the oven to 350°.

In a medium skillet, sauté the onions in the butter until pale yellow.

Mix in the beans, sour cream and salt and pepper. Place in an ovenproof casserole and bake for 15 to 20 minutes.

Yield: 4 servings.

Wacky Cake

Back before the era of mixes, this cake was popular. It's as fast as a mix, it's made right in the pan and is moist and chocolatey enough for the most avid chocolate addict. Delicious sprinkled with powdered sugar, chocolate heaven with the fudgy Dobos Torte frosting (see p. 136).

1 ½ cups flour
1 cup sugar
3 tablespoons unsweetened cocoa
1 teaspoon baking soda
½ teaspoon salt
1 tablespoon vinegar
6 tablespoons oil or melted butter
1 teaspoon vanilla
¾ cup cold water

Preheat the oven to 350°.

Put the flour, sugar, cocoa, baking soda and salt in a sifter or strainer and sift into an 8" x 8" x 2"
cake pan. Level it off. With the back of a wooden spoon make 3 holes equal distances apart. Into one hole pour the vinegar. Pour the oil or melted butter into the second and the vanilla into the third. Pour the cold water over everything and stir thoroughly with a table fork.

Bake for 30 to 35 minutes or until a cake tester inserted in the center comes out clean.

Yield: 8 servings.

The Adventurous Chef: For a fudgy texture use 2 tablespoons less flour.

Tasty Sauces From a Can

You don't have to turn in your gourmet badge if you cheat with canned soups. These sauces may not be the fancy originals, but they're good. When it's a choice between an interesting meal that says "eat me" and one that lies naked on the plate staring sullenly up at you, I come down on the side of the fast sauce. These use a 10½ ounce can of condensed soup.

Quick White Sauce: To 1 can cream of chicken or cream of mushroom soup add ¼ to ½ can milk or water, depending on how thick you want the sauce.

Curry Sauce: Fry 2 teaspoons curry powder for 30 to 60 seconds in a little oil or butter to mellow the flavor. Stir into Quick White Sauce.

Quick Cheese Sauce: To Quick White Sauce add 1 cup or more of cheese, or use 1 can of cheese soup plus ¼ to ½ can milk or water.

Quick Mushroom Sauce: Heat 1 can cream of mushroom soup with 2 tablespoons butter and ⅓ cup milk or sherry. Optional additions: ½ cup canned sliced mushrooms and ¼ cup grated cheese.

Mom's Spanish Pound Cake Sundae

This dessert justified my mother's reputation as an unflappable hostess who could produce an impressive meal on the spur of the moment.

⅓ cup water
1 cup sugar
1 cup frozen orange juice concentrate
8 1" slices of frozen pound cake, thawed
8 scoops of ice cream

Combine the sugar and water in a small saucepan and bring to a boil over high heat. After the sugar has dissolved, boil for 1 minute. Remove from heat and add orange juice concentrate. Toast the pound cake slices until their edges are nicely browned. Place a slice on each serving plate. Top with a scoop of ice cream and ladle on some warm orange sauce.

The Adventurous Chef: You already thought of this one but I'll note it anyway. Substitute chocolate or hot fudge sauce for the orange sauce. Maybe some chopped nuts on top?

Vegetable Ideas

Perfect garden-fresh vegetables need only salt, pepper and a little butter. But the high seasons are short so during the rest of the year give them a little extra attention with a sauce (see the previous and following pages), an herb, a topping—or all three. Here are some ideas:

Vegetable	Sauces	Herbs & Spices	Toppings
Artichokes	Lemon or chive butter	Chives, oregano	Parmesan cheese
Asparagus	Hollandaise, lemon butter	Oregano, parsley, chives	Chopped hard-cooked egg, grated cheese
Beans: green, wax, lima	White, chive butter	Dill, chives	Crumbled bacon, nuts, minced onion, cheese
Beets	Orange butter	Chives	Orange marmalade, sour cream and dill
Broccoli	Cheese, lemon butter	Thyme, basil	Buttered crumbs, nuts
Brussels sprouts	Mushroom, orange butter	Caraway, nutmeg	Sautéed nuts, plumped raisins, green grapes
Cabbage	Chive butter	Caraway, dill, paprika	Sour cream and poppy seeds
Carrots	Orange or lemon butter	Dill, tarragon	Chopped pecans, green grapes
Cauliflower	Hollandaise, white or cheese	Nutmeg	Buttered crumbs, Parmesan
Corn	Chive butter, stewed tomatoes	Chives, parsley, thyme, chili powder	Crumbled bacon, chopped black olives
Eggplant	Cheese, tomato	Basil, oregano	Buttered crumbs, Parmesan
Fennel	Cheese, chive butter	Snipped fennel tops, nutmeg	Crumbled bacon, Oriental sesame oil
Greens	Cheese, lemon butter	Mustard, thyme	Hard-cooked egg, crumbled bacon, vinegar
Mushrooms	Herb butter, chive butter, white	Rosemary, oregano, tarragon	Sweet sherry, sour cream

Vegetable	Sauces	Herbs & Spices	Toppings
Onions	White or cheese, tomato	Nutmeg, tarragon, thyme	Buttered crumbs, bacon, sherry, peanuts
Peas	Chive or orange butter	Mint, rosemary	Water chestnuts, nuts, sliced green onions
Potatoes, white	Butter, white or cheese	Rosemary, thyme, dill	Cheese, sour cream
Spinach	Herb butter, white or cheese	Nutmeg, thyme, mustard	Buttered crumbs, cheese, crumbled bacon
Squash, winter	Lemon or orange butter	Cinnamon, allspice, nutmeg	Maple syrup, brown sugar and cinnamon
Squash, summer	Herb butter, lemon butter, cheese	Dill, basil, oregano	Poultry stuffing mix, bacon, nuts

More Quick Sauces

For green vegetables, rice and potatoes.

Butter Sauces

Basic Butter: In a small pan combine ½ cup butter and other ingredients. Cook until butter melts.

Nut: Sauté 2 tablespoon sliced or slivered almonds or chopped pecans or walnuts for 2 to 3 minutes or until golden. Add 1 to 2 teaspoons lemon juice (optional).

Lemon: Add 2 tablespoons lemon juice.

Chive: Add 2 tablespoons lemon juice and 1 tablespoon fresh or frozen minced chives.

Orange: Add 1 tablespoon grated orange rind.

Cheese Sauces

Chive: Melt ½ of an 8-ounce package cream cheese with chives with 2 to 4 tablespoons milk. Makes ½ cup.

Sour Cream: Over low heat blend 1 cup sour cream with 1 cup any shredded cheese, stirring constantly. Stir in 2 tablespoons lemon juice. Add salt to taste.

Yellow:

1 tablespoon butter
1 tablespoon flour
½ cup chicken broth
¼ cup whipping cream or evaporated milk
¼ cup grated Swiss, Parmesan, or Cheddar

Melt butter, stir in flour and let it bubble up for a minute. Gradually stir in broth, then cream. Cook, stirring, until thickened and smooth. Stir in cheese.

Try Soup Tonight

There is something very soothing and basic about soup. A good soup can make your reputation and satisfy your soul. Some of the soups in this chapter are almost hearty stews, loaded with savory chunks of meat, poultry, vegetables, seafood. Make a specialty of soup meals. Give them an intriguing hot bread from the boxes sprinkled throughout the book. Assemble a wardrobe of pottery bowls and mugs. Get a tureen or handsome cooking pot so you can ladle your soup out at table, steaming and aromatic. For a gourmet treat, serve soup in individual, toasted bread bowls. They're easy to make and the crunchy outsides and soup-soaked insides are scrumptious. Serve soup to company. Set your table with a bright cloth and pottery dishes. Start with an interesting nibble, add a crisp salad, an unusual bread and a comforting dessert like chocolate mousse or cherry crunch. This is cozy, relaxed dining that guests will remember with pleasure. For quickly-prepared soups that look elegant and taste like loving time and wizardry, look at the nifty chart that tells how to combine canned soups of different flavors with a significant other ingredient and a spiffy garnish.

"Get a pretty tureen or handsome cooking pot so you can ladle your soup out at table, steaming and aromatic."

Bacon and Leek Soup with Brie

This is comforting and warming on a cold night: thick and hearty, tinged with smoky bacon and topped with gooey, melting cubes of Brie. Serve with a crisp French bread and a green salad with lots of crunch.

Prep Time: 10 minutes
Cooking Time: 30 minutes

6 slices bacon, in 1" pieces

1 leek, sliced

1 medium onion, sliced

1 tablespoon vegetable oil

1 medium boiling potato, peeled and sliced

2 cups grated cabbage

4 cups chicken broth

½ teaspoon dried oregano

3 ounces Brie cheese, rind removed, cut into ½" cubes

salt and pepper to taste

chopped parsley as a garnish

In a large, heavy saucepan fry the bacon, leek and onion in the oil until softened. Don't let the onion brown. Add potato and cook until the bacon begins to brown. Add the cabbage and mix well. Add chicken broth, oregano, and salt and pepper to taste. Cover and simmer for 20 minutes. Cool slightly.

Place the soup in the blender or food processor and purée. Return it to the pan and heat to boiling. To serve, divide the cheese among 4 soup bowls and pour the hot soup over. Sprinkle with parsley.

Yield: 4 servings.

❧ Bread Bowls ❧

If you serve soup to guests and want to fuss a little, serve it in these individual bread bowls. You eat the soup from the bread bowl and tear off pieces of the bowl, which will be impregnated with the soup flavors, to eat with your salad. Fun and dramatic.

Preheat the oven to 350°.

Use big rolls or small round loaves, about 6" in diameter. Stick the point of a sharp knife into the top of each loaf near the edge and cut off the top. Hollow out the center leaving a ¾" wall. Rub the inside with the cut side of a clove of garlic (optional). Brush the inside with about a teaspoon of olive oil and sprinkle with a half-tablespoon of Parmesan cheese (optional again).

Place the bread bowls on a baking sheet and bake for 15 minutes or until they are golden and crusty and the cheese has melted. As you can see, you have made a big, hollow crouton.

Spoon a serving of soup or filling into it and sprinkle with whatever garnish you are using.

The Adventurous Chef: It's fun to use the cut-off lids. Top each with garlic, oil and cheese and bake them alongside the bread bowls. Set askew on the filled bowls they look very jaunty, and you'll get a reputation for being a food stylist.

Spanish Clam and Shrimp Soup

The Spaniards inexplicably call this "Quarter of an Hour Soup" which, as you can see, it isn't quite. But it's a nifty seafood soup, a rich broth jam-packed with ham, shrimp, clams, rice and peas, topped with chopped hard-cooked egg and pimento. Before you start, put the eggs in to boil for the garnish so they will be ready. Give them 10 minutes at a very low simmer.

Prep Time: 10 minutes
Cooking Time: 30 minutes

½ cup diced ham

2 tablespoons olive oil

1 cup chopped onion

2 cloves garlic, crushed

1 cup shrimp, peeled and deveined

2 medium tomatoes, peeled, seeded and chopped

1 teaspoon paprika

6 cups chicken broth

2 cans (7 ounces each) minced clams

½ cup uncooked rice

1 cup peas, fresh or frozen

2 chopped hard cooked eggs and 2 bottled roasted red peppers, cut in strips as garnishes

In a medium saucepan, combine ham, oil, onion, garlic and shrimp. Cook and stir for 5 minutes. Lift out shrimp to a dish and reserve. Add tomatoes and paprika. Sauté until the tomatoes soften, 3 to 4 minutes. Add the chicken broth. Hold a sieve over the pot and empty the opened cans of clams into it so only the liquid goes in the pot. Put the clams with the shrimp.

Cover the pot, raise the heat and bring the soup to a boil. Uncover and stir in the rice. Lower the heat and simmer uncovered for 15 minutes. Add the peas and cook for 5 minutes more. Add the shrimp and clams and cook briefly to heat through but not cook. This will keep the seafood juicy and tender. Too much heat makes it tough. Garnish each portion with chopped eggs and pimento.

Yield: 6 servings.

The Clever Chef: If you use cooked frozen or canned shrimp, don't give them the initial sauté. Add them at the end to heat through. Remember to rinse canned shrimp well. They have a briny taste.

The Social Chef: To make this into a meal for lunch or supper guests, add garlic toasts and a salad with flamenco overtones: greens with artichoke hearts, black olives and sliced oranges. A flan would give a very Spanish ending.

❧ A Cook's Motto ☙

A British country saying to remember when you wield the saucepan: *Kissin' don't last. Cookin' do.*

Reuben Soup

This is for Sunday night or a night when you want to feel soothed and snuggled. Make some rye croutons to float in it (bake buttered rye cubes at 400° for 5 to 10 minutes) or serve it with buttered rye toast.

Prep Time: 8 minutes
Cooking Time: 20 minutes

½ cup chopped onion
½ cup chopped celery
2 tablespoons butter
2 cups chicken broth
2 tablespoons cornstarch
2 tablespoons water
2 cups cooked corned beef, chopped or in ribbons
2 cups light cream or half-and-half
¾ cup sauerkraut, well rinsed and drained
1 teaspoon tomato paste
1 teaspoon sugar
1 cup shredded Swiss cheese
salt and pepper to taste

In a large saucepan sauté the onion and celery in butter until tender. Add the broth.

In a small dish mix cornstarch with water and stir into the pan. Bring the soup to a boil over high heat and cook for 2 minutes, stirring occasionally.

Add the corned beef, cream, sauerkraut, tomato paste and sugar. Return to a boil, then reduce the heat to medium low and simmer gently for 15 minutes. Stir in the cheese and heat only until the cheese starts to melt. Add salt and pepper to taste.

Yield: 4 servings.

The Skinny Chef: Substitute lite cheese and skim milk. If you use milk, increase the cornstarch by ½ teaspoon to replace the thickening effect of the cream.

Menu

Reuben Soup

Green Beans Vinaigrette with
Hard-Cooked Egg

Buttered Rye Toast

Fruit Cobbler

Canned Soup Wizardry

It's easiest if you first combine the canned soups in your pot with a whisk or wooden spoon and gradually whisk in the liquid before you start heating them. All recipes serve 4 to 6.

The Basic Steps:	Combine these canned soups:	Heat with this liquid and seasoning:	Add this garnish:
Asparagus Cheese *Rich flavor with a hint of curry.*	Cream of asparagus and Cheddar cheese.	2 cans milk; 1-2 table-spoons curry powder (sauté in butter first for a mellower taste) and ½ teaspoon sugar.	Coarse chopped roasted peanuts.
Crab Bisque *Flavored with sherry, this is an elegant starter.*	Cream of asparagus and cream of mush-room.	½ cup light cream; 1½ cups milk; ½ cup dry sherry and 8 ounces crabmeat, flaked; or a 7-ounce can, well rinsed.	Croutons; chopped parsley or chives.
Southwest Bean and Cheese	Bean with bacon and nacho cheese.	1 can milk and ½ can water.	Crumbled bacon and crushed corn chips.
Mushroom Cheese *A lovely luncheon dish.*	Cheddar cheese and cream of mushroom.	1½ cans milk; ⅓ can dry white wine; and a pinch *each* savory, thyme and mace.	Sliced sautéed mush-rooms and paprika.
Shrimp Bisque *Delicious! No one flavor dominates.*	2 cream of tomato and 1 cream of green pea.	½ - ¾ cup sherry; 1 cup cooked, shelled medium shrimp, sautéed in butter for 2 minutes and chopped; ⅛ tea-spoon nutmeg and hot cayenne pepper to taste.	½ cup whipping cream, salted and whipped.
Tomato Cheese *A lunchtime favorite.*	Cheddar cheese and tomato.	2 cans milk; ¼ cup minced onion and a big pinch *each* of basil and oregano.	Minced chives.
Potage *Different and delightful.*	Cream of mushroom; beef broth and tomato.	½ can water; 1 can milk; ⅓ can sherry and ¼ teaspoon dried thyme.	Spoonful of sour cream swirled in each bowl.

Sausage and Green Chili Soup

This is a thick soup with lots of things in it. The Polish sausage and green chilies give it a rich, spicy flavor. Use mild or hot chilies.

Prep Time: 5 minutes
Cooking Time: 30 minutes

1 can (16 ounces) diced tomatoes

6 ounces Polish sausage, sliced thin

1 cup onions, sliced thin

1 cup carrots, quartered lengthwise, then sliced as thin as possible

1 can (4 ounces) diced green chilies

4 ounces small mushrooms, halved

1 cup chicken broth

salt and pepper to taste

Put tomatoes into a large saucepan along with the sausage, onions, carrots, green chilies, mushrooms and broth.

Bring the mixture to a boil over high heat. Cover, lower the heat and simmer for 25 minutes. Add salt and pepper to taste.

Yield: 4 servings.

✃ The Speedy Chef ✃

Chop peppers, onions and garlic and freeze them separately in plastic bags or small containers. This way they're ready when you need them. Remember, when they thaw, peppers and onions will be soft, so you can use them only in cooking. But they're fine for that.

    Keep frequently used ingredients near where you cook. A small tray can hold salt, pepper, spices, vegetable oil, flour and vinegar. It saves time when you don't have to dig through the cupboards for things you use every day.

Minestrone

Here is a gem: a minestrone you can make in 20 minutes. The secret is to use canned vegetables. This recipe makes a big pot of soup, enough for dinner and a couple of containers for the freezer.

Prep Time: 5 minutes
Cooking Time: 25 minutes

1 pound ground beef
1 tablespoon olive oil
1 large onion, chopped
¼ medium cabbage, shredded
1 can (15 ounces) carrots with their liquid
1 can (14 to 16 ounces) tomatoes
1 can (15.5 ounces) kidney beans, drained and rinsed
1 can (15.5 ounces) cannellini beans, drained and rinsed
1 can (15 ounces) corn, drained
6 cups water plus 6 chicken bouillon cubes
1 can green beans, drained
¾ cup small elbow macaroni
½ teaspoon salt, or to taste
½ teaspoon dried oregano
½ teaspoon dried thyme
¼ teaspoon pepper
grated Parmesan cheese for garnish

In a large pot, sauté the ground beef in the olive oil until it is no longer pink.

Add the onion and cabbage to the meat and stir and cook over medium-high heat until the vegetables start to wilt, about 5 minutes. Add the remaining ingredients. Bring the soup to a boil, lower the heat and simmer for 20 to 30 minutes.

Swirl 1 tablespoon Parmesan cheese into each serving.

Yield: 12 servings.

The Unhurried Chef: If you cook it for an extra 10 minutes the flavors will mellow.

The Clever Chef: If you substitute canned broth for the bouillon cubes, use 5 cans low-sodium chicken broth.

Freeze Flat

Here's a trick from my friend Judy for freezing soups and sauces. Ladle them into pint or quart freezer bags. Put the bag in a square freezer container while filling so it stays upright. Squeeze out all the air, seal. Freeze flat on a baking sheet or other flat surface. When frozen, sauces will stack flat or on end like books. Neat.

Ham and Corn Chowder

A creamy soup whose velvety richness is studded with little nuggets of smoky ham and sweet corn kernels. Serve it with Quick Corn Bread, p. 163.

Prep Time: 7 minutes
Cooking Time: 20 minutes

2 cups diced cooked ham
1 cup chopped celery
½ cup chopped onion
¼ cup butter
2 cans (16 ounces each) cream-style corn
1 cup milk
½ teaspoon celery salt
½ teaspoon garlic powder
½ teaspoon pepper

In a large saucepan sauté the ham, celery and onion in butter until tender. Add the corn, milk, celery salt, garlic powder and pepper.

Bring to a boil. Reduce the heat, cover and simmer for 20 minutes. Serve hot.

Yield: 6 servings.

Salad with Hot Brie Dressing

The Brie sauce that adorned the chicken of p. 70 is also a knockout dressing for salad. The contrast of crisp greens and hot dressing is nothing short of dazzling. This is too good to be a side salad. Serve it as a first course or a salad course. It has to star.

1 small bunch curly endive
½ head iceberg lettuce
1 small head romaine
¼ cup olive oil
2 teaspoons shallots or green onions, minced
1 teaspoon garlic, minced
¼ cup sherry or other wine vinegar
1 tablespoon fresh lemon juice
2 teaspoons Dijon mustard
5 ounces ripe Brie cheese, rind removed
pepper to taste
garlic croutons as a garnish

Put the washed, dried and torn greens in a serving bowl and chill in the refrigerator while you finish the salad.

Warm the oil in a large, heavy skillet over low heat. Add shallots and garlic and cook for 4 to 5 minutes or until softened, stirring now and then. Stir in the vinegar, lemon juice and mustard. Cut the cheese into small pieces and stir into the mixture. When it is smooth, season with pepper to taste. Toss the *hot* dressing with the *cold* greens and serve topped with croutons. This makes a real impression.

Yield: 4 servings.

Tortilla Soup

Hearty and good. You can omit the tortilla strips and pass a bowl of crushed corn chips along with the Cheddar and sour cream. This is delicious on a chilly winter evening.

Prep Time: 5 minutes
Cooking Time: 20 minutes

½ pound lean ground beef

¼ cup chopped onions

1¾ cups water

1 can (14 to 16 ounces) chopped stewed tomatoes, undrained

1 can (16 ounces) pinto beans, drained and rinsed

1 can (8 ounces) tomato sauce

2 tablespoons taco seasoning mix (half a package)

shredded Cheddar cheese and sour cream as garnishes

In a large saucepan cook the beef and onion over medium heat until the meat is browned. Add water, tomatoes and their liquid, beans, tomato sauce and seasoning mix. Cover and simmer over medium-low heat for 15 minutes.

Pass bowls of cheese and sour cream to top each serving.

Yield: 4 to 6 servings.

Cheese Pan Biscuits

1 package (10.8 ounces) refrigerated biscuits
½ cup grated processed cheese
¼ cup melted butter

Preheat the oven to 450°. Place biscuits close together in 9" pie plate. Stir cheese and butter together until smooth. Spread over the biscuits. Bake for 15 minutes.

Yield: 4 to 6 servings.

Borscht

All you have to do here is slice an onion and wield the can opener—a real dump and cook recipe. It's a delicious soup, thick with a rich, sweet-sour tang. Serve with Garlic Bread, p. 55. Hearty appetites might want a cheese or ham sandwich added to the meal.

Prep Time: 5 minutes
Cooking Time: 25 minutes

6 cups packaged coleslaw mix (cabbage and carrot)

1 can (10½ ounces) condensed beef broth

1 can (8 ounces) tomato sauce

1 can (14 to 16 ounces) diced tomatoes, with liquid

1 can (14 ½ ounces) sliced beets with liquid

1 large onion, thinly sliced

2 tablespoons sugar

2 tablespoons vinegar

¼ teaspoon pepper

salt to taste

sour cream as a garnish

In a 4-quart Dutch oven combine coleslaw mix, beef broth, tomato sauce, tomatoes and beets, both with their liquid, onion, sugar, vinegar and pepper. Bring to a boil.

Cover and simmer for 20 minutes. Add salt to taste.

Serve with a bowl of sour cream to spoon onto individual portions.

Yield: 6 servings.

❧ Instant Gateau ❧

When you want to nestle in a chair with a cup of coffee and nibble on something delectable, here's the answer.

1 boxed cake mix, any flavor
jam, any flavor
whipped cream
ice cream
chocolate sauce

Prepare cake batter according to the package directions. Bake 1 cup of batter at a time in a heated waffle iron. Cool the waffle cakes slightly and top with any of the following combinations:

• jam
• jam and whipped cream
• ice cream and chocolate sauce

Freeze extra waffle cakes and thaw them in the toaster oven before serving.

Yield: 6 to 8 waffle cakes.

Try Salad Tonight

Salad, once a first course, a side dish, or a light ladies' lunch, has become a beloved main dish—not just for the summer months when we want something light and quick, but year round. The salads in this chapter are different, hearty and delicious with seductive flavors that will tempt the most determined meat-and-potatoes eater. They include favorites like Tortellini with Ham, Olives and Blue Cheese; sophisticated combinations like Belgian endive with shrimp, ham with walnuts, and delectable mixtures from the Orient, Latin America and the Mediterranean. Try the Sushi Salad with its enchanting mix of chewy, sweet-tart rice, shrimp, sesame seeds and vegetables; the exotic Thai and Oriental salads; or the Mexican chef's salad dressed with warm Cheddar cheese sauce. To keep your tossed salads up to date, there is a chart that describes the greens you'll find at the market, what they taste like and how to combine them. Remember, be flexible. Don't let a recipe bully you. If you don't have a major ingredient, go ahead and substitute. Make a chicken salad with pork, a beef one with chicken. The sky won't fall and you'll eat very well.

"The salads in this chapter are different, hearty and delicious with seductive flavors that will tempt the most determined meat-and-potatoes eater."

Chicken Salad Olé

Spicy sautéed chicken on a bed of corn, black beans, lettuce and crunchy corn chips. Don't let the ingredient list discourage you. A quick stir-fry of the chicken, a couple minutes of chopping and you're ready to call the family.

Prep Time: 8 minutes
Cooking Time: 10 minutes

1 tablespoon chili powder

1 teaspoon ground cumin

½ teaspoon lemon pepper seasoning

½ teaspoon garlic salt

1 pound skinless, boneless chicken breast halves cut into ½" strips

2 cups canned or frozen corn

1 can (15 ounces) black beans, rinsed and drained

1 can (4 ounces) sliced black olives

1 avocado, diced

1 cup onion, diced

4 cups lettuce in bite size pieces

½ cup plus 1 tablespoon olive oil, divided

2 tablespoons red wine vinegar

1 tablespoon lemon juice

1 teaspoon black pepper

1 jalapeño pepper, seeded, deveined and diced

½ teaspoon dried oregano

¼ teaspoon grated lemon rind

4 cups corn chips

as a garnish, any or all of these: sliced black olives, slices of avocado, papaya, mango

Sprinkle chili powder, cumin, lemon pepper and garlic salt over the chicken strips and work the spices into the meat with your fingers. Set aside.

In a large bowl combine the corn, beans, olives, avocado, onion and lettuce.

Dressing: In a small bowl whisk together ½ cup of the olive oil, vinegar, lemon juice, black pepper, jalapeño, oregano and lemon rind. Add it to the lettuce mixture and toss. Place an equal portion on 4 plates.

In a medium skillet heat 1 tablespoon oil over medium-high heat and stir-fry the chicken until it is deep brown, 8 to 10 minutes.

Place an equal portion of chicken on each mound of salad. Top with corn chips and garnish with olives, avocado, papaya or mango.

Yield: 4 servings.

Chicken Salad with Rice Noodles

The Thai are artists at harmonizing textures and flavors. Witness this exotic blend of soft noodles, tender chicken, crisp vegetables and crunchy peanuts in a vaguely sweet, lemony dressing.

Prep Time: 12 minutes
Cooking Time: 17 minutes

Chicken:

3 cups chicken broth

½ cup white wine or vermouth

4 skinless, boneless chicken breast halves

*12 ounces oriental rice noodles or
1 pound angel hair pasta*

1 tablespoon Oriental sesame oil

Dressing:

¾ cup rice or wine vinegar

½ cup soy sauce

¼ cup sugar

2 tablespoons Oriental sesame oil

2 tablespoons minced fresh ginger

1 to 2 teaspoons hot red pepper flakes

2 cloves garlic, minced

salt to taste

Salad:

1 large seedless cucumber, slivered

12 ounces bean sprouts

*¾ cup green onions, sliced thin (include
the green tops)*

¾ cup chopped cilantro leaves

½ cup chopped basil leaves

¾ cup minced roasted salted peanuts

lemon wedges as a garnish

In a medium saucepan bring broth and wine to a boil. Add the chicken and return the liquid to the boil. Lower heat and simmer gently until chicken is springy to the touch and cooked through, about 12 minutes. Remove the chicken to a plate.

Return the broth to a boil, add the noodles and cook for 3 minutes or until done. Drain. Fill a bowl with cold water, add the sesame oil to the water and put the noodles in it to cool them quickly. Shred the chicken.

In a small bowl mix the vinegar, soy sauce, sugar, sesame oil, ginger, pepper flakes, garlic and salt to taste.

When the noodles are cool, lift them out and place them on a serving platter. Place the chicken, cucumber, bean sprouts, green onions, cilantro, basil and peanuts in individual bowls. Set out a bowl of the dressing. Diners make their own salad by placing some noodles on their plate and topping them with the other ingredients, then the dressing.

Yield: 4 servings.

Beef Salad Orientale

This is real flavor. Beef marinated in spicy-sweet hoisin, salty soy, and smoky sesame is sautéed for a crisp outside, then laid on mixed greens and bathed in a dressing of orange and lime. It's super quick despite the number of ingredients, most of which just get a spin in the processor.

Prep Time: 15 minutes
Marinating Time: 30 minutes
Cooking Time: 3 minutes

Salad:

4 teaspoons dark soy sauce (see note)

4 teaspoons hoisin sauce

4 teaspoons tahini

*1 pound beef tenderloin or chuck steak
    tenders (see box p. 88)*

8 cups bite-size mixed greens

Dressing:

1 large clove garlic

¼ cup chopped basil leaves

1 strip orange peel, 4" x ½"

7 tablespoons olive oil, divided

¼ cup lime juice

4 teaspoons light soy sauce

2 tablespoons honey

*1 teaspoon Chinese chili-garlic paste or
    chili oil*

½ teaspoon nutmeg

For the salad: in a medium bowl combine the dark soy, hoisin sauce and tahini. Cut the beef into ⅛" thick slices, then in half, and toss with the mixture. Cover and leave at room temperature for 30 minutes.

For the dressing: Put the metal blade in the food processor, start the motor, and drop the garlic through the tube. Add the basil and pulse once or twice. Add the orange peel, 6 tablespoons of the olive oil, lime juice, soy sauce, honey, chili-garlic paste and nutmeg. Let the motor run for about 2 minutes.

Arrange the salad greens on 4 individual plates.

In a large skillet heat 1 tablespoon olive oil over high heat. When the oil looks wavy, add the beef. Cook and stir for 2 to 3 minutes or until it is golden brown on the outside, but still pink inside.

Place equal portions of the meat on the greens. Give the dressing a whisk and spoon it over the meat.

Yield: 4 servings.

The Clever Chef: Tahini is a Middle Eastern sesame paste. You'll find it in the international or health food section of the grocery store. Dark soy sauce is heavier and richer than the standard soy sauce because it has caramel added, but use the light variety if that's what you have.

Shrimp Pecan Salad

W ith the crunchy sautéed pecans, soft avocado and salty feta cheese, these shrimp are indeed glorified. This is a bright, imaginative, utterly scrumptious salad.

Prep Time: 10 minutes
Cooking Time: 10 minutes

1 pound raw jumbo shrimp (see note)
2 tablespoons lemon juice
1 ½ teaspoons sugar
½ teaspoon seasoned salt
½ teaspoon seasoned pepper
½ teaspoon dried oregano
¼ teaspoon garlic powder
¼ cup olive oil
½ cup large pecan halves sautéed in 1 tablespoon butter with ½ teaspoon dried rosemary (see note)
1 tablespoon chopped chives
1 tablespoon chopped parsley
3 radishes, thickly sliced
3 black olives, thickly sliced
3 stuffed green olives, thickly sliced
1 large fresh tomato, in wedges
½ large avocado, sliced
⅓ cup feta or Monterey Jack cheese
lettuce

Drop the shrimp into rapidly boiling water and cook for 3 to 4 minutes or until they turn bright pink. Plunge into cold water. Shell, devein and place in a large salad bowl.

In another bowl whisk together lemon juice, sugar, seasoned salt and pepper, oregano, garlic powder and olive oil. Pour the dressing over the shrimp.

Mix the pecans, chives, parsley, radishes, olives, tomato, avocado, and feta with the shrimp. Arrange on salad greens.

Yield: 4 servings.

The Speedy Chef: Save time by buying the shrimp already cooked.

The Clever Chef: To sauté pecans, melt butter in a heavy skillet over low heat. Cook pecans for 8 to 10 minutes or until lightly toasted. Stir often and watch carefully. Once nuts start to darken they cook very fast.

Couscous and Chicken Salad with Orange Dressing

This has a subtle orange flavor which goes so well with the olives, roasted peppers and chick peas. This is just the ticket when you want something special for a potluck supper.

Prep Time: 10 minutes
Cooking Time: 8 minutes

1 box (10 ounces) quick-cooking couscous

1 teaspoon salt

1 cup raisins

½ cup orange juice

*2 tablespoons balsamic vinegar or
red wine vinegar*

2 tablespoons grated orange peel

2 teaspoons ground cumin

6 tablespoons olive oil

*2 cups roasted chicken or turkey breast,
in bite-size cubes*

*¾ cup bottled roasted peppers, drained
and diced*

1 cup canned chick peas, rinsed

½ cup Kalamata olives, chopped

*3 green onions, green and white parts,
chopped*

¼ cup chopped fresh cilantro leaves

romaine lettuce

salt and pepper to taste

Bring 2¼ cups water to a boil in a saucepan. Add couscous, salt and raisins. Cover, remove from heat and let stand 5 minutes. Fluff the couscous with a fork and set aside. In a small bowl mix the orange juice, vinegar, orange peel, cumin, olive oil and salt and pepper to taste.

Place the couscous in a large bowl. Add the chicken, peppers, chick peas, olives, green onions and cilantro. Pour the dressing over and toss. Check for salt and pepper—couscous absorbs a lot of seasoning.

Line a salad bowl with romaine and spoon the couscous over it.

Yield: 4 servings.

The Speedy Chef: Buy a rotisserie chicken for this recipe.

Beyond Iceberg and Romaine

Salads are a lot more fun when you vary the greens. Head lettuce (iceberg) and romaine are gradually losing place to the magnificent assortment of shapes and colors you find in today's produce sections. Greens range in flavor from the mild to the slightly bitter assertive. These last make marvelous accents, but can be delicious on their own if you use a dressing that has enough spunk to stand up to them.

Make salads with a single green or a combination. In a mix of assertive and mild, you want a lot of mild and just enough assertive to provide punctuation. Here is a list of greens in case hurried shopping threatens to put you in a salad rut.

Mild Greens

Bibb: Small, tender head with crisp leaves. Best on its own with a light vinaigrette. Try it with sliced radishes and chopped hard cooked eggs.

Boston (Butter): Light green, very tender leaves with a subtle, sweet flavor.

Red-Edged Ruby Leaf Lettuce: Large, loosely-packed, red-tipped leaves. Crisp, delicate texture with a mild and sweet flavor. Good for color. Use with sturdier greens.

Oak-Leaf Lettuce: A delicate green with a nutty flavor. You can make this the whole salad—which is a good idea because it doesn't keep as long as the sturdier lettuces.

Mâche (Corn Salad, Field Lettuce, Lamb's Tongue): Dark green leaves in small clusters about 2 to 3 inches long, very delicate texture. Sweet flavor. Best in combinations.

Iceberg: Sweet, crunchy, good for texture. Break, don't cut it.

Romaine: The workhorse of salads, with good reason. Long heads, crunchy, mild, sweet, nutty. Can take a strong vinaigrette.

Spinach: Use the young, tender leaves. Texture coarse and hearty, sweet and musky flavor. Good with blue cheese and bacon.

Mesclun: A mixture of all sorts of young leaves. Expensive but so good. I like to buy a bag and toss a little into salads of more mundane greens. Of course it's marvelous on its own.

Napa Cabbage: Very mild and crunchy. Needs spicy aromatics like garlic and ginger to set it off.

Assertive Greens

Escarole: Broad-leaved cousin of curly endive. Pleasantly bitter flavor and crisp texture.

Arugula: Addictive, chewy texture, pungent flavor. Smaller leaves are best. Use in combinations or on its own. Delicious with sweet vegetables like red onions or red bell peppers or with tomatoes and mozzarella. Needs a strong vinaigrette.

Belgian endive: Pale green or yellow in color. Wonderful crunch. Good with oil, vinegar and chopped walnuts. The little hard bit at the end is especially bitter. Cut that off.

Curly Endive: A firm, nubby bundle with curly little leaves. Adds a wonderful texture and tang. Try it with walnuts and sliced apples.

Dandelion Greens: Refreshing, tart taste. Must be young and fresh. Good alone or in combination.

Watercress: Peppery, with a refreshing bite. Nice with sliced pears, crumbled mild goat cheese or feta, and toasted almonds.

Radicchio: Round, tightly packed little wine-colored heads. Chewy texture. Wonderful color accent.

✃ Speedy Tiramisu With Raspberries ✃

Chocolate and raspberries mixed with coffee-flavored cream cheese and cream soak into pound cake layers to produce a dessert as wickedly delicious as the real thing.

1 square (1 ounce) semisweet chocolate
1 container (4 ounces) whipped cream cheese
2 tablespoons coffee-flavored liqueur (Kahlua or Tia Maria)
½ teaspoon vanilla
¾ cup whipping cream
⅓ cup powdered sugar
½ teaspoon espresso coffee powder mixed with 1 teaspoon hot water
1 cup coarsely crumbled pound cake
½ box frozen raspberries, thawed

Grate the chocolate and set aside 1 tablespoon. In a medium bowl, using a whisk or fork, beat the cream cheese with the coffee liqueur, vanilla and the grated chocolate. Blend well.

In a small bowl whip the cream with the powdered sugar until it makes stiff peaks. Set aside 1 cup and fold the rest into the cheese along with the espresso mixture.

Divide half the crumbled cake among 4 dessert glasses. Set aside 4 whole raspberries. Spoon half the remaining berries with their syrup onto the cake. Top with half the cheese mixture, covering completely. Add the remaining cake crumbles, berries and juice, and cheese mixture. Top with the reserved whipped cream, sprinkle with reserved tablespoon of chocolate and put a raspberry on each.

Yield: 4 servings.

The Clever Chef: To halve a box of raspberries easily, either cut the box in half while still frozen, or thaw it and measure out a generous ½ cup which includes juice.

Favorite Vinaigrettes

Plain Vinaigrette

Use this on everything. It's especially good on delicate salad greens.

2 tablespoons wine vinegar
¼ cup oil
salt and pepper to taste

Whisk together all ingredients. Refrigerate any extra in a covered container.

Yield: About ⅓ cup.

Mustard Vinaigrette

This is good on assertive greens and on mixes of greens and other vegetables.

1 tablespoon Dijon mustard
2 tablespoons red wine vinegar
¼ cup oil
¼ cup chopped parsley
salt and pepper to taste

Whisk together all ingredients. Refrigerate any extra in covered container.

Yield: About ½ cup.

Louis's Vinaigrette

This has been the standard in our house for the last 20 years. I learned it from our cook in Cotonou who cooked like an angel. Use it for salads, spoon it over red-ripe tomatoes or add it to salads made of cooked vegetables.

1 cup finely chopped onion
2 minced cloves garlic
4 teaspoons Dijon mustard
½ cup red wine vinegar
1 cup vegetable oil
salt and pepper to taste

Put all ingredients into a screw-top jar. Shake or whisk. This keeps for at least a week in the fridge and gets better as it ripens.

Yield: About 2 cups.

Hot Ham and Green Bean Salad

This differs from the usual salads in that it has no vinegar or lemon, just the clean crunch of beans and succulent mushrooms bathed in the sweet smoky flavors of ham and bacon. You'll love it. It's a supper dish with rice and corn bread, also a lovely first course.

Prep Time: 15 minutes
Cooking Time: 10 minutes

1 ½ pounds young green beans
1 teaspoon salt
4 ounces bacon in 1" pieces
6 ounces country or other ham, sliced ¼" thick
1 - 3 tablespoons butter
1 bunch green onions, in ½" pieces
1 cup sliced portobello or other mush-rooms
1 cup chopped parsley

Trim the beans and cut them into 2-3" lengths. In a large saucepan bring 2 quarts of salted water to a boil. Add the beans and boil for 6 minutes. Drain. Immediately place them in cold water to stop the cooking. Drain again and place them on a double thickness of paper towels.

In a large skillet, cook the bacon and ham in the butter. Add the green onions, mushrooms and parsley. Stir-fry for a few minutes. Add the beans. Cook just to reheat.

Yield: 4 servings.

❧ Quick Risotto ❧

This has a lot of the rich taste of the risotto on p. 143 but doesn't require any stirring. I think you'll like it.

½ medium onion, chopped
1 tablespoon olive oil
1 cup rice
2 tablespoons butter
1 ½ cups chicken broth
½ cup grated Parmesan
salt and pepper to taste

In a heavy saucepan over medium-high heat sauté onion in olive oil for 5 minutes or until softened. Stir in rice, butter, broth and salt and pepper to taste. Turn the heat to low, cover and cook for 10 minutes. Uncover and cook until remaining liquid boils off and the rice is done, about 10 minutes. Stir in the cheese and serve piping hot.

Yield: 4 servings.

Tortellini Salad with Ham, Olives and Blue Cheese

P lump little cheese-filled pasta cushions hobnobbing with ham, mushrooms and blue cheese. How can you go wrong?

Prep Time: 15 minutes
Cooking Time: 8 minutes

1 package (8 to 9 ounces) cheese-stuffed
fresh or frozen tortellini

1 cup sour cream or plain yogurt

1 tablespoon white wine vinegar

2 tablespoons crumbled blue cheese

6 large mushrooms, trimmed and thinly
sliced (about 3 cups)

6 ounces baked ham, thinly sliced and cut
into narrow ribbons

½ cup minced parsley

½ cup chopped black Kalamata olives

½ cup thinly sliced celery

salt, pepper and sugar to taste

Cook the tortellini in boiling water according to package directions. Drain in a colander, then transfer to a mixing bowl.

While the tortellini cook, in a medium bowl mix sour cream and vinegar until smooth. Fold in the blue cheese. Add salt and pepper to taste. It may need a pinch of sugar.

Add the dressing to the tortellini along with the mushrooms, ham, parsley, olives and celery. Toss gently.

Yield: 4 servings.

🍲 Jazz up a Can of Soup 🍲

Cream of Tomato: Top with a fat dollop of whipped cream and a sprinkle of chives or parsley.

Chilled Cream of Tomato: Chill the soup icy-cold (15 minutes in the freezer). Top as above. Good for summer lunches with a green salad, Bel Paese or Gorgonzola cheese, and some crusty rolls. Add a glass of white wine for a treat.

Minestrone: Stir in sliced smoked sausage or diced ham and top with lots of grated Parmesan.

Chicken Broth: Heat with a little soy sauce and minced fresh ginger root. Top with chopped green onions. Try a few drops of Oriental sesame oil.

French Onion: Stir in a little Dijon mustard. Top some ½"-thick rounds of French bread with grated Swiss cheese and run them under the broiler until the cheese melts. Float them on the soup. A French friend does this with butter crackers instead of French bread. It works!

Cheese Soup: Add canned chopped green chilies, ground cumin, oregano, and some corn kernels. Top with crushed corn chips.

Shrimp Soup: Make a chowder by adding a box of frozen, chopped spinach and a can of minced clams.

Greek Pasta Salad

Chewy pasta is enlivened by crisp cucumbers, tomatoes sweet and cool to the bite, creamy salt-tinged feta, and rich black Mediterranean olives with their almost smoky taste. This is eating!

Prep Time: 10 minutes
Cooking Time: 15 minutes

8 ounces rotini, fusilli or other sturdy pasta

⅔ cup plus 2 teaspoons olive oil, divided

3 tablespoons white wine vinegar

1½ teaspoons dried oregano

1 large clove garlic, minced

½ teaspoon salt

1 sweet onion, thinly sliced

1 medium cucumber, peeled, seeded and diced

1 green pepper, sliced into ribbons

4 large ripe tomatoes, peeled, seeded and cut into coarse chunks

16 black Kalamata olives

6 ounce feta cheese in 1" cubes

pepper to taste

Cook pasta according to package directions, al dente. Drain, rinse with cold water. Drain again. Toss in a bowl with 2 teaspoons olive oil.

Place the vinegar in a small bowl and, with a fork or whisk, beat in the oregano, garlic, salt and pepper to taste. Whisk in ⅔ cup olive oil. Taste and add more vinegar, salt or pepper if needed.

In a large bowl combine onion, cucumber, green pepper, tomatoes, olives, feta and pasta. Pour the dressing over the salad and toss gently until everything is well coated. If the salad stands a short time before it's served, it will be even better. Serve at room temperature.

Yield: 4 servings.

❧ Mild Garlic Bread ❧

Garlic cloves become very mild when simmered and will peel easily. Try stirring 1 tablespoon dried oregano into the garlic mixture for extra flavor.

6 cloves garlic, unpeeled
¼ cup melted butter or olive oil
1 loaf (1 pound) Italian bread

Simmer garlic cloves in water to cover for 20 minutes or until soft. Rinse under cold water, drain and peel. Place in a small bowl, mash with a fork, and stir in the butter.

Preheat oven to 350°. Slice bread into 1" slices, cutting almost but not quite through to the bottom. Spread each cut surface with garlic mixture. Wrap loaf in heavy-duty aluminum foil. Bake for 15 minutes or until heated through. Serve warm.

Yield: 8 to 10 servings.

Ham, Shrimp, Endive and Walnut Salad

This is a beautiful and unusual salad. The white, crisp, fresh-tasting Belgian endive is perfectly balanced by the ham, walnuts and shrimp. The yogurt sauce has a lovely, soft, tart quality. Make this one when you want to feel pampered.

Prep Time: 12 minutes
Cooking Time: None

8 ounces medium to large shrimp, cooked, peeled and deveined

8 ounces mild-flavored ham

4 heads Belgian endive (about 1 pound)

½ cup coarsely chopped walnuts

⅓ cup plain yogurt

3 tablespoons fresh lemon juice

¼ cup vegetable or light olive oil

¼ cup chopped chives

salt and pepper to taste

watercress or parsley as a garnish (optional)

To Toast Nuts

It takes only a minute to toast walnuts or other nuts called for in a recipe. Browned nuts are delicious and have a delightful crunch. Toss them into a skillet over medium heat and stir for 2 to 3 minutes only.

Cut the shrimp into large dice and place them in a mixing bowl.

Cut the ham into ribbons 2" long and ½" wide and add them to the shrimp. Wash the endive and dry it well. Cut it into lengthwise ribbons about the size of the ham strips. Add endive and walnuts to the shrimp-ham mixture.

In a small bowl whisk together yogurt and lemon juice, adding the lemon juice gradually and checking the taste. If lemon juice is very sharp, you may want to use less. Slowly beat in the oil a few drops at a time so that a thick cream is formed. Fold in the chives and add salt and pepper to taste.

Toss the dressing with the salad. Mound it on individual plates and decorate with watercress or parsley if you wish.

Yield: 4 servings.

The Clever Chef: The little piece at the bottom of the stem end of the endive is bitter, so cut it off.

Warm Scallop Salad with Bacon Dressing

S callops, bacon and a touch of apple on watercress with a hot vinegar-bacon dressing—what a combo!

Prep Time: 10 minutes
Cooking Time: 7 minutes

2 bunches (3 to 4 ounces each) watercress

½ medium tart green apple (Granny Smith or Pippin)

1 tablespoon fresh lemon juice

¾ pound bacon, cut into 1" pieces

1 pound bay scallops, or sea scallops, halved horizontally

2 tablespoons shallots, finely minced

⅔ cup white wine vinegar

½ teaspoon sugar

black pepper

Wash and dry the watercress. Remove the big stems and arrange the greens in mounds on 4 individual plates. Peel and core the apple and cut long, ⅛" thick slices. Toss them with the lemon juice to keep them white.

Place the bacon pieces in a cold 10" skillet. Cook over medium heat for 4 minutes. Raise the heat to high, add the scallops and cook for 2 minutes. Add the shallots, vinegar and sugar and cook for 30 seconds. Add black pepper to taste.

With a slotted spoon lift out the bacon and scallops and divide them among the plates. Drizzle each salad with some of the mixture in the skillet (you may not need it all) and serve immediately while topping is hot.

Yield: 4 servings.

The Clever Chef: Substitute any vinegar for the wine vinegar. It won't taste the same, but it will be good.

❧ To Pit Olives ❧

To pit olives easily, press down on them with the heel of your hand. The pit is then very easy to separate from the flesh—often it actually pops out.

From top to bottom, clockwise: Ginger Peach Chicken Stir-Fry, page 53; Japanese Pancakes, page 168; and Sushi Salad, page 206.

From top to bottom, clockwise: Quick Cassoulet, page 154; Shrimp Scorpio Style, page 29; and Caramel Brie with Fresh Fruit, page 69.

Mexican Salad with Chili con Queso

What a fun idea. A crisp chef's salad with all the usuals plus hot chili-laced cheese sauce poured over it. It's different and delicious.

Prep Time: 20 minutes
Cooking Time: 5 minutes

4 cups torn romaine or head lettuce
⅔ cup coarsely shredded carrot
⅔ cup diced celery
⅔ cup cooked ham, cut into thin strips
⅔ cup cooked chicken or turkey breast, cut into thin strips
1½ medium tomatoes, diced
2 tablespoons sliced green onions, including the tops
1⅓ cups (5 ounces) sharp processed American cheese (not cheese spread)
6 tablespoons milk
2 tablespoons chopped, seeded canned green chilies (hot or mild)
2 tablespoons sliced ripe olives
corn chips as an accompaniment

Combine the lettuce, carrot and celery in a large salad bowl. Top with the ham, chicken, tomatoes and green onions.

Cut the cheese into cubes. In a medium saucepan over low heat combine the cheese and milk. Cook, stirring constantly, until the cheese is melted and the mixture is smooth. Stir in chilies and olives.

When you are ready to serve, pour the hot cheese sauce over the salad and toss lightly. Serve immediately. Pass corn chips to sprinkle on top.

Yield: 4 servings.

The Adventurous Chef: Make the cheese sauce and use it cold. To do this, increase the milk to ⅔ cup.

English Muffin Pizzas

These are good with soup or salad—or both.
4 English muffins
olive oil
garlic salt
2 tablespoons (approximately) tomato sauce
8 small strips mozzarella cheese
toppings such as anchovies (soaked first in milk for 5 minutes), sliced black olives, etc.

Preheat the oven to 375°. Split the English muffins and toast as usual. Brush the cut sides with olive oil, sprinkle with garlic salt and spread with a little tomato sauce. Sprinkle generously with oregano. On each half put 2 strips mozzarella and a flat anchovy fillet, sliced black olives, whatever strikes your fancy. Bake for 10 minutes or until cheese melts.

Yield: 4 servings.

Sushi Salad

If you're not a sushi addict now, this salad will start you on your way. Sushi rice is pickled in a mix of sugar and light rice vinegar, mingled with ginger and horseradish and topped with shrimp and avocado. A seductive combination.

Prep Time: 15 minutes
Cooking Time: 10 minutes

1⅓ cups rice
1 pound large shrimp, raw or cooked
½ cup seasoned rice vinegar
2 tablespoons minced ginger root
2 tablespoons prepared horseradish
2 teaspoons sugar
½ teaspoon salt, or to taste
⅛ teaspoon Oriental sesame oil
2 cups diced seeded cucumber
1 cup thawed frozen peas
½ cup thinly sliced radishes
¼ cup sliced green onions
fresh spinach leaves
1 avocado, sliced
salt to taste
2 to 3 tablespoons toasted sesame seeds

Cook rice according to package directions. Immediately turn out onto a baking sheet, give it a minute to stop steaming and refrigerate until it reaches room temperature, 3 to 5 minutes.

If using raw shrimp, bring a pan of salted water to a boil, drop in the shrimp and let them boil for 3 minutes or until they turn pink. Drain and run cold water over them. Shell and devein them.

In a large bowl combine the rice vinegar, ginger, horseradish, sugar, salt and sesame oil. Add the cucumber, peas, radishes and green onions. Remove the rice from the refrigerator and gently mix it into the salad. Fold in the shrimp. Taste and add salt if necessary.

Arrange the rice in a mound on a bed of fresh spinach leaves. Garnish with avocado slices. Sprinkle with sesame seeds.

Yield: 4 servings.

The Adventurous Chef: Substitute cooked crabmeat or salmon for the shrimp.

The Clever Chef: To toast sesame seeds, put them in a hot skillet and stir them for 3 to 5 minutes or until light brown. Remove immediately. The oil in the seeds will keep them cooking after they leave the heat.

Don't Cook Tonight

There are times you just don't feel like cooking but you still want to eat well. Here are some ideas for meals to assemble rather than cook. The whole dinner can be found on the supermarket shelves and at the deli counter. These are ethnic meals. I find that when a meal is assembled, it's a good idea to have a theme so things go together. Besides, it's fun.

This section won't just get you through a night of not wanting to cook. It can help you build a reputation as a relaxed party giver who knows good food. One of the unhappy casualties of a busy schedule is entertaining at home. With a few additions, none of which require you to turn on the stove, you can turn these menus into parties which look lavish and imaginative and which you can put together after work. So dust off your social calendar and dazzle your friends.

For a family meal select from the items in the "What To Buy" list. For company, go all out and serve most of them. When you want to put on a real extravaganza, I've suggested other recipes in the book that would be smashing additions.

"The whole dinner can be found on supermarket shelves and at the deli counter. These meals can help you build a reputation as a relaxed party giver who knows good food."

Greek Mezze

A Greek meal is eaten slowly: a bite of this, a taste of that, a swallow of retsina wine. Provide a delicious assortment and enjoy.

What to Buy

Choose some or all of the items below, and see the directions at right for how to prepare.

Canned stuffed grapevine leaves
Feta cheese
Canned small beets, whole or sliced
Celery and carrot
Green onions
Fennel
Green and red peppers
Zucchini
Fresh tomatoes
Potato salad
String cheese
Kalamata olives
Hummos, p.210
Pistachio nuts
Pita bread

Optional:
Rotisserie chicken
Cooked shrimp

The Adventurous Chef: Be sure to try the delicious, quintessential Greek dessert, which is yogurt drizzled with honey that thickens and turns chewy and caramel-like on the cold yogurt. Sprinkle chopped walnuts on top. For a party, buy a richer yogurt than the fat-free. If fat-free is all that is available, stir in a little sour cream.

What to Do

Put each item on a separate plate.
Garnish stuffed grapevine leaves with lemon wedges. Serve with plain yogurt or Yogurt Mint Sauce (p. 209).
Cut raw vegetables in slices, sticks or rings. Serve with Skordalia (p. 209), Tahini Sauce (p. 97) or Cucumber Garlic Sauce (p. 209).
Cut feta into cubes. Drizzle feta and sliced tomatoes with olive oil and sprinkle with oregano.
Perk up deli potato salad with fresh or dried mint, olives and a few drops of olive oil.
Sprinkle hummos with paprika and a drizzle of olive oil.
Set out plates or bowls of pistachio nuts, olives, string cheese.
Cut pita bread in wedges to use as a scoop for dips.
Garnish cooked chicken or shrimp with parsley and lemon wedges. Serve with any of the dips.

Add a Dessert

Yogurt drizzled with honey and sprinkled with chopped walnuts (see left)
Baklava

To Make It a Party

Add any of the following:
Beets with Walnuts, p. 210
Greek Meatballs, p. 97
Rotisserie chicken or cooked shrimp
Cannellini Bean and Black Olive Salad, p.210
Red or white Demestica or Retsina wine

❧ Greek Mezze ❧

Tahini Dip

Serve this creamy sesame dip with pita bread, raw vegetables or seafood.

1 to 2 cloves garlic
½ cup tahini
¼ cup lemon juice
½ teaspoon salt
minced parsley as a garnish

Crush the garlic into a bowl. Stir in the tahini and whisk in ½ cup cold water, lemon juice and salt. Beat in more water, 1 tablespoon at a time, until the sauce has the consistency you prefer. Garnish with parsley.

Yield: About 1½ cups.

Yogurt Mint Sauce

Nothing tastes so fresh on the palate as yogurt infused with mint. Use this as a sauce or dip with stuffed vine leaves, meats, vegetables and fruits.

1 cup plain yogurt
¼ cup fresh mint or 1 tablespoon dried
1 clove garlic, minced

In a small bowl, mix yogurt, mint and garlic. This is best served at room temperature.

If you use dried mint, let it stand 15 minutes so the mint has time to release its flavor.

Yield: About 1 cup.

Skordalia

This garlic almond dip is the Greek version of Aioli. It's a delicious sauce or dip for meatballs, seafood, raw vegetables or pita bread.

1 cup mayonnaise
1 to 2 cloves garlic
2½ tablespoons breadcrumbs
2 tablespoons ground almonds or walnuts
1 tablespoon chopped parsley
salt and pepper to taste

In a bowl mix mayonnaise, garlic, bread crumbs, nuts and parsley. Season to taste with salt and pepper. Let ripen at room temperature for 30 minutes.

Yield: About 1 cup.

Cucumber Garlic Yogurt Sauce

Eat this cucumber yogurt sauce as a salad or scoop it up with pita bread. It's also delicious with meatballs, chicken, fried zucchini, eggplant or seafood.

2 cups plain yogurt
1 medium cucumber, peeled, seeded and diced
2 to 3 teaspoons olive oil
2 teaspoons lemon juice
⅓ cup finely chopped onion
1 tablespoon minced garlic

Combine all the ingredients in a bowl and chill 30 minutes or more to develop the flavor.

Yield: About 2½ cups.

The Adventurous Chef: For a delicious mint variation of this sauce, see p. 97.

❧ *Greek Mezze* ❧

Beets with Walnuts

Beets turn exotic and mysterious beneath this silken purée of walnuts and prunes.

⅓ cup walnuts
1 clove garlic
3 tablespoons white wine vinegar
⅓ cup water
1 teaspoon lemon juice
8 drops hot sauce
2 teaspoons vegetable oil
¼ teaspoon ground coriander
¼ teaspoon salt
2 dried prunes, pitted and chopped
1 can (1 pound) sliced beets

⅓ cup minced onion
1 tablespoon chopped parsley

Grind walnuts and garlic in a food processor. In a small bowl, mix the vinegar, water, lemon juice, hot sauce, oil, coriander and salt. Add this to the walnuts along with the prunes. Process to a silky puree. Drain the beets and mix with the onion and parsley. Pour the sauce over the beets, mix to coat and refrigerate 2 hours to ripen.

Yield: 4 or more servings.

Cannellini Bean and Black Olive Salad

A salad with so many contrasts for the eye and the tongue: soft white beans, tangy purple-black olives and juicy red tomato bathed in lemon and olive oil.

⅔ cup olive oil
⅓ cup lemon juice
⅓ cup Kalamata olives, halved
1 ripe tomato, sliced
3 cups canned cannellini beans, drained and rinsed
salt and pepper to taste

In a bowl, beat the olive oil and lemon juice until thick. Add the olives, tomato and salt and pepper to taste.

If the beans are wet, turn them onto paper towels and pat dry. Add beans to the dressing and mix to coat well. Let stand at room temperature so the beans soak up the flavor.

Yield: 6 servings.

Hummos

This is thick and garlicky and you scoop it up on triangles of pita bread.

1 can (15 to 16 ounces) chick peas, drained
2 cloves garlic
3 tablespoons lemon juice
3 to 8 tablespoons tahini
½ teaspoon salt
⅛ teaspoon pepper
¼ teaspoon cumin
2 tablespoons olive oil
parsley or paprika

In a blender or food processor, place chickpeas, garlic, lemon juice, 3 tablespoons tahini, salt, pepper and cumin. Process to a smooth purée. With the motor running, pour in the olive oil. The mixture should be soft. Add a little water or olive oil to get the texture you want. Add more lemon juice and tahini to taste. Pour hummos into a bowl and sprinkle with chopped parsley or mint.

Yield: About 1½ cups.

Hors D'Oeuvres Variés

This was a standard guest luncheon of our cook, Louis, when we lived in Benin in Africa. It looked gorgeous and everyone loved it. I serve it often as a summer dinner. As you can see, it is infinitely expandable.

What to Buy

Choose items from each category. See the directions at right for how to prepare.

Vegetables

Cucumbers
Tomatoes
Canned beets
Avocados
Canned asparagus, drained
Julienned carrots
Radishes
Black olives
Minced fresh parsley

Seafood

Cooked shrimp
Crab meat (cooked or canned)
Sardines

Meats and Cheese

Salami, ham or pâté
Assorted cheeses
French bread

What to Do

Wash and slice the raw vegetables. Mix each with a little of Louis's Vinaigrette (see p. 199). Don't omit the julienned carrots—they're a must.

Mix the shrimp or crab meat with mayonnaise and a little tarragon or dill. Spoon vinaigrette and minced parsley over the sardines.

Roll thin slices of salami, ham or other cold meats. Cut the cheese and pâté into slices or sticks.

On a very large platter, arrange little mounds of the vegetables in vinaigrette and the seafood. Intersperse the mounds with rolled up slices of ham, salami, fingers of cheese and slices of pâté.

Decorate the platter with radishes and black olives. Sprinkle the top with lots of parsley. Serve a basket of French bread.

Add a Dessert

Choose one of the following:
Fresh fruit and cheese
Peaches in Wine, p. 71
Lemon Raspberry Napoleon, p. 153
Instant Chocolate Mousse, p. 54
Raspberry sorbet
Any fruit dessert (see Hidden Treasures, front of book)

To Make It a Party

Add any of the following:
Zucchini Rémoulade, p. 212
Navy Bean Salad in Herb Vinaigrette, p. 212

✣ Hors D'Oeuvres Variés ✣

Zucchini Rémoulade

A tangy salad to accompany the hors d'oeuvres.

¾ pound zucchini (4 small ones)
6 tablespoons mayonnaise
1½ teaspoons Dijon mustard
2 teaspoons chopped parsley
1½ teaspoons capers, drained and chopped
¼ teaspoon salt
⅛ teaspoon dried tarragon

In the food processor using the medium grater or the julienne disk, cut zucchini in julienne. If you don't want to get out the processor, cut each zucchini in ¼" slices. stack them up and cut into ¼" wide sticks.

Squeeze the zucchini in paper towels to remove moisture, then place in a bowl. stir in the mayonnaise, mustard, parsley, capers, salt and tarragon. Toss to mix.

Yield: 2 to 2½ cups.

Navy Bean Salad in Herb Vinaigrette

This combination of beans in an herby vinaigrette is irresistible.

1 can (15 ounces) navy beans
1 cup sweet, mild onion, finely chopped
1 teaspoon garlic, finely minced
2 tablespoons parsley, finely minced
2 tablespoons fresh basil, chopped
1 tablespoon fresh mint, chopped
¾ teaspoon salt
1 teaspoon sugar
freshly ground black pepper
¼ cup red wine vinegar
¼ cup fruity olive oil

Drain the beans, discard the liquid and rinse with cold water.

In a 1-quart saucepan, combine the onion, garlic, parsley, basil, mint, salt, pepper, sugar, vinegar and olive oil. Mix well. Add the beans and mix lightly so you don't crush them.

Yield: 4 servings.

Antipasto Dinner

L ike the other menus in this section, this would make a dynamite cocktail party. An antipasto meal is something you can often assemble from what is already in your pantry and refrigerator. Everyone likes Italian flavors. Like the other meals, there is little work to do here. Arrange and enjoy.

What to Buy

Choose some items from each category. See directions at right for how to prepare.

Vegetables
Lettuce
Canned garbanzo beans
Roasted red peppers
Fresh tomatoes
Raw or marinated mushrooms
Marinated artichoke hearts
Peperoncini
Olives, green and black
Fennel, cut into sticks
Radishes
Green onions
Celery and carrots
Parsley and other fresh herbs

Other Ingredients
Solid pack canned tuna
Hard-cooked eggs
Anchovies and sardines
Vinaigrette dressing (purchased or
Louis's Vinaigrette, page 199)
Crunchy bread sticks
Italian bread

Meats and Cheese
Ham or prosciutto, in thin slices
Roast beef, in thin slices
Turkey breast or cold cuts, in thin slices
Mozzarella or provolone cheese, sliced

What to Do

On a large platter, arrange green lettuce leaves as a base. On the lettuce, make attractive mounds of the vegetables: garbanzo beans, roasted red peppers, sliced or wedged tomatoes, mushrooms.

Drain the tuna well and place it in the center of the platter. Drizzle vinaigrette over everything and sprinkle with minced parsley. Roll slices of assorted meats and cheese and arrange them around the edge of the platter.

Add other vegetables: fennel sticks, radishes, green onions, marinated artichokes, celery and carrot sticks, black and green olives. Decorate the platter with fresh parsley, basil, thyme or other fresh herbs.

Serve with bread sticks and Italian bread.

Add a Dessert
Choose one of the following:
Fresh fruit and cheese
Italian Cassata, p. 215
Fresh figs with cream and brown sugar
Peach Mousse with Pound Cake
Fingers, p. 215

To Make It a Party
For a party, add the following:
Melon with Prosciutto, p. 214
Shrimp Cauliflower Salad, p. 214
Cheese Stuffed Celery, p. 214
Espresso, p. 24

❧ *Antipasto Dinner* ❧

Melon with Prosciutto

This combination of juicy sweet melon and salty prosciutto is irresistible. Serve this to begin a summer luncheon.

1 ripe honeydew or cantaloupe melon

¼ pound sliced prosciutto

Peel the honeydew or cantaloupe melon, scoop out the seeds and cut the melon in skinny wedges.

Wrap each wedge of melon with a slice of prosciutto. You can also use quartered pears or whole ripe figs. Allow one to two wedges per person.

Shrimp Cauliflower Salad

Taste the lemon juice before you add it, as lemons vary in tartness and you may need more or less. This salad makes a lovely starter for a dinner party.

½ cup mayonnaise

1 tablespoon minced onion

1 tablespoon fresh lemon juice

salt and pepper, to taste

2 cups cooked shrimp, shelled and deveined and chilled

2 cups cauliflower florets, cooked crisp-tender and drained

In a small bowl, mix mayonnaise, onion and lemon juice. Arrange the shrimp and cauliflower in alternate layers on a large plate. Top with the mayonnaise sauce. Serve chilled.

Yield: 4 servings.

Cheese Stuffed Celery

This is crunchy, creamy and tangy. Cut into 3-inch lengths, these make a lovely addition to any hors d'oeuvres assortment.

2 ounces Gorgonzola or other blue cheese

1 tablespoon butter

1 tablespoon olive oil

½ teaspoon paprika

1½ teaspoons Worcestershire sauce

12 narrow celery stalks

Using a fork, mash the cheese and butter in a shallow bowl. Mash in the olive oil, paprika, pepper and Worcestershire sauce. Stir to make a smooth, soft paste.

Stuff the mixture lightly into celery ribs. Sprinkle with paprika.

Yield: 12 stuffed celery ribs.

♣ *Antipasto Dinner* ♣

Italian Cassata

Not too rich, not too sweet, the pound cake layers of this luscious cake are lightly soaked with orange juice and liqueur, then sandwiched with a creamy mixture of ricotta, chocolate chips almonds and orange peel.

16 ounces ricotta cheese
¼ cup sugar
⅔ cup chocolate chips
1 tablespoon orange rind
¼ cup chopped toasted almonds
2 tablespoons orange juice
¼ cup orange-flavored liqueur
1 frozen pound cake (1 pound), thawed

Place ricotta and sugar in the bowl of a food processor and process with on/off turns until smooth. Pour into a bowl and stir in the chocolate chips, toasted almonds and orange rind.

In a small bowl, mix the orange juice and orange liqueur.

Cut the pound cake into 4 lengthwise layers. Brush each layer with one fourth of the orange juice mixture. Assemble by spreading one third of the filling on the first three layers and topping the cake with the fourth. Place in the freezer for 10 minutes to set, then store in the refrigerator.

Yield: 6 to 8 servings.

Peach Mousse With Pound Cake Fingers

Celebrate the peach season with this gloriously fresh-tasting dessert: peach purée folded into cream with no other flavors getting in the way. Use the toasted pound cake fingers as dippers or accompaniments.

3 peaches, peeled and pitted
1 cup whipping cream
4 slices pound cake, cut into fingers
½ to ⅔ cup sugar

Purée the peaches in the blender or processor. Pour them into a medium size bowl and stir in sugar to taste. In another bowl whip the cream until it makes soft peaks. Fold it into the peach purée.

In a toaster oven or under the broiler, toast the pound cake fingers until the edges are golden brown and caramelized. Put the peach mixture into 4 individual dessert dishes and surround with pound cake fingers.

The Adventurous Chef: Bananas or raspberries are good in this. Out of season, use frozen peaches.

Aioli

The Grande Aioli was long the traditional Friday dinner in Southern France. A big bowl of creamy garlic mayonnaise eaten with a variety of boiled vegetables and cold poached fish or chicken.

What to Buy

Choose items from each category below. See the directions at right for how to prepare.

Seafood and Meat
Large cooked shrimp
Solid-pack white tuna
Rotisserie chicken

Vegetables
Canned chick peas, drained
Sliced canned beets, drained
Canned artichoke hearts
Carrots, peeled and sliced lengthwise
Fresh mushrooms
Green onions
Fennel, separated into stalks and rings
Cherry tomatoes
Fresh or frozen green beans (optional)

Other Ingredients
Hard-cooked eggs
French bread

What to Do

In the center of a large platter, arrange the seafood and/or sliced chicken. Surround with vegetables and hard-cooked eggs.

Green beans (cooked, drained and cooled to room temperature) are a nice addition to the platter.

Make the aioli sauce (below) and spoon into small dishes, one for each diner. Each bite of vegetable, seafood or chicken is accompanied by a little dollop of aioli.

Add a Dessert
Choose one of the following:
Fresh fruit and cheese
Mediterranean Oranges, p. 61

To Make It a Party
Add the following:
Canned artichoke bottoms
Chick peas in Louis's Vinaigrette, p. 199
Hot Herb Loaf, p. 133
White or French rosé wine
Coffee with liqueur, p. 85

Aioli

This is the beloved garlic mayonnaise sauce of Southern France. Try it with fried fish or spoon it in a baked potato.

4 cloves garlic, pressed
½ teaspoon salt
1 tablespoon lemon juice
1 cup mayonnaise

Mash garlic and salt in a mortar or use a dish and crush with the bottom of a glass. Whisk in the mayonnaise, olive oil and lemon juice.

Yield: About 1 cup.

Scandinavian Smørbrød

S morbrød are open-faced sandwiches to eat with a knife and fork. You can prepare them before the meal, but it's more fun to let diners make their own combinations.

What to Buy

Choose from each category. See the directions at right for how to prepare.
Potato salad
Sliced rye and pumpernickel bread
Assorted hard rolls, cut in half
Sliced hard-cooked eggs
Butter, plain or flavored, p. 218
Herbed cream cheese
Sour cream
Capers and anchovies, as garnishes

Vegetables
Lettuce
Fresh dill
Sliced tomatoes
Thinly sliced cucumbers
Minced parsley
Thinly sliced red onion rings
Sliced green pepper rings

Seafood, Meat and Cheese
Ham, salami, roast beef or bologna
Herrings in cream or wine
Smoked salmon
Cooked shrimp
Sardines
Jarlsberg, Camembert, Brie or blue cheese
Anchovies

What to Do

Perk up store bought potato salad with a little olive oil, chopped onion and chive, dill or other fresh herbs.

Set out a basket of bread and rolls.

Put out little dishes with hard-cooked eggs, butter, herbed cream cheese, sour cream, capers and anchovies.

Place the vegetables, seafood, meat and cheese on platters .

Add a Dessert

Choose one of the following:
Instant Chocolate Mousse, p.54
Fruit and cheese
Danish Apple Cake, p. 219

To Make It a Party

Add the following:
Herring Salad, p. 218
Beet, Celery and Apple Salad, p. 219
Russian Salad, p. 142
Ham, Tomato and Cheese Tart, p. 134

✌ Scandinavian Smørbrød ✌

Let diners make their own sandwiches or serve them ready-made. Either way, they are very pretty. Here are suggested combinations:

- Butter, smoked salmon, sliced red onion and dill
- Garlic butter (see below), lettuce and herring
- Herbed cream cheese, shrimp and fresh dill
- Butter, salami and sliced radishes
- Horseradish butter (see below), roast beef, lettuce and tomato
- Butter, herring salad, green pepper rings and sliced hard-cooked eggs
- Bologna with cucumbers in Louis's Vinaigrette, p. 199
- Smoked salmon, herring salad and parsley
- Mustard, mayonnaise, sardines, tomato and sliced hard-cooked egg

Garlic Butter

Try this with lettuce and herring.

½ cup butter
1 clove garlic, mashed
2 tablespoons minced onion

In a small bowl, place butter, garlic and onion. Mash and stir to combine.

Yield: ½ cup.

Horseradish Butter

A zesty spread that's good with roast beef, lettuce and tomato.

½ cup butter
1 tablespoon well drained horseradish

In a small bowl, place butter and horseradish and stir to combine.

Yield: ½ cup.

Herring Salad

This is good on buttered pumpernickel bread.

1 jar (13 ounces) herring in wine
1 unpeeled apple, cored and diced
2 small green onions, finely chopped
⅓ cup mayonnaise
⅓ cup sour cream

Drain the herring and pat dry in paper towels. Strain the onions out of the herring marinade; reserve onions and discard marinade.

In a bowl, combine herring, onions from marinade, apple, green onions, mayonnaise and sour cream. Chill before serving.

Yield: 4 to 6 servings.

❧ *Scandinavian Smørbrød* ❧

Beet, Celery and Apple Salad

The beets and apples are sweet, the apples and celery fresh and crunchy and the smooth cream that binds is tangy with horseradish and lemon.

1 cup sour cream

2 tablespoons whipping cream

2 tablespoons lemon juice

2 tablespoons minced onion

2 tablespoons bottled horseradish, well drained

1 teaspoon salt

2 cups canned, diced beets, drained

2 cups peeled, diced apple

1 cup diced celery

minced green onions, as a garnish

In a medium bowl, combine the sour cream, whipping cream, lemon juice, onion, horseradish and salt. Stir in the apple, beets and celery. Toss gently.

Garnish with the minced green onions.

Yield: 4 servings.

Danish Apple Cake

Don't think that because this calls for bread crumbs it will be dull. Those crumbs are toasted to a crispy caramel in butter and sugar, layered with applesauce and topped with whipped cream. A superb combination.

2 cups dried white breadcrumbs

2 Tablespoons sugar

½ cup butter

2½ cups applesauce

1 cup sweetened whipped cream

¼ cup grated chocolate, optional

In a bowl, combine the crumbs with the sugar.

In a heavy 10-inch skillet, melt the butter. Add the crumbs and stir and cook over medium heat until they are browned and crisp, about 4 to 5

minutes. Watch carefully—they brown fast. Cool briefly.

Put a third of the crumbs into a 1-quart serving bowl. Carefully spread on half the applesauce. Add another third of the crumbs, the remaining applesauce and top with the remaining crumbs. Chill at least 30 minutes. Before serving, cover the top with sweetened whipped cream. Decorate with grated chocolate if desired.

Yield: 6 servings.

The Pantry

A well stocked pantry takes a lot of stress out of your kitchen life. There are three lists in this chapter to help make cooking fun and carefree. *The Pantry List* contains all the staples you'll need to make any recipe in this book. If you buy the meat or fresh vegetables, the rest is on your shelves. *Pantry Shelf Recipes* tells you all the dishes in the book that can be made using only pantry shelf ingredients. You'll be surprised how many there are. This is your magic wand when you haven't had a chance to shop and the freezer is empty. Presto! Flip through the list and head serenely for your pantry. *Emergency Menus for Company* suggests wonderful, imaginative meals that use the pantry shelf recipes. This is your lifesaver when unexpected company drops in and you would love to offer dinner. With your well stocked pantry and the menu ideas there's no sweat. How about Italian Seafood Stew with garlicky Rouille Sauce, French Bread Sticks, Green Salad Vinaigrette and Pears in Chocolate Fluff? You'll become known as the least flappable, most hospitable, best-cooking host in town. Read through the chapter, make your shopping list, stock the shelves and relax. You're in control.

"With a well stocked pantry, you can make a surprising number of the super recipes in this book at the drop of a hat."

Herbs and Seasonings

basil, dried
bay leaves
chili powder
cinnamon, ground and sticks
coriander, ground
cumin, ground
garlic powder
mint, dried

nutmeg, ground
oregano, dried
paprika
red pepper flakes
rosemary, dried
tarragon, dried
thyme, dried
vanilla extract

Sauces and Condiments

A-1 sauce
capers
chili sauce
chutney
Dijon mustard
hoisin sauce
horseradish
ketchup

mayonnaise
salsa
sesame oil
soy sauce
Tabasco sauce
Worcestershire sauce

Staples

baking mix
baking powder
baking soda
bouillon cubes and granules
chocolate: un-sweetened, chips, syrup
cocoa
coffee
corn syrup
cornbread mix
cornstarch
flour
honey

jam: apricot, pineapple, raspberry
milk: evaporated and condensed
oatmeal
oil: olive and vegetable
pepper, black and cayenne
sugar, white, brown and powdered
tea
vinegar: red and white wine

Canned, Bottled, Boxed and Bagged

anchovies
beans: kidney, navy, black, large butter
breadcrumbs
clams
clam juice
chili with and without beans
cocktail onions
coconut
coconut milk: sweetened and unsweetened

corn chips
couscous
crabmeat
fruits, canned: mandarin oranges, pears, peaches, crushed pine-apple
fruits, dried: dates, raisins (light and dark)
gingersnaps
herring in wine

juices: orange, tomato
lentils (red cook fastest)
maraschino cherries
marinated arti-choke hearts
miniature marsh-mallows
noodles
nuts: almonds, pecans, wal-nuts, pine nuts

olives: black, green, ripe
pasta, dried
peanut butter
puddings, instant
rice
roasted red pep-pers
soups, a variety of cream-style, especially mushroom
stuffing mix

Canned, Bottled, Boxed and Bagged

tamales
tomato paste
tomato sauce
tuna
vanilla wafers
vegetables,
    canned: arti-
    choke hearts,
    beets, corn
    (cream-style and
whole kernel),
    chilies, green
    beans, mush-
    rooms, pota-
    toes,
sauerkraut
tomatoes (1-pound
    and 28-ounce
    cans)
water chestnuts

Fresh

apples
bacon
bell peppers
carrots
celery
cured sausage
dairy products
    (see below)
eggs
garlic
ginger
green onions
lemons
onions
oranges
parsley
potatoes
salad greens

Dairy

butter
cheese: Cheddar,
    feta, mozzarella,
    Parmesan
cream: light,
    whipping and
    sour
cream cheese:
    plain and
    herbed
milk
plain yogurt

Freezer

breads (see below)
ice cream
orange juice
    concentrate
peas
pound cake
raspberries
ready-to-eat crumb
    crusts
ready-to-bake pie
    crusts
spinach, chopped
strawberries
whipped topping

Breads

bagels
English muffins
French and Italian
    loaves
pita
refrigerated
    biscuits
refrigerated pizza
    crust
sandwich bread
tortillas, corn and
    flour

Alcoholic Beverages

bourbon
cognac
dry sherry
liqueurs
madeira
port
red and white
    table wines
rum
white vermouth

❧ Pantry Shelf Recipes ❧

If you have a moderately well stocked pantry (see previous pages) you can make a surprising number of the recipes in this book. Here is my list of off-the-shelf recipes. At the most, you may have to omit a minor ingredient or substitute dried, canned or frozen ingredients for fresh. Scribble the names of any other recipes you think of in the margins, and delete the ones that use ingredients you don't normally keep on hand.

Beverages

Fun Dessert Coffees, 24
Fun Dessert Coffees II, 85
Fun Dessert Coffees III, 147
Mexican Mocha, 173
Perfect Iced Tea, 73

Breads

Crostini, 56
French Bread Sticks, 15
Garlic Bread, 55
Herb Toasts, 100
Herbed Butter Sticks, 66
Hot Herb Loaf, 133
Mexican Biscuits, 101
Mild Garlic Bread, 202
Parmesan Cheese Bread, 29
Pita Wedges with Herb
    Butter, 36
Quick Cheese Loaf, 141
Quick Cornbread, 163
Savory Slices, 10
Toasted Onion Puff Bread,
    123

Desserts

Bananas in Yogurt, 76
Betsy's Tart, 28
Chocolate Fondue, 59
Easy Dobos Torte, 136
Fruit Romanoff, 135
Ginger Pears, 8
Ice Cream Parfait, 35
Ice Cream with Toppings,
    34
Instant Chocolate Mousse,
    54
Mom's Spanish Pound
    Cake Sundae, 177
Pears in Chocolate Fluff, 41

Hors d'Oeuvres

Aioli (with selected
    dippers), 216
Antipasti (selected), 213
Bagna Cauda (with
    selected dippers), 160
Beets with Walnuts, 210
Elegant Pizza, 172
Herring Salad, 218
Skordalia, 209
Summer Meal (vegetables
    with tonnato sauce), 79

Navy Bean Salad in Herb
    Vinaigrette, 212
White Pizza, 172
Yogurt Mint Sauce (as
    dip), 209

Main Dishes

Aioli (with selected
    dippers), 216
Artichoke Linguini, 20
Bagna Cauda (with
    selected dippers), 160
Cheese Chick Pea Stir-Fry,
    165
Cheese Soufflé, 175
Chili Avocado Tostada, 110
Chili Pie, 108
Crab Artichoke Pasta, 12
Elegant Pizza, 172
Herbed Cream Cheese
    Pasta, 19
Huevos Rancheros, 169
Italian Seafood Stew
    (Pantry-Shelf variation),
    42
Kidney Beans in Sour
    Cream, 176
Macaroni and Cheese, 8
Pasta Alfredo, 12

❧ Emergency Menus for Company ❧

If you stock your pantry according to the suggested list, you can produce any of the meals below at the drop of a hat. If you're out to impress unexpected guests, add a fancy coffee, fold the napkins invitingly, make a quick garnish and light some candles. These little extras are the difference between eating and dining.

Antipasti, 213
Rigatoni with Tuna in Pimento Garlic
Sauce, 16
Betsy's Tart, 28

Russian Salad, 142
Artichoke Linguini, 20
Green Salad with Mustard Vinaigrette, 199
Herbed Butter Sticks, 66
Ginger Pears, 8

Italian Seafood Stew, 42
Rouille Sauce, 23
French Bread Sticks, 15
Green Salad with Vinaigrette, 199
Pears in Chocolate Fluff, 41

Two Bean Chili, 163
Corn Casserole, 124
Hot Herb Loaf, 133
Tossed Green Salad
Chocolate Fondue, 59

Mushroom Polenta, 161
Tossed Salad with Louis' Vinaigrette, 199
Garlic Bread, 55
Vanilla Ice Cream with Hot Melba Sauce, 34

Cheese Soufflé, 175
Tossed Green Salad with Accents, 131
Herbed Butter Sticks, 66
Instant Chocolate Mousse, 54

Sunflower Nacho Pizza, 108
Sour Cream
Garbanzo Beans or Artichoke Hearts Vinaigrette, 127
Fruit Romanoff, 135

Tamale Casserole, 109
Quick Cornbread, 163
Chocolate Cinnamon Parfait, 35

Elegant White Pizza, 172
Green Salad with Roquefort Dressing, 175
Mom's Spanish Pound Cake Sundae, 177

Crab Bisque, 185
Pasta Puttanesca, 6
Green Salad with Croutons
Toasted Onion Puff Bread, 123
Bananas in Yogurt, 76

Chilled Cream of Tomato Soup, 201
Crab Artichoke Pasta, 12
Tossed Green Salad with Accents, 131
Parmesan Cheese Bread, 29
Easy Dobos Torte, 136

Tonnato Sauce, 79
Hard Cooked Eggs
Boiled Potatoes
Roasted Red Peppers
Artichoke Hearts
Cooked Green Beans
Italian Bread
Mediterranean Oranges, 61

Index

About the Author

Polly Clingerman is the author of five cookbooks: *Fast and Fabulous Hors D'Oeuvres, Holiday Entertaining, A Passion for Pasta, Red Raspberry Recipes* and the new cooking classic, *The Kitchen Companion*, which was a 1995 James Beard award nominee. She also wrote *Fast and Easy Garnishes* for The Pampered Chef, and starred in the video that accompanied it. She has written articles on cooking and travel for *Vogue, Mademoiselle, The Washington Post, The Chicago Tribune, The Stars and Stripes* and *The Foreign Service Journal.* In 1987 she was a featured cook in Bon Appetit's Great Cooks series. Polly graduated from Michigan State University with a BA in English Literature and studied for a year at the Sorbonne in Paris.

As the wife of a foreign service office, she spent thirty years traveling the world, living, cooking and entertaining in the capitals of Nepal, Zaire, France, Benin, Belgium, Zambia and Lesotho, where her husband, John, was the Ambassador. After John retired, the Clingermans lived for two years in Germany, England and Greece where John taught foreign affairs on Air Force bases and Polly wrote travel articles and worked on *The Kitchen Companion*—a book that grew out of the notebooks she kept during her years as cook and hostess. *The Kitchen Companion* is a bestseller that has provided needed kitchen lore and encouragement for cooks across the nation, with more than 50,000 copies sold in less than two years. Polly has become a popular television personality promoting her cookbooks. The Clingermans now make their home in Northern Virginia and spend part of each year abroad.